Professional Rabbit

A Complete Book on Rabbit Snaring
For
Gamekeepers,
Professional & Amateur Trappers,
& Field Sportsmen

*How to Catch Rabbits
by the Thousand*

By

G. S. Waters
(Snareman)

International Edition

"DEDICATION"

This book is dedicated to my

> Mother and Father
> Thomas and Janet Waters
>
> My wife Winnie and my family
>
>
> Others who helped further my career
>
> Late Jimmy Waterson
>
> Late Sandy Livingston - Gamekeeper
>
> Late Willie McMaster - Gamekeeper
>
> Late Alex Chisholm - Gamekeeper
>
> Andy White - Pro Rabbit Trapper

ISBN 978-0-9558535-3-1

Copyright © 2016 Glenn Waters

Cover design by Ragdog (www.ragdog.co.uk)

Published by Fourteenacre Ltd

Contents

Preface

Glenn Waters is well known in the UK and abroad as a trapper and hunter of skill, knowledge and great ingenuity. Although just as handy with the trap, net or dog, it is the development and championing of humane snaring for which Glenn is probably best known.

In 2006 Glenn wrote a series of articles for the internet forum 'The Hunting Life' which explained his 'large loop, wire tealer' method of snaring rabbits. This was a method Glenn had been using for many years and this was an early step in trying to share it with a wider audience. It was an approach to snaring which he knew worked far better than much of the advice being given at the time. It was well received and for many people who'd been struggling for years, it was the key to being able to snare effectively.

Glenn continued to develop his method, experimenting with stops and breakaways to make the snares more humane and more selective. As pressure against snaring grew, Glenn lobbied the government departments in England, Scotland and Northern Ireland to try and convince them that snaring was a highly effective method that needed to be preserved.

In 2009 Glenn rang and asked me to collate his original articles into a simple printed book, A4 and 34 pages long. Just 11 copies of this book were printed, each copy numbered and signed by Glenn before being distributed to various government bodies and friends. Six years later Glenn approached me again to help publish this second book - the most comprehensive book on rabbit snaring ever written.

Glenn is a prolific writer and illustrator who is able to capture the essence of any snaring problem or technique in a clear freestanding commentary. What began as a very large box full of Glenn's original handwritten articles, drawings and photographs has been reproduced here with minimal editing. This book remains very much in Glenn's 'voice' with the articles arranged within a loose structure and using the original hand drawn illustrations that Glenn produced.

For anyone who knows Glenn the style will be unmistakable. For those who don't then welcome to a wealth of knowledge and let's hope that your ears aren't *"painted on your head"*.

John Bryan,
Fourteenacre
May 2016

The Rabbit

Wee rabbit weel its understood,
That guid grass is your favourite food

Tae live we ken that thou mon steal
And wreak havock in the farmers field
While the poor old farmer canna sleep
For thinking o his hungry sheep
And prays the day will come Tae pass
When you'll stop eating his precious grass

We ken poor beastie thou mon Thieve
But alike the mouse thou tae mon live
Although in some harsh mens opinion
You've nae place on their dominion
And doomed Taedie a horrid death
Denied a bite, denied a breath
The result o a monstrous devilist plan
An insult tae the integrity o man

We've tackled you before today
And some of the weapons brought to play
Were snare & net & trap & gun
Tae pay you back for you've terrible sin
The best o brains against you pitted
A beast sae timid and dimwitted
And the thing that conquers wi such ease
Is a fiendish ill thought up disease

And so you'll die an unmourned death
Tae leave this world a place of evil
Denied the place god gave on earth
By a band of shameless human devils
While a crown of thorns adorns mans brow
We know the voice spoke true
When he said "O'Lord forgive now
They know not what they do"

Author Unknown

Introduction

Six decades have now passed since the arrival of myxomatosis in the UK and although rabbit numbers have increased in general they are not quite to pre-myxy levels. There are still annual outbreaks of this filthy disease even today. Man has tried every devious method to try to eradicate the humble coney but to no avail. This creature is a born survivor and can adapt to practically any type of habitat. It really has to be admired for its sheer tenacity to survive and although extensive damage can be incurred to crops, trees and undermining of buildings and roads etc, why they try to exterminate this creature is a mystery. Man is the most destructive being on God's earth today and causes more destruction to the environment through pure greed and ignorance than any other animal on the planet. Control the animals to an acceptable level as many other species depend on the rabbit for their survival.

Commercial field sports businesses thrive due to the sale of equipment for rabbit control, many countrymen and pest controllers gain their livelihood from rabbit control. Cutting the import of rabbit carcasses and boneless meat from foreign countries would help create employment for people in our own country and increase sales of our own organic wild rabbit population. Rabbit snaring is a legitimate pursuit which many countrymen partake in, but many who pursue this activity lack any real knowledge of the snaring game. This is due to the fact they still harbour old traditional practices therefore obtaining poor results and have eventually given it up.

The setting of snares may appear to be a simple task in itself; good equipment, skill in handling and proper setting technique all play an important part in either success or failure. To become really successful in this art is only achieved through many years of practical experience. The professional trapper knows his quarry, its habits and characteristics intimately. This knowledge will only be acquired through much time being spent outdoors in all types of inclement weather conditions and various types of terrain. The knowledge given in this book has not been gained through second hand hearsay but from a lifetime's practical experience and fieldwork. Therefore the reader will gain a large amount of true practical information from the illustrations I have personally hand drawn. Along with all the written instructions to accompany them, these illustrations will bring attention to the exact details I want to portray, far better than any pictures could capture.

Many difficulties will be overcome after the reading of this text, as I have shown the faults and recommended the correct solutions to solve many of the problems which the reader will encounter once the practical snaring operations begin. In the following chapters various different snares and techniques will be referred to and their most practical setting methods. I will cover how to construct and assemble snares and volumes of instruction are given in their use and how to apply them properly. I will bring beginners and amateurs up to an acceptable standard in snaring very quickly, due to the fact that throughout these chapters I have cut many corners and years of frustration and trial and error for them to become adept in a much shorter period of time.

Snaring is a fascinating and interesting activity and very necessary in rabbit and fox control as well as in a survival situation. It is a highly effective method by which large numbers of rabbits or foxes can be culled quickly in a very short period of time. Many people portray it as a cruel method of capture and those who know the least about a subject usually talk the most. Life in general is cruel, nature itself is totally ruthless in ensuring only the fittest survive and culls the weak through disease and starvation. The professional trapper reduces cruelty to the very minimum by applying his snares properly to make them almost one hundred percent species specific. It is only people who are inexperienced, lazy or ignorant who set snares and don't or won't check them in compliance with the law who cause much unwarranted attention to the genuine law abiding field sports fraternity. Remember one snare in the hands of a fool can cause more problems than enough. The simple fact is if you can't be bothered to check them don't set them.

Scotland now leads the way in humane snaring in the UK due to the fact that I have devised the breakaway rabbit snare with the larger 6" stop loop. This snare system has practically eliminated 100% of all the problems associated with rabbit snaring over the years. We now have strict snaring laws whereby a snaring course must be attended where an exam is held to gain the necessary certificate. Then a police reference number must be applied for to tag every snare with the said number. I developed the first breakaway rabbit and fox snares in the UK, along with the larger stop loop system, which have improved animal welfare in the country immensely by allowing non target species to activate the breakaway link and free themselves.

Rabbit damage to a crop field. Snares can be pegged along the edge of a field or they can be set further out. Look for the meadow grass growing further out, 8-15 yards between the rows of crops. Follow along a row and you will find a beat every so many yards along the length of the row. Set every beat and your markers are all in line.

All along crop fields rabbits can do serious damage to cereals as they eat down large areas all around the field edges. They have a habit of eating in half-moon shapes along a hedge or fenceline and woodland edges where barley, wheat and other cereal grows. These patches can vary in size from 5 yards to over 25 yards in length.

Look for and set parallel runs that connect these patches of eaten crops a few yards out from the field edge itself. I call these runs 'visiting runs' due to the fact that the rabbits run back and forth on a daily basis between cropped locations and good catches may be taken from these runs. They are also good for snaring foxes.

Why I Use Snares

I use snares to control rabbits for the simple fact that I can snare all year round no matter the weather. They never sleep and work twenty-four hours a day all day and all night long, I don't have to dye and wax them like traps or even camouflage them and temperature and inclement weather conditions do not affect their performance. Due to the simplicity of snares, problems effecting their working performance and catching ability are practically nil. The snare sits quietly and runs silent therefore animals do not associate them as a danger to be avoided as they do with traps on occasions. Except in certain circumstances, I can set far more snares in a day than traps and know that they will still be working regardless of weather conditions and temperature out with our control. In my opinion it's one of the best all round method of rabbit control we have encountered.

Weathered snares are very hard to see when set even to the trapper who sets them. At times they blend into their surroundings very well which cuts down on theft problems. Very seldom do I lose any snares even in high risk areas and losing a few is nothing in comparison to losing steel traps which are most expensive in our country compared to the price of snares. I can make a pegged snare for a few pence where a steel trap, depending on the type, can vary from seven pounds upwards. The tools I carry with me on the snareline are simple and weigh practically nothing. A hundred pegged snares weigh nothing against one hundred steel traps. There is no digging or sifting dirt involved with snaring. Once again if there were no access to the trapping area by vehicle steel traps and equipment would be a burden compared to snares.

The pegged snare is an all in one piece of equipment used to catch the animal on its line of travel unaware of the snare's presence as no bait or lure is needed to attract him like in cage trapping. The snare catches the rabbit on his line of travel where he is going anyway out to his feed ground exactly where he wants to go. This makes the job of catching much easier than trying to entice him into a cage baited with carrot and maybe lured with urine. In my opinion using cages is a waste of time, as a well set snare is deadly as the rabbit is unaware of its presence until it's too late. His environment has no sign of change to alert it to any sudden danger as they do not recognise a snare loop as a trap as it sits and also runs silent even if one slips a noose and escapes. It does not relate to it as a danger therefore he will be captured the following night unless poor snares and poor snaring techniques are applied, e.g. human odour, other abnormal odours and poor equipment.

Snares don't need a great deal of attention as long as they are checked and maintained after every operation especially the brass cable itself. Check for kinks and broken strands, check for frayed and chewed twines, also for split and broken pegs, which are normally the main problems found. Therefore if the latter faults are rectified and nooses, twines and pegs are replaced before each outing to the field, very little in the way of faults occur. Snaring is one of the easiest methods of capturing animals as it's less expensive, less work as they weigh less, are far quicker to set out in vast numbers, work in all weathers around the clock and outperform more expensive and bulky traps any day for simplicity and easier handling out in all weathers. All you have to do is set the snare on the line of travel and just sit back and wait. What could be more simple than that?

Snaring and the Law

This is a practical book of successful snaring techniques intended to improve the effectiveness, proficiency and professionalism of snarers worldwide.

It is written for an international audience who are subject to a wide variety of snaring law and best practice which differ from country to country and sometimes even between states and counties with a single country. Even in the UK the laws are complicated by the different government bodies having independent jurisdiction in England, Wales, Northern Ireland and Scotland.

To try to cover all the worldwide legislation would be simply too difficult and potentially misleading as laws are being updated all the time.

If you are going to set snares it is **your responsibility** to know, understand and abide by the law and current best practice guidance in the place where you are setting them.

Recommended further reading for UK snarers:

- Defra Code of Practice on the Use of Snares in Fox and Rabbit Control
- The Snares (Scotland) Order 2010
- SNARING IN SCOTLAND A PRACTITIONERS' GUIDE

A prominent, well used rabbit run in pasture grass. The beats were padded into mud. I set two snares on this run and took 3 rabbits over two mornings.

Section 1 - The Professional Pegged Rabbit Snare

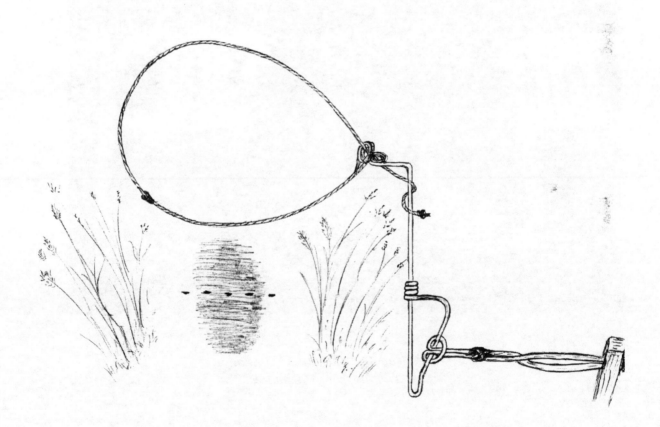

Back from the snare line with Lady
69 rabbits from 100 snares.

Chapter 1 - Why People Struggle to Snare Rabbits

The snare, a device which is so simple yet so efficient, is used by countrymen through the UK for the controlling of rabbits. It provided many a hungry family with a dinner in pre-war years before the spread of myxomatosis. Even with today's high tech pest control techniques, the noose still plays an important role in rabbit control when used in the skilled hands of a competent snareman. Rabbit control is carried out in the British Isles on a year round basis. There is now an abundance of rabbits due to a series of mild winters and a wide variety of winter cereal crops now being planted. There is no shortage of food in the agricultural belts of the country and crop damage by rabbits runs into millions of pounds annually. Although the consumption of rabbit meat declined after the onset of myxy, the demand has now started to steadily increase as people realise that rabbit is lean and high in protein. Much of this increase is taken by boneless rabbit meat and frozen carcasses being imported from foreign countries, some of which still use pesticides that are banned in the UK. Far better to increase the sales of healthy organic home-grown wild rabbits, which would also create jobs for trappers in our own country.

The complete snare is made up of five components; the firmly twisted brass wire noose, the brass eyelet, 9 ½ inch galvanised 2.5mm wire tealer (which holds the attached noose in position), double strands of thick baling twine and an 8" ash wood securing peg with a $^3/_{16}{}^{th}$ hole drilled almost 1 ¼ inches from the top of the thick end. Although snare nooses can be purchased commercially professional snaremen usually make their own equipment. This is simply because many commercial nooses are inferior often designed for maximum profit rather than maximum efficiency and therefore not suitable for professional use. Wire tealers are also hand made from 2.5 mil galvanised steel fence wire (not HIGH TENSILE) as they are usually unavailable to purchase commercially. Tethering pegs are also cut by hand, as the commercial ones I have viewed personally are of the old fashioned tent peg style big and clumsy and would do more justice to staking out a field marquee than snaring. The mere thought of having to carry fifty of these monstrosities never mind 100 of them would bring any self respecting trapper out into a cold sweat just looking at them. It would be too much like hard work - now there's an ugly word.

The key to any type of work is simplicity even when snaring. Many people have a tendency to make life difficult for themselves as they seem to have this habit of complicating every task they approach. Many would-be snarers work in their own light day after day and getting nowhere fast. The older generation set in their ways are the worst, reluctant to change in any shape or form, with their old-fashioned antiquated ideas of '*my father showed me*' and '*that's how it's done*' type of attitude. People with the latter type of attitude rarely if ever will they advance forward due to their stubbornness and being unwilling to admit they are wrong. Although they sit back they are quick to criticise and condemn new snares and snaring techniques but will never submit any new methods or ideas themselves for the simple fact is that they lack real knowledge and good practical experience.

Forget all of the old-fashioned nonsense that's been written on rabbit snaring over the many past decades and antiquated methods. Keep an open mind. Use professional snares and equipment and new techniques and you will become proficient in the art of snaring by keeping it simple.

Shop Bought Snares

The following illustration denotes a typical shop bought snare which consists of a snare noose around 18-19" long.   It has no brass eyelet at the running end of the snare noose, the formed eye is constructed from just the wire strands with a wind down of an inch to one inch and a half below the eye loop. Depending on the manufacturer some do have an end eyelet inserted between the three double strands holding it in place which is better than a plain loop, which starts to distort by elongating and twisting out of shape. This causes the person using these type of snares to waste time poking a nail into the wire eye to straighten it up to make it capable of running again. These snares are made without eyelets to save money, along with their short length. The brass wire strands are usually only half spun making them more prone to kinking and weakening, therefore instead of six strands taking the equal strain you may only have three as the other three are kinked causing weakness and breakages on a regular basis.

The long wind down under the eye also impedes the snare's running action. Some even have eight or ten strands - just a pure waste of brass wire which could really have been put to a better use to make them longer and spun tighter with no wind down. But they are not produced by trappers so they really don't know any better or how to make a good quality snare noose. The eight and ten strand snares are poor when it comes to fast closure. There is cheap 10" long double green hairy type cordage attached to these nooses which does not last any length of time and frays and snaps due to inclement weather conditions. They were being sold at the game fair at Scone in 2013 with no stops on them which is illegal since 2010. These snares are of inferior design compared to the real professional snares produced by real trappers.

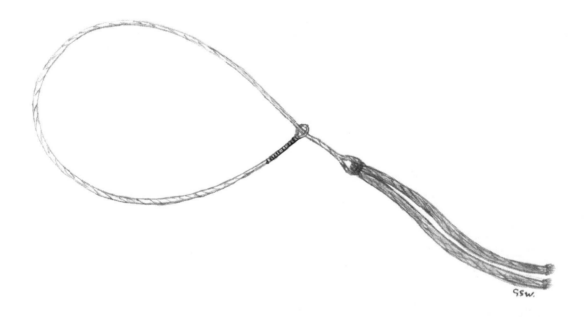

A Typical Amateur Snare Set

The illustration (A) below shows how amateurs set their snares. I have seen this all too often and there are some who are still setting snares like this today. First of all let's look at the placement of the snare loop - it is all wrong. You do not set snares on the jump which is in between the beats as shown here. Next look at the size of the snare loop - a 4" diameter loop which half of the country still snare with. It is not tensioned properly due to fact that the large majority of people can't do it so what they do instead is open up the small 4" loop and make a kink in front of running eyelet to hold it open. Should this snare get knocked by a bird like a crow, pheasant or partridge, or by hedgehog bumping the bottom of the snare loop as it trundles past, the snare loop will spring forward, half close and catch nothing. If the snare loop had been tensioned properly the loop would have reset itself back into the catching position.

This drawing also shows the type of old fashioned securing peg which some still use today - like a big old tent peg that would hold a lion. It would need an elephant and forty troops to carry a hundred of these monstrosities. The hazel tealer served the real professional rabbit trappers well for many decades until the first double wire tealer was invented up here in Scotland by Tam Stratton from Perthshire. The single wire tealer with the central loop was devised by Willie McMaster, an old mentor of mine from Kirkliston in West Lothian.

(B) Shows a rabbit beat with a dotted line across the middle which is where the large snare loop should be placed at the proper height.

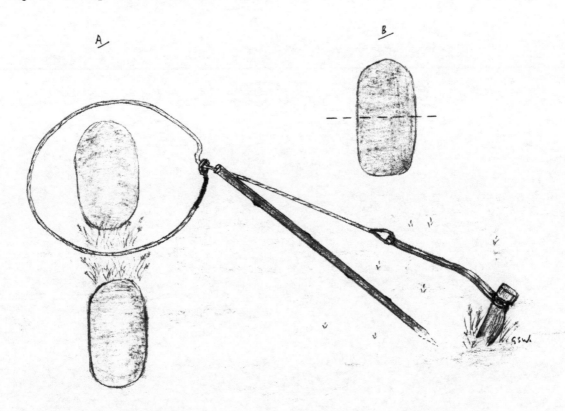

Common Snaring Mistakes and the Problems That They Cause.

Mistake 1

Do not set rabbit snares between the beats at any time, especially with small loops set low to the ground. What happens is this; as the rabbit bounds along the run he springs from one beat to another, therefore it strikes the wrongly placed and low set snare loop with its chest as the rabbit is now in mid jump towards the forward beat. The small low set snare loop is now lying in a flat position under the rabbit's belly, as its front feet land on the first half of the forward beat. The problems now occur when the rabbit pulls his back feet in behind it, as these then trip the small snare loop. Therefore it's a costly mistake for the amateur who continually set in this manner, as you will have many tripped and empty snares each morning.

(A) - shows the open snare loop lying under the rabbit's belly as its front feet land on the first half of the forward beat.

(B) - showing how the shape of your tripped and empty nooses look every morning.

(C) - showing the rabbit which may be caught by the hind foot as it pulls its back feet in behind it. Never ever sets snares between the beats.

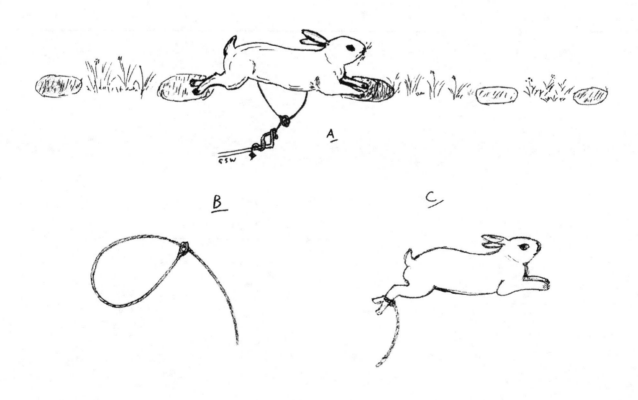

A

B

C

Mistake 2

There is another costly problem of setting snares with a small loop and low to the ground even when you place the snare correctly, directly over the middle of the beat. The rabbit comes along the run with his ears erect and hits the underside of the top of the small snare loop set too low, with his nose. The noose then closes around its face between the eyes and its nose. The rabbit then jumps around and rolls and tumbles, flinging the noose from its face. All that remains is an empty snare pulled taught with a tiny kinked loop at the end about the size of a two penny piece. You will catch very few rabbits, more by good luck than skill, but you will certainly have a big catch of empty nooses every morning. So get smart and set high with a big noose or you can remain a dunce and catch nothing.

All these faults have been caused by setting silly little snare loops low to the ground. If you set snares the way I show you in this book your catch rate will go up by tenfold overnight.

The illustrations below and on the following page

(A) - Shows the rabbit travelling along the run and striking the underside of the top of the small, low set snare loop, even though the snare has been set correctly over the middle of the beat.

(B) - Rabbit has been caught around the muzzle, between the eyes and the nose. The odd rabbit is held occasionally in this manner.

(C) & over page - Shows the shape of the empty snare loops each morning. The term used to describe a snare loop of this shape is 'frying panning'.

G.S.W.

This photo taken by Phil Lloyd shows a rabbit caught around the muzzle. The snare was properly set across the middle of the beat but needed to be set higher in the longer grass.

The rabbit's face has struck the underside of the top of the snare loop.

Professional Snare Set

This is the standard snare set my old mentor used many decades ago to great effect. Millions of rabbits all over the country were caught using this old system which consists of a large noose and a peg with a hazel wand as a tealer. Like everything in life there are odd problems that crop up now and again; the rabbits would chew the hazel tealers in cold weather, the split at the top of the hazel tealer would start to widen as the wand dried out after a period of time and an another minor problem that occurred on a regular basis was that you had to look the grass to retrieve the wooden tealer which would be flung from the snare wire when a catch was made.

To combat this problem William Mac would wind a couple of turns of rabbit snare wire around the top of the tealer so that it became a permanent fixture on the snare. This trick saved the trapper time as he no longer had to search for the tealer pin or star pin or set pin as they were sometimes referred to. A thinner type tealer was best due to lower visibility in short cover. I'm sure it was 1948 that the first wire tealer became available devised by Tam Stratton from Perth in Scotland.

(B) - Showing snare wire held firmly in the tealer with a couple of strands of brass wire wrapped around the tealer top.

(C) - Some trappers tapered their tealer top as shown for easier insertion of the snare wire.

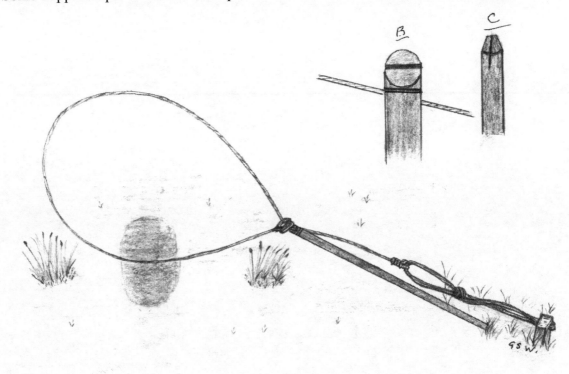

Willie Mac devised the single wire tealer system and set his snares from the side of the rabbit run as shown. High catches will be obtained when snares are set with big loops at the proper height over the rabbit run regardless if set at a 45 degree angle or in a vertical setting.

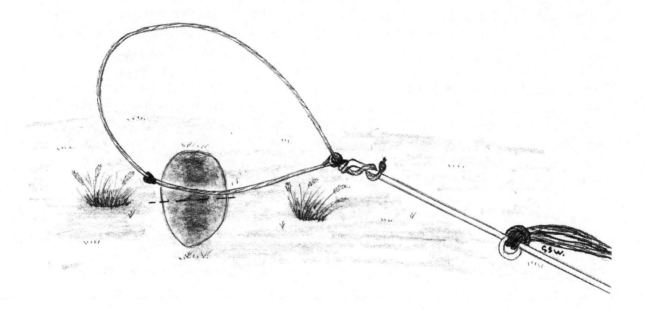

I have shown many rabbit snarers what was the cause of their problems. Many of them had become so frustrated by the sheer numbers of sprung and tripped snares which they were getting each morning, genuine lads who were trying their best but getting nowhere fast. The problem stems from the amount of books and articles written over the years where practically every scribe copies each other about setting small loops, between the beats and four fingers high nonsense. Another piece of nonsense that's written is about setting extra snares to compensate for the misses you get. Anyone who makes statements like this tells me straight away that they really know nothing about snaring, in my opinion they are incompetent snarers.

The reason I have drawn these articles and penned this information is to weed out the imposter and the so called snaring expert, remember it was experts who built the Titanic. If you set the snare the way I do you will have very few misses, over the years I've caught 97 out of a 100 (3 times) and over 190 out of 200 in the morning. I do not disturb the rabbits at night with a silly torch and I set no extras to compensate for misses. There are lads that I have taught over the years who can snare over 10,000 rabbits a season. Therefore I must have done something right.

So remember if you get small kinked nooses as shown in the earlier illustrations, set your snares up higher.

Rabbit tracks crossing a frozen canal in a hard winter to reach the bark on trees in a woodland planting.

Things to Avoid

1. Do not bury snares in a dung heap for two weeks.

2. Do not soot snares over a candle.

3. Do not set a big noose at a wide part of the run and a small snare noose at a narrow part of the run, this is utter nonsense.

4. Do not set runs only in the shadows of trees in the moonlight, (set them all)

5. A snare does not break a rabbit's neck as it bounds along a run, as some amateurs make you believe.

6. Do not set on large beats about 10 inches to 12 inches long with droppings on them, as the rabbits sit on them.

7. Another misconception is that rabbits can't be caught in a snare when hopping along an edge slowly, not in a small low set noose you won't!

8. Do not use 8 & 10 strand snares they are like tow rope, a 6 strand snare holds hares and even fox cubs.

9. Shop bought snares are poor quality design they are only half spun, bad for kinking and breaking with thin cheap twine that just rots.

10. Do not use tethering cords 12 inch long it's far too long and unnecessary.

11. Forget all about hops and trods as this is most confusing for beginners, just remember one thing. Set on a small beat and you won't go wrong.

12. Do not check snares 1hr after darkness, all you are doing is causing disturbance, check the snares only on the following morning, giving the rabbits peace, unless there is a bad fox problem or control the fox first, set some good rabbit runs with fox snares also to eliminate this problem.

Chapter 2 - The Right Snare

The pegged snares pictured in all the sets and illustrations throughout this book are all handmade by myself. The originator of this type of design was one of my old mentors Andrew Whyte, a professional rabbit trapper now 86 years of age. A lot of thought went into the snare system as it's specially designed and in my opinion there is no other rabbit snare can compare with it. It has the simplest and most ingenious swivelling system used to attach it to the wire tealer which makes it almost impossible for a rabbit or hare to pull it apart. On many occasions this snare system has held full grown adult foxes. The snare is made in two different sizes to hold both rabbits and hares. The whole system and construction of this snare is designed to correspond to the target animal's size and weight, the length of the snare cable is such that when formed into a loop the diameter is perfect in size in comparison to the characteristics of the rabbit's head.

The brass snare cable is of the very best quality available, every snare loop, tealer, twine and tethering pegs are all cut and measured to the same length and size. It has a light tension set into the snare loop, the brass eyelet slightly cocked forward and sits straight with no right or left twist - this ensures that it's designed to close with relative ease and lightning speed. This is a very important feature in all types of snares to be set lightly so that the slightest pressure exerted on the noose will ensure an immediate response of instant closure. The actual swivelling system consists of nothing more than a double knot pulled together tightly on the end of the brass snare cable.

The tealer pin is made from galvanized steel fencing wire 2.5 mil in diameter and will not cut or damage the brass cable as there are no sharp edges. The eye of the tealer consists of two and a half turns of wire at the end of a tight right angle bend, the smooth wire turns of the tealer eye allows the double knot to swivel freely but unable to be pulled through the smaller diameter hole. Thus allowing free movement of the snare cable to centre itself in any direction it is being pulled by the animal in the snare which will ensure the proper maximum swivelling action.

The snare cable itself plays a most important part in the capturing of rabbits. It must be tightly wound but not over tight so as to make it too stiff and non-pliable when forming the loop. If the cable is slack and not wound properly it's soft and flexible, is weaker in strength and does not close as quickly which causes a lot of displacement of wire strands making the snare more prone to breakages and constant rewinding.

This snare design is most compatible with the animal it is made to capture, everything about it is geared for maximum efficiency from the loop to the tealer to the twine and the peg every single item is measured and cut to the exact details they look as if they were cloned. It is a complete balanced system that guarantees excellent results in the snaring fields. This system used in areas of high rabbit concentration catches of nine rabbits out of every ten snares set is not uncommon, that is why I use this simple and highly effective system.

Another addition that I added to my pegged snares was a large sized fishing swivel this component was added to the tealer pin just before its completion. The end of the twine attached to the securing peg was slipped through the other swivel eye and the peg was then dropped through the end loop completely securing the whole system together now making it a triple swivelling unit.

All my hare snares are made like this to help safeguard from kinking, it also helps take the strain of the snare noose and allows for 360° rotation allowing the animal freedom of movement in any direction.

Important first points, always use marker pins for every snare as to not lose track, also check snares at first light. Always use a marker pin to every snare so that you don't leave any behind.

Always use quality brass wire, do not use inferior brass wire as used in picture frame wire as it's too springy, snaps easily and is no use whatsoever to the experienced trapper.

If doing pest control in the summer months check your wires morning, afternoon and evening. If you have limited time and are unable to check on a regular basis, use another method of control to keep your trapping humane and reduce any risk of suffering.

Over the decades practically every writer who has penned an article on rabbit snaring has stated that the snare should be set at either a fist high or 3 to 4 fingers high, on an average man's hand a closed fist measures 3.5 inches high, they also often say that the snare should be set between the beats, they never mention the terrain, or the height of the grass or crops, or the time of the year, or the distance between the beats etc. By their shallow coverage and detail this tells me they have snared most of their rabbits from the comfort of an armchair in front of the fire. There is nothing more frustrating for the beginner than to follow these old fashioned instructions, then go out the following morning with great anticipation of a big catch and all he finds are knocked or tripped snares and maybe one or two rabbits caught more by luck than good skill. He then resets in exactly the same way and the same places in the hope of better things the next morning. This does absolutely nothing for a beginner's confidence and can be so frustrating to the point of making him give up altogether.

Colin 'Woodga' Woodhall with 52 rabbits from 100 peg snares in a single night.
Selkirk 2006

The Complete Pegged Rabbit Snare

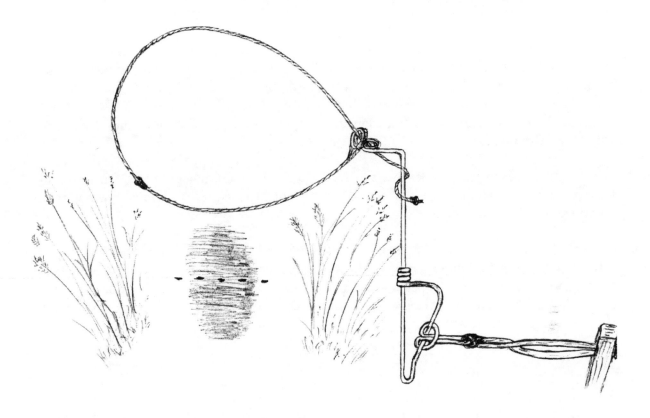

This illustration portrays a fully assembled and function professional pegged rabbit snare with the large 7.5" x 5½ " snare loop. The total length of the snare loop is 22½" long which consists of six strands of .457 diameter brass wire. The components of the brass consists of 70% copper and 30% zinc which makes a nice strong soft pliable wire to be used to spin up and form a nice noose. When spun the six strands of snare wire must be twisted into a nice firm cable - do not over tighten the cable otherwise it becomes hard with a brittle feeling about it with no stretch or play to it. It feels rough to touch and practically unworkable when it comes to setting the tension into the loop and shaping it - due to its rigidity it will not perform well and breakages do occur. An eyelet can be inserted part way along the loop between the six strands of wire, three on either side before the wire strands are spun into a cable. This extra eyelet acts as a stop system fixed to the snare cable to prevent full closure of the snare loop.

I came up with an idea how to make cheap and every effective snare stops, using car brake pipe and a mini pipe cutter purchased from Screwfix for less than £4. The government recommends a 5" stop loop. In my opinion due to vast experience it's too small. I make my stops and place them on the cable at 6" along the snare cable from the running end eyelet. This larger stop loop increases animal welfare far better than a 5" stop loop which does cause rubbing on large winter rabbits over 5 to 6 lbs in weight where the 6" stop loop eliminates this problem altogether due to the larger diameter of the stop loop which leaves ample space between the rabbit's neck and the snare cable. There is no trauma around the animal's head that too has been eliminated. With the addition of the breakaway snare link I devised a number of years ago it too has totally eliminated woodland deer losing afoot due to necrosis due to a broken snare noose around a leg in an accidental catch by the foot.

The wire tealer system which stabilises and holds the big noose in place over the run is made from 2.5 mil galvanised fenceline wire. The regular tealer length is 9½" long to be used in normal conditions. When used in high flora tealers can be made to suit these conditions 10½"-11" long which is pure common sense due to the fact in higher grass, (and also where the beats are more distant), the rabbits are springing up and over the high growth to land on each beat. These can be up to 14" 18" to 2 ft apart depending on the height of the high standing flora at different locations. Therefore the snares must be set around ten inches high to the bottom of the loop to get results. Ask yourself this how are you going to catch rabbits in a silly little 4" noose set at four fingers high in growth almost wellie height ? You're not ! The sooner you waken up to this fact the better, get the snares up higher and your catch rate will increase dramatically.

For attaching pegs to snares baler twine is the cheapest strongest material to use. It's also waterproof and lasts for many years. To cut twines quickly I use a little template which is described in detail in Chapter 5.

Once all the twines have been knotted, insert the loop end through the peg hole and pull its full length through until double knot touches peg. Then make another knot in the double twine three-quarters way along from peg leaving a larger space to insert hammer shaft or wooden toggle through between the twines when uplifting the snares. When attached to the tealer pin the total twine length is 8" between peg and tealer. When using longer securing pegs twines will have to be cut longer also to suit longer tealer length between the grip and the top of tealer eye.

The securing peg can be cut any size from 6" heeling pegs to 8" average length, even to a foot long when snaring in soft ground, pure commonsense once again. Drill the twine hole in pegs one inch down from the top of peg, a 3 to 4mm hole will suffice. Remember to chamfer the top of snare pegs which helps repel water otherwise it will become damp and wet, then the peg top is liable to mushroom and will be prone to rotting and weakening. Another good tip here is to make a longer tapering point on your pegs due to the fact when inserting them into the damp ground the longer tapering point will slide down into the soil more tightly creating good suction for holding power. Do not cut a short snub point on your snare pegs for the simple reason is when hammering the pegs into the ground the blunt snub peg nose is forcing the soil down underneath the peg all the way down its full length instead of cutting through the soil which is clinging to the longer tapered peg as it slides into the soil tightly like a glove all the way down its full length, as I've said before, giving greater holding power due to the tight suction created.

The snare tealer is placed to the side of the run with only the large snare loop sitting over the middle of a small beat with the striking curve sitting in the middle of the bottom wire of the snare loop ready to take a rabbit under the chin when it travels along the run. Notice the twine between the tealer and the securing peg is straight but not over-taut allowing no play in the system which is sitting tensioned from the loop to the tealer to the twine and the peg. The whole system is tensioned ready for the strike as the strain is taken immediately a rabbit hits the noose. This is how a high catch rate is attained if you set your snares in this manner.

This next illustration shows how to carry your snares. Slip all the snare pegs through the loops from the same side, this keeps your snares neat and tidy when carrying them on your arm and stops any entanglement. My snares are all tied and hung up in bundles of 25 making for easy carrying, counting, setting, lifting.

The pegs seen in this illustration is made from elderberry, it is 6 inches long, 3/8 of an inch thick and approximately 1 ¼ inches broad. This little peg is a heeling peg used out in pasture grass, it has great holding power and once inserted into the ground, being broad and flat, it does not turn in the ground.

Elderberry pegs can also be made 8 inches long and this type of wood is most common in the countryside. Once cut into logs of the desired length and stripped of its bark it is easy to split and work with. The beauty of this wood is that once the pegs are cut, shaped and left to dry, they become hard as iron and very light to carry. My friend Woodga uses elderberry pegs on a regular basis. The normal pegs I use are made of ash and are cut half and inch square by 8 inches long. They are strong and robust and last for many years.

The parts of a Large Loop & Tealer pegged snare

The illustration opposite shows the elements of a professional pegged snare

A Professional size noose, 7 ½ inches by 5 ½ inches

A1 Copper snare stop

B The striking curve is dead centre of the big loop to sit over the middle of the small beat, to take the rabbit cleanly under the chin.

C Double eye of the tealer pin.

D Neck of the tealer pin

E Double knot in the end of the snare wire to act as a simple, but highly effective swivel system under the double eye of the wire tealer when a rabbit is caught.

F Shaft of tealer made from 2.5mm thick galvanised wire, not high tensile. English Tinsley is the best if you can get it.

G The grip with which to push the tealer into the ground in a vertical position, to hold snare loop at the proper height.

H Double knot in baler twine three quarters of the way along from peg allows excess space to slip a wooden toggle or hammer shaft through when extracting snare peg from the ground.

I Waterproof baler twine - cheap, reliable and very strong.

J Ash snare peg to secure the complete snare in the ground. Length can be cut to suit various types of ground.

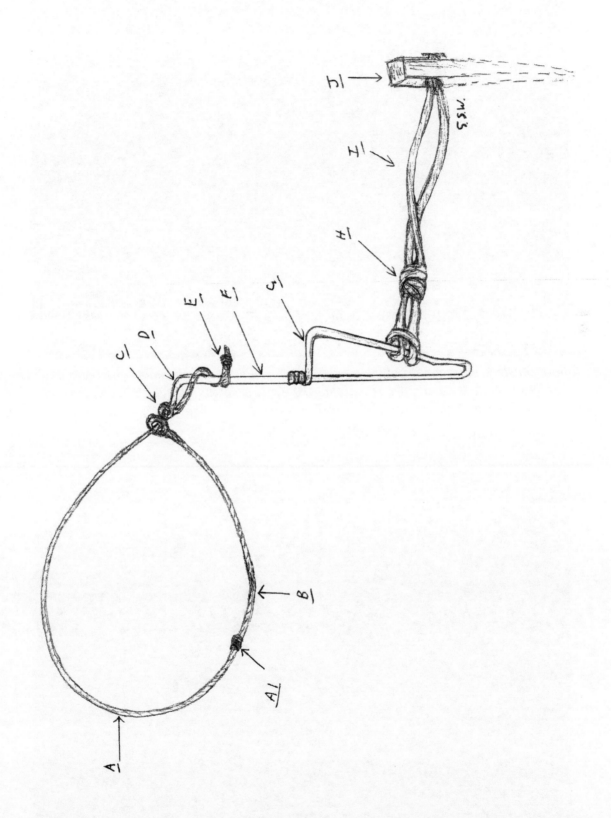

A fully constructed pegged rabbit snare set over a small beat, seen under the bottom of the snare loop. Note the extra swivel and that the twine is straight between the tealer and the securing peg- tensioning the whole system from snare loop to peg, ready for a strike. Snaring like this allows for a high catch rate.

Close up of the breakaway system in use.

Chapter 3 - The Right Size Loop

The illustration on the following page portrays the front elevation of a rabbit's head although the ears are not exactly vertical when travelling along a run the ears are up. This is where many authors and field sports scribes got it wrong, because everyone looked at a rabbit's head minus the ears attached to it. It's amazing the amount of people over the years who have told me that they didn't know that a rabbit runs with its ears up, (which they do of course), hence the constant use of the small 4" loop. They also forgot about the length of the whiskers across the face. It's almost as if it's been written in stone over the last century to set rabbit snares with a small loop at a height of three or four fingers to a fist high and usually to set between the beats which are all totally wrong. This is not just a national problem it's universal, how many times on the internet do you see video footage of people still setting silly little snare loops close to the ground and building stupid little stick fences to force the rabbit through - the simple fact is we have been shown and told how to do it wrong for decades.

Look at the size of a large adult rabbit and look at its head. It measures approximately 6" from under the chin and the whiskers, which are the sensors across the face, are 7½" long across the face. As I have said before there are locations where every rabbit weighs five to six pounds. Do you really think you are going to make large catches of rabbits of this size and weight with small 4" loops, at around a fist high? Whether they are set between beats which is the wrong placement, or the proper placement across the middle of the beat makes no different, there's absolutely no way. You won't even make a decent catch of normal rabbits at 3 ½ to 4 lbs in weights.

The big loop system is the way to go it's not nearly any means as the real old pro rabbit trappers have been using it over many decades, obviously for good reason they would not show anyone how to do it PROPERLY because they earned their living FROM SNARING

The noose size is 7 ½ inches across by 5 ½ inches deep.

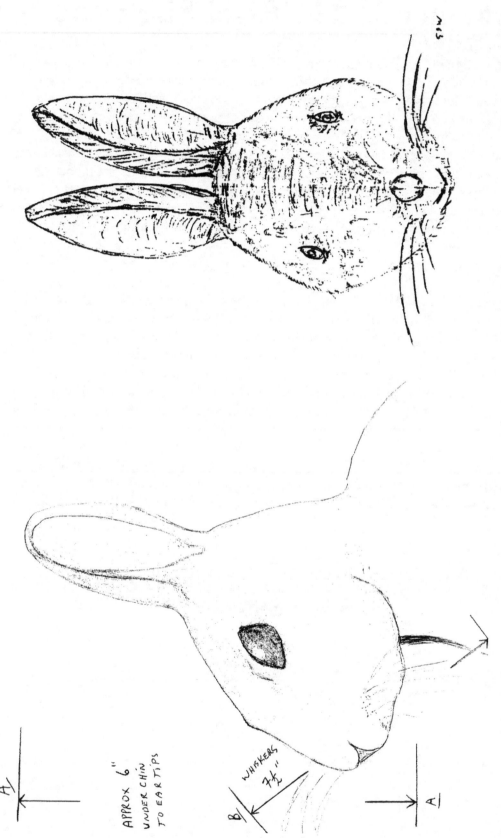

A rabbit has a large head and runs with its ears up. The height from under its chin to the top
of its ears is approximately 6 inches. The width of its whiskers is approximately 7½ inches.
Your snare loop needs to be large enough for this to fit!

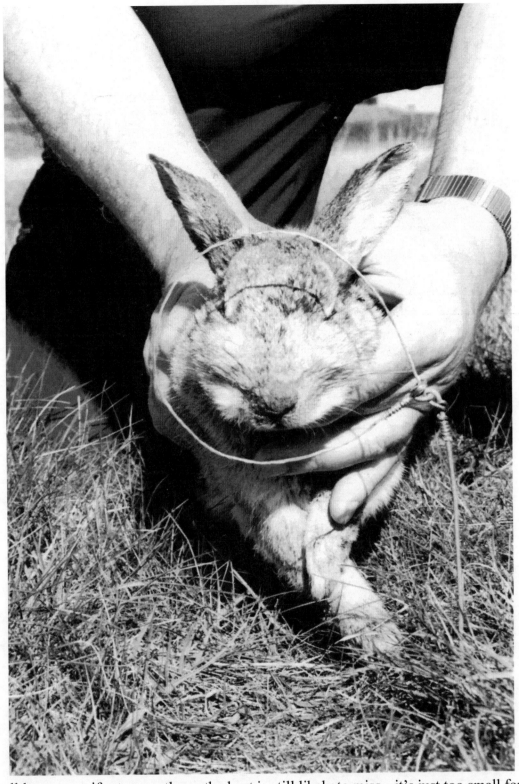

A small loop, even if set correctly on the beat is still likely to miss - it's just too small for a rabbit's head

Large Loop System

The illustration below shows the large loop system and how it correlates effectively with the dimensions of a rabbit's head. It shows a front elevation of how a rabbit is approaching the kill area inside the large noose, first of all the animal is looking through the loop not at it. The 5 ½" deep loop is the same measurement from under the rabbit's chin to the tops of the ears, the length of the loop correlates with the length of the whiskers which are the sensors across the rabbit's face, the size of this loop covers the run properly by itself allowing for any margin of error. Therefore taking any large rabbit travelling along a run with relative ease even in the wildest and darkest of nights as the wind sways the large noose to and fro it's still very capable in catching rabbits going on their outward travels and also when they are incoming.

Three main points to remember when snaring rabbits is to set across the middle of a small beat, with a large loop with the striking curve in the middle of the bottom of the loop, in conjunction with the proper height of the snare to the bottom of the loop whether set in pasture grass or in higher growth. The real old professional rabbit catcher who worked the large loop system over many decades like my old mentor kept very quiet about the effectiveness about this system as they earned their living at this game. Therefore no outsiders where shown how to snare properly, the amateurs were left to plod on still using the old traditional methods of setting with small loops low to the ground through no fault of their own. They had read so much false information on how to set snares over the years.

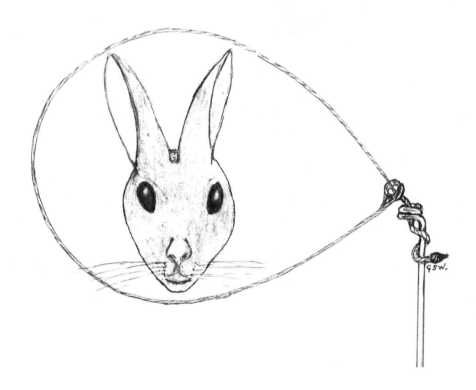

Advantage of Using a Longer Snare Noose.

First of all, before I elaborate on the illustration on the next page, the length of my completed snare nooses are 22½" long once fitted to the tealer pin and the double knot being formed at the end of the noose. This gives me loop size of 7½" x 5½" as mentioned before, these dimensions correlate with the characteristics of a large adult rabbit's head including erect ears and whiskers. On setting a location with higher types of flora when using 9½" tealers one must cock the snare loop upwards in a more elevated position. Due to this higher level of the snare you now lose the benefit of the striking curve normally situated in the middle of the bottom wire of the snare loop found in normal setting positions.

Many years ago Whyte said to me that you get more slipped snares and misses using a 24" long snare loop. I made fifty pegged snares with the larger sized noose and tried them. Whyte was right. What I did in future settings using these snares was to twist the end of the snare noose around the tealer shaft twice therefore reducing the snare loop back to its normal size. When working with the normal 22 ½" noose there is only one turn tightly around the tealer shaft . To compensate when setting in high growth make longer tealer pins around 11" long. This helps immensely as it is also pure common sense and it helps retain the striking curve on the bottom of the snare loop.

Look carefully at the illustration which follows on the next page. What you see here is a tealer pin of a normal length 9 ½ " length attached to it is a 24" snare loop with a double knot formed at the end protruding lightly from the tealer shaft. At the top of the tealer eye you will see around an inch or more protruding upwards before the actual formed snare loop, you may think that the loop has not been tensioned properly and that is has sprung partly closed but this is not so. As I have previously mentioned about using 24" long nooses on normal 9½" tealers you do get misses, if you remember I said to wind the end of the snare noose twice around the tealer instead of once to reduce excess wire length.

Well this is where you can put this snare to good use in fact making it dual purpose by winding the tail of the snare only once around the tealer shaft then using the extra length to gain more height for your snare loop. By holding the snare wire an inch or so above the tealer eye then forming and tensioning the snare loop it sits as seen an inch or so more in height and helps to retain in the striking curve in the bottom of the snare loop whilst still retaining a decent size snare loop, still capable of making good catches of rabbits.

When Whyte needed extra height at times he would take his little hand axe and cut out approximately a 3" square of turf with soil attached, place it beside the run , press it down slightly to stabilise it with his foot then stick the tealer into it to gain immediate extra height. All of these little tricks work well at different locations at certain times. It's just a case of putting a little thought into what you are doing to overcome small problems that occur now and again on the snareline.

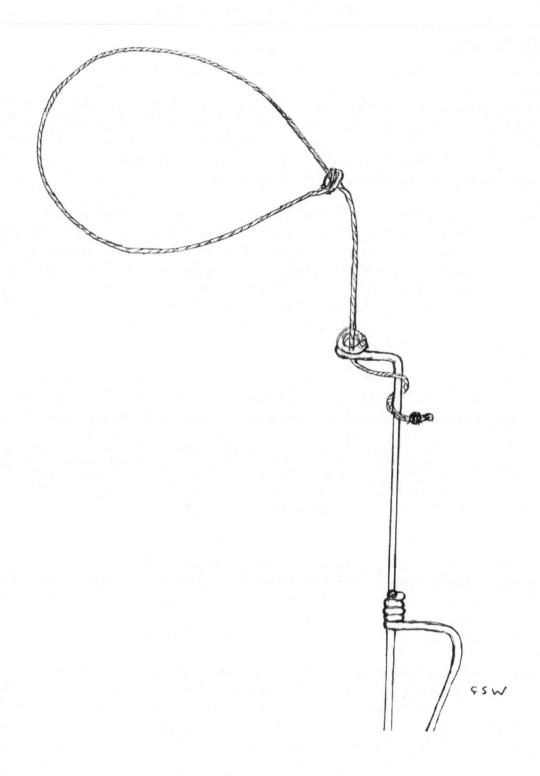

Chapter 4 - The Tealer

Snare Stabilizers

For a rabbit snare to function properly it must be set with the loop suspended over the run which an animal is expected to use on a nightly basis. Although the brass cable is firm and pliable it cannot provide enough support to hold the open snare loop in the proper catching position. Before the wire tealer came into use in the 1940s the main and most common type of snare support was made from natural wooden branches, hazel wands being the most favoured due to its suppleness strength and its natural straight growth. Prickers, as they were called, were cut to approximately 9" long and ½" thick, and sharpened at one end for easy penetration into the ground. The opposite end or top of the pricker was split with a knife to a depth of approximately an inch, so that the snare wire could be inserted into the split end of the stick and held tightly and firmly in position.

Although these natural prickers served the purpose well in their day they had a few faults, such as not being weatherproof. Being continually worked and set out on a daily basis and subjected to the ever changing elements they would dry out and the split on the top of the tealer would become slack and open, losing its tight holding ability. On occasions the trapper would have to search for it amongst the grass. To overcome this problem a single strand of snare wire was wound around the neck of the pricker making it a permanent attachment to the end of the snare loop. Set out in flat open ground the rabbits could see them especially in daylight hours and avoid them. In cold weather the rabbits would sit and chew on them.

Like in any profession we must learn to adapt and advance with time, if you don't you stay static. New and more modern materials are available and being produced therefore we must use them to our advantage if they are more suitable to our use. By far the most efficient means for supporting a snare loop and keeping it in position is to use galvanized wire. The main advantage in using wire is that it is supple enough to work with, stiff and strong enough to hold the snare loop at any required height and angle. It is also waterproof and weatherproof and can withstand all of the elements and continual abuse, it is cheap, light, non bulky, practically invisible when set and will outlast anything else and give you a lifetime of use. Wire snare stabilizers are called by different names in certain parts of the country, such as prickers, tealers, set pins, star pins etc.

The best type of wire to use when manufacturing them is galvanized steel fenceline wire, not the high tensile as this is too hard to work with. Just use the ordinary pliable wire which is more supple to work with there are different types of wire that can be purchased from various wholesale suppliers, such as farm supplies, ironmongers, builder supplies and fencing contractors. When purchased wholesale it is very reasonably priced like all items when the middle men are eliminated. My friend is a fencing contractor and a 1,000 meter roll is twenty pounds which will give a rabbit trapper a lifetime supply for his own personal use. The different types of wire that can be purchased are English, Italian and Spanish. The latter two are cheaper and softer, the galvanized coating tends to flake on occasions when twisting the tealer eyes and at the grip area when winding it round the stem of the tealer pin. The English wire is the best quality, the wire itself if 2.5mm in diameter it is a fraction thicker than the European wire which can be seen with the naked eye when comparing them together although they are also 2.5mm thick. The English manufactured wire does not flake when twisted and is of superior quality and strength, being far more robust which is most evident when it is being cut and twisted to make stabilizers. There are four various types of tealers that I have made and used over the latter years. The very first type I worked with was the single wire tealer which was devised by Willie McMaster one of my old mentors. It is a very simple device which can be made very quickly, a single eye loop is constructed at the top with a half inch loop twisted into the middle of the single stem of wire. McMaster used 3mm diameter wire; the tealer was 9½" long, the central half inch loop allows the twine to be attached firmly to the back of the loop catching the double wires together giving a more secure and stronger grip to hold the struggling quarry once captured.

The single tealer constructed with the 3mm diameter wire was strong and pretty robust allowing for easier penetration into hard ground, the thicker diameter wire was to give it a firmer grip and more stability and it worked very well but it also had a couple of faults which came to light. Due to continual daily use faults can be found with most working implements and tools. Being of a single wire construction and inserted into the ground it would on some occasions turn in softer type ground if the snare was knocked by a deer, birds or foxes. It would also turn when set in certain bare open areas void of any cover, especially when facing into a very strong wind. I have actually seen it happen when in the process of setting the snares. A large sycamore leaf blown by a strong wind and striking the snare noose would also turn the snare to the side. These latter faults have also been commented on by other trappers.

There are trappers who use this type of wire support today and retain good results. The earlier style of double wire tealer I used was constructed with thinner wire it was 9" long with a single eye loop the same as the single tealer, the bottom had a 4½" long narrow double base to which the twine was attached, when inserted into the ground the double narrow base penetrated quite easily and held the big snare loop in a very secure position and was very resistant to high wind force the only problem found was that it was prone to bending due to being constructed from a lesser diameter wire. Many trappers still use this type of tealer today.

The wire hoop is one of the simplest and most deadly forms of wire tealers ever to be constructed its design is simply a length of 4mm galvanized fence line wire cut into 44" lengths and bent into a U shape. There are no hard and fast rules on length, just cut the wire to suit the type of ground density. I use the normal type of pliable fence wire, although the high tensile can be used it's much harder to work with and it won't bend at all, once it has been inserted into the ground it takes a secure grip and is not affected by the elements, the double wire legs give it great stability and holding power more will be said later on the hoop snare the late Alex Chisholm another of my mentors taught me how to make and use the latter two types of tealers.

The most favoured tealer I use at the present time on my pegged snares was the brainchild of professional rabbit trapper Andy Whyte another of my mentors, to whom I am extremely grateful for sharing his vast wealth of knowledge with me. This tealer is constructed from 2.5 mil galvanized fenceline wire, I make them 9 ½ inches long with a double eye at the top on a small tight right angled bend with a straight shaft and a V shaped double base which narrows at the bottom for easier ground penetration. This tealer is strong and very robust and strong. It can hold larger creatures than which it was designed and intended for such as hares, foxes and cats, it will take extreme abuse and last a lifetime the same as the wire hoop. Remember the wire stabilizer is a very important part of the snare system, many people do not realise this and fashion their tealers out of thin cheap materials. If you skimp on good material you are selling yourself short.

A good tealer pin constructed from the proper wire when inserted into the ground firmly is secure and allows no slack or movement to take place. It holds the big loop at the proper height and position ready to take the immediate strain once the intended quarry strikes the loop. On occasion I have heard people speak of using bicycle spokes from old wheels, do not use these spokes for snare tealers, for starters they are far too thin and will not give proper stability to hold a snare loop in position. The wire of these spokes are as hard as iron and absolutely useless to work with, use the 2.5 mil English galvanized fenceline wire if you can get it, as I have said it makes an excellent snare support which is just perfect in every way for the job it is required for and will stand any amount of daily abuse with a lifetime's use. To make good snares use good materials to construct them if you want top class results out in the snaring field. In this game good quality handmade snares are a must for beginner and professional alike; they are a pure killing machine. Treat your equipment with care and check them over after every operation and the snares will never let you down.

Benefits of the Adapted Single Tealer System

What you see here is a drawing of a large sycamore leaf and an ash stem with leaves attached. These items can be a nuisance when snaring in fields around woodland, especially when using the single wire tealer system in windy and blustery conditions. Where the peg snares are set out and the big nooses of the snares are being constantly buffeted by the windy conditions, these large leaves and stems are also blown around regularly striking the large snare loops. This causes the single wire tealer system to be turned in the ground so that the big snare loop is now facing parallel along the run rendering the snare loop ineffective and unable to make a catch. To combat these types of conditions I developed a single tealer with a cast in the wire near the base. This tealer has a dual purpose - it is 10 ½ inches long and works well in firmer ground conditions and good for snaring in high grass. When snaring in normal pasture grass the tealer is pushed into the ground until the underside of the central wire loop touches the grass this gives you the true height of the snare loop to catch rabbits in these locations - 6 ½ inches high to the bottom of the loop.

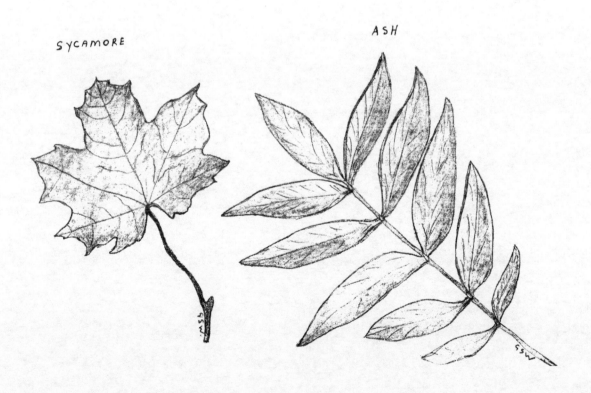

SYCAMORE   ASH

Different Types of Wire Tealer

The simple wire tealer has been made and used in many different forms, although the basic principles have stayed the same. These are examples (shown opposite) of different styles which I know of.

1) An old Scottish type of wire tealer devised by Tam Stratton of Perthshire. It is made from thinner 1.5mm diameter galvanised wire.

2) A single tealer devised by Willie McMaster, my old mentor. Willie made these tealers 9 ½" long from 3mm galvanised fenceline wire and they had good stability.

3) This tealer I devised myself. It is made from galvanised 2.5mm semi-high tensile wire and is 10.5 inches long. It was designed to set in high grass in harder type ground but is dual purpose. It's good for beginners as it gives the exact height in pasture grass when pushed into the ground in a vertical position until the base of the centre loop touches the ground. Just tweak the snare loop slightly up or down and you have the perfect height of 6 ½ inches in pasture grass. The cast in the bottom stops the tealer from being turned in the ground when struck by windblown objects e.g. leaves, stems or ends of thin branches

4) The Figure 4 tealer made from 2.5mm galvanised wire, devised by A. Whyte another mentor of mine.

5) This type of tealer was used up around the Dundee Kirriemuir area. This was a short tealer, 8.5 inches long and made from 1.5mm berry wire, (the wire used between posts to support raspberry canes). The end of the snare loop was pushed down through the double eye and tied onto the loop on the shaft. In my opinion it was a silly idea as it wasted wire that could have been used to make the snare loop larger, which makes the snares catching ability far more productive. I wouldn't have used it.

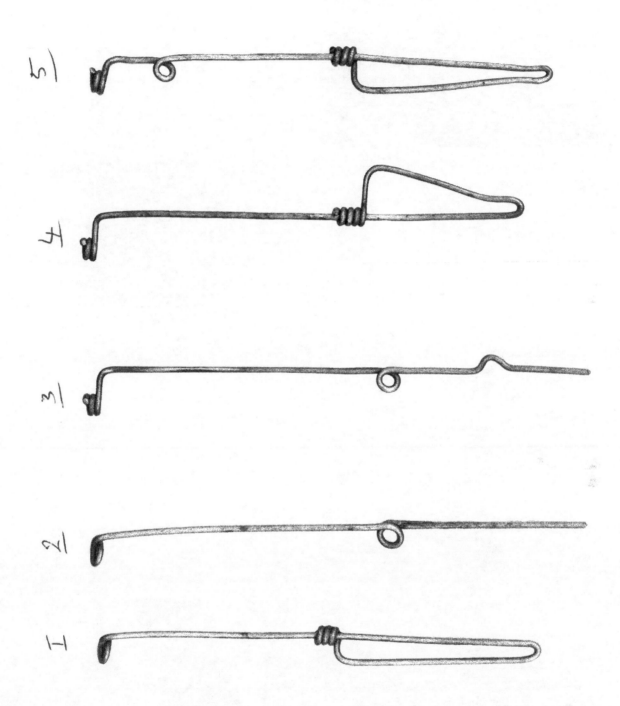

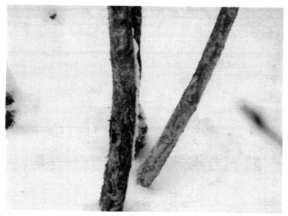

*Rabbit damage to ash trees and a rose
bush by stripping bark in a hard winter*

Chapter 5 - The Peg & Twine

Securing Pegs

Like any device designed and meant to hold an animal, a snare must be properly secured in place and this is particularly important to remember when setting rabbit snares. The movement of an animal captured and restrained in a snare is somewhat restricted by the wire around its neck. But an animal caught in a pegged snare out in open ground, where entanglement is impossible, has the full use of body weight and the power of all four feet to fight against the snare and its securing system. This must be remembered and taken into consideration. Take for instance a good prime adult winter rabbit around 5 lbs caught in a snare but due to the length of twine plus the length of the tealer and snare wire it will be at least two feet in length away from the central securing point. Now take into consideration its body weight and the speed in the opposite direction of your approach. The quarry now has a total distance of four feet to travel away from you in the opposite direction; two feet in length to the securing point and two feet past it. So take the total mass and speed and distance and strike of four feet covered and that rabbit when it hits the end of the total length of the snare puts a fair bit of shock and tension all the way down the whole system to the peg, which must always be embedded securely to retain the quarry.

There are various types of ground densities in various locations and different parts of the country, therefore securing pegs come in various shapes, lengths and different types of wood to suit each individual trapper's personal choice. Natural wooden securing pegs are generally most preferred due to an ample and readily available supply from local woodland from which the professional will select to cut and fashion his pegs to the preferred and required shape. Many of the older generation of trappers used snare pegs made from elderberry or boon tree as it is referred to on occasion. The stakes were made from green freshly cut elder shaped like a wooden tent peg, the wood is easily cut and pared to the preferred length and shape with a sharp knife. After the latter requirements have been completed, the trapper will store them to dry and harden up.

Chisholm used a lot of elder wood as he worked with a thousand snares, when the pegs were dry they became very tough and resilient, and lightweight which made the snaring operations easier when setting hundreds of snares in a day. Chisholm pegs were of an unusual design, they were cut six inches in length and shaped like a commando dagger blade an inch and one quarter broad and a half inch thick this flat pointed peg had great holding power in grass fields and would not turn in the ground once they were inserted. McMaster used larch pegs seven and a half inches long. They were cut from the lateral branches on the trees with a hand axe or they would be selected and cut from the branches that had been trashed by the foresters. With a razor sharp little hand axe Willie would cut, shape and shave the bark of the pegs in no time, right there and then in the woods using an old log left behind after felling for support. The overall finished pegs would all be cut to the same length of seven and one half inches long, slightly less than three quarters of an inch thick, chamfered at the top to repel water, with a neat long tapering point and straight as an arrow. They were so neat the pegs looked as if they were cloned. When left to dry naturally, the larch peg was smooth, round and neat and very hard, also a smooth peg retains practically no soil on it being pulled from the ground. Old Willie Mac as he was known to everyone was clever and extremely knowledgeable and a top class rabbit and fox trapper, he used to say to me *"keep it simple son"*, he was right as his pegs were all cut there and then in the woods with no cuttings or wood chips to clear up behind him, he only had to drill a hole for the twine once the pegs were dried.

Hazel pegs are also widely used south of the border, they will be more favourable as the trees seem to be more abundant down south and more readily available. The hazel sticks grow very straight and make easy cutting and many can be gathered in a short time. I have never used hazel pegs due to its scarcity in our locality although I used ¼" thick hazel wands which are supplied to me by Phil Day when he visits. These thin hazel sticks are used as marker pins to each snare. I have found due to continual use out in the fields the weather conditions take their toll as they are constantly getting wet and drying out they peel and become brittle and snap. Phil told me that they were prone to splitting at times when being hammered into the ground.

Ash is one of the most popular woods used in the country for the manufacture of snare pegs. It is one of our common woodland hard woods that is readily available to trappers. Although I have split green ash logs for snare pegs up to a hundred can usually be obtained from nine inch diameter log but my old mentor Andy White a professional rabbit trapper of 84 years of age also a very clever and knowledgeable man in this profession taught me a lot about ash. He showed me a tree that he had felled and cut into seven foot lengths - it was matured and between forty and fifty years old and straight as a dye. The lengths of mature ash were left until the month of August when they were put into a trestle then measured exactly 7½" long and cut into perfectly straight logs with the chain saw. The logs were then split with a large heavier felling axe into quarters, then into smaller sliced sections to be finished into neat pegs with a small hand axe. The grain was absolutely beautiful in these older mature logs and they split perfectly straight - at this moment I have a thousand of these ash pegs cut and ready for use with chamfered tops and nice tapered points. Once matured and dried the ash pegs are quite light and very hard and strong and they can stand a lot of abuse and last a long time. My Thorr Number Two hammer with the rolled hide at both ends of the head is ideal for knocking in snare pegs and causes no damage to them at all. In my opinion the ash makes a good all round snare peg that is totally reliable and will penetrate extremely hard ground.

All tools regardless of what job they are designed for have their strengths and weaknesses. Always construct them with the best available materials that can be acquired. Wooden snare pegs are nationally employed throughout the United Kingdom for staking and securing rabbit snares and there are a few tips I would like to share with you about snare pegs. First of all as I have previously mentioned a smooth round peg holds very little soil on being extracted from the ground. But it does have a fault of being pulled from the ground in wet weather conditions, especially when operating snares out in web stubbles and softer ground because the snared rabbit runs around in a circle tugging and pulling at the snare. Even more so if the quarry is caught in front of the hips it has more leverage and a stronger more effective pulling power gaining from all of its four feet on the ground. Due to these actions the top of the peg hole widens out considerably like the top of an ice cream cone and occasionally a peg will be pulled free from the ground. This can also happen when inserting a peg into the ground and the peg being diverted at an angle due to it striking a hidden stone, so always check that your peg is secure by giving it a couple of tugs to make sure it is properly embedded.

A peg with a longer tapering point holds better in the ground than a peg with a blunt short snub tapered point, when the ground is moist the longer tapered pointed peg cuts into the ground pushing the soil up tightly to the sides of it making a nice tight fit all round and the suction holds the peg firmly. A blunt thick tapered point packs the soil all the way down in front of it. When the ground becomes and dry and parched watch the weather forecast for rain coming and lift your snares. If you don't you can lose quite a number of them if it rains heavily through the day or even a heavy downpour for a few hours at night you will find that the securing peg will pull freely from the ground usually with a small clod of dirt clinging like a doughnut around the peg. When setting snare throughout the summer months in dry hard ground I use my steel bricklayer's double edged line pin to break the hard top surface of the ground. I knock it in at a vertical angle then I insert the peg and hammer it in this helps protect the points of the snare pegs once again lift the snares if rain is forecast.

Some trappers will heel their pegs in with their foot but a lot of pegs will angle instead of a straight insertion, again snares can be pulled out, so I always use a hammer which is safer. If a snare is pulled free check along the woodland fence line or if the perimeter is a dry stone dyke (or wall) check both sides, as the peg can become jammed between the stones, sometimes the rabbit will get through the front of the wall and stuck at the back so check both sides. Many times they will be resnared with the first snare trailing from their neck. All my own snare pegs are cut square to ½ an inch square and to a length of eight inches.

Do not use soft white wood for pegs as it just splinters and breaks. Always chamfer the edges at the top of your snare pegs to repel any water in wet and damp weather. Check all snares over after every snaring operation and repoint any snare pegs with a splayed point, drill the twine hole <u>no less</u> than 1 inch down from the top of the peg.

Phil Day, with over 150 rabbits snared in one morning using my method.

Elderberry logs cut and shaved ready to cut into pegs.
When dried out they are very light, robust and become every bit as hard as ash.

Professional Rabbit Snaring

Wooden Snare Pegs

The illustration on the following page shows the four most common types of snare peg.

(A) This little heeling peg is made from elderberry wood, 6" long $1^1/_4$" broad and $^3/_8$" thick with the hold drilled one inch down from the top. Similar to the shape of a small commando dagger it also tapered from the centre of the blade to the edges making very streamline for the job required. It was Chisholm who introduced me to this style of peg in the seventies when he used to work a thousand pegged snares. The pegs made from elderberry were hard and very robust and extremely light to carry, important when working the amount of snares he was using. These little pegs held very well, when heeled or hammered into grassland in normal ground conditions, due to the suction caused by the dampness in the ground. Another benefit was the breadth of $1^1/_4$" - these pegs would not turn in the ground and took a good grip. Also with the longer tapering point they slid TIGHTLY into the ground giving great holding power.

Another wood which I discovered, that is practically made for snaring and are ready for use in minutes, is these little rolls of border fencing made from flat pointed mature bamboo. Used in gardens they can be bought in Poundland and also in Wilkinsons and they are $8^1/_2$" long. There are 28 pegs to the roll held together by thin wire, just cut the wire and the pegs fall out. Give them a little paring and smoothing you will have 28 pegs at your disposal ready to drill one inch down. I gave some to Colin when he came up to visit me and he has snared a lot of rabbits with them as mature bamboo is extremely hard and robust and a very tough material. Should anyone just want to make and keep only 25 pegged snares to catch one or two for the freezer buying a roll of bamboo edging for a pound will save you sawing logs and a lot of chopping. They are practically readymade and good in pasture grass.

(B) The McMaster larch pin peg, as described at the beginning of this chapter. It was McMaster who devised the single wire tealer with the central loop. He used 3 mil wire to make his tealers $9^1/_2$" long. The slightly thicker wire gave his snares better stability than the single 2.5 mil wire as he was well aware of the snares being struck by flying leaves, small twigs and ash stems when setting out in open ground in very windy conditions. A single snare tealer was prone to turning slightly if the loop was struck by some flying debris in high winds, stopping the noose from functioning properly making it non-operational.

(C) The ash peg is an all round favourite with the a majority of snaremen, mine are cut 8" long, chamfered at the top to stop if flattening and holding water which would eventually cause it to rot, so by chamfering the top helps repel water. They are half an inch square with long tapering points for good tight gripping power in the ground. The hand cut pegs have better gripping power than smooth sawn pegs. The ash is hard and tough once dried out and will last many years. Don't use coppice ash as it is really not good for quality pegs. Coppice ash are trees that have sprung up from old ash tree roots, they have a poor root structure and the centre of the trees at times are black in colour. What you want is a good ash straight tall and smooth around ten inches diameter - a nice mature tree. Ash trees are best cut in winter months December-January as the sap is down the pores are closer together, the fibres are harder you can feel the strength in the wood. It has a tighter and more firmer grain. In the summer months there is too much life in the wood. The pores are open with the sap risen therefore the fibres are much softer.
The best logs to keep for your self are the first five or six up from the tree base as the wood is more fibrous and stronger, due to the lower base taking the strain in strong winds over the

years. Another point to look for is to see if there is a nice pinkish hue in the wood, if so you've cracked it with a nice mature tree that indicates it has grown in ground with lime in it. If your tree is cut into five foot lengths do not go too high up near the branches. These five foot lengths should be covered at each end with a bag and kept in a dark cool place and no wind available to help stop spider cracking at the ends. They can be taken out months later and checked at the ends. If need be a couple of small slices can be cut with the chain saw from each end to remove any damage and to square the logs up. Then measure every 8 inches and cut straight through and neatly - not at an angle but straight. When hit with the felling axe this mature wood splits up into lovely slices just like cheese with a beautiful grain smooth as silk. Once cut into slices use the hand axe to cut and finish good quality pegs. Whyte taught me all about the ash, he had a sharp eye and his logs were all cut to exact perfection. Get yourself a chopping block made from a pine log around 16"-18" long a good foot in diameter you can sit out on the garden seat on a good day and chop hundreds of pegs while passing the hours - listening to the birds singing, giving you great satisfaction by making your own pegs and snares. I have snare pegs approximately 12" long for use up on the shale bings where they are needed and I keep 100 of these snares for his sole purpose. Therefore use a longer peg for soft ground conditions.

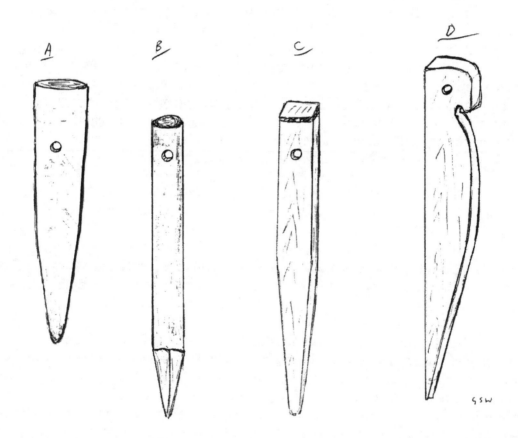

(D) This was the old fashioned type ash snare peg that was used for years with hazel tealers and hairy bender twine. The peg was approx 10" long and $^3/_4$" thick a heavy monstrosity that would look more at home staking out a marquee at a funfair. It would take an elephant and 40 troopers to carry a hundred of these snares, I often wondered to myself what size of rabbits these people were catching as these pegs would have held a lion. In all my years of snaring I never saw any of my mentors ever use an ugly snare peg of this size they were all sharp and very smart men. I'm afraid I would not recommend this size of snare peg for use.

Double Hitch Knot

(A) This illustration shows an old fashioned type snare peg.

(B) Shows the way the end of the twine was looped to attached it to the peg to stop it slackening off you can either turn the two loops back to back or one loop.

Some smart trappers cut and carried pegs with a similar notch to the one seen on this peg but their pegs were made from elderberry. Long and slim but extremely light to carry the elder dries extremely hard and makes a very robust peg cut the length of pegs you require to suit various types of ground.

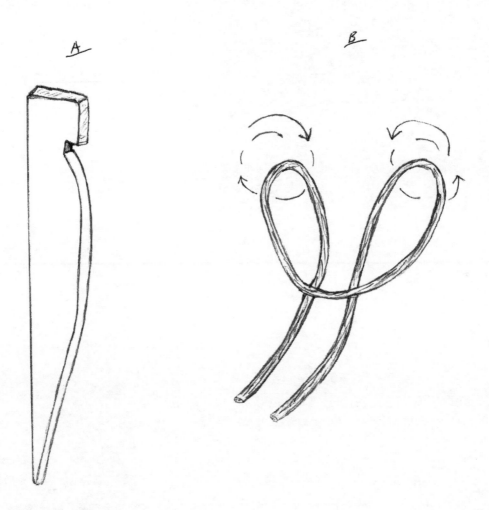

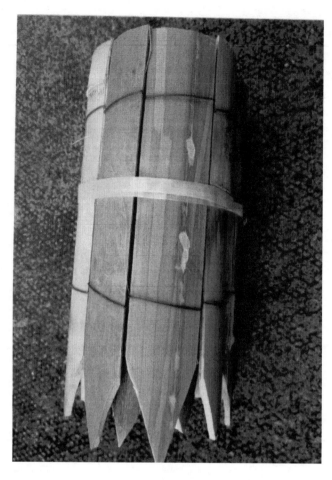

A roll of Bamboo edging from Poundland - approx 32 pegs can be made for the cost of £1

Finished and shaped bamboo pegs 8 inches long - light and robust in normal conditions out in pasture grass. Points heated to harden

Wet Ground Conditions -
A fault with round snare pegs

The illustration below shows a rabbit caught in a pegged snare but if you look carefully you will see a problem with the securing peg. Everything else is perfect except for the peg - it is a round peg. Now this is only a minor problem that occurs occasionally but I am mentioning this to help you the reader avoid it. My old mentor Willie McMaster told me about this problem 40 yrs ago as he snared with round pegs 7 ½ inches long. Old Willie Mac as he was known would take a little hand saw and a nice sharp little axe. He and I would go into a larch wood where Willie would select the lateral branches which protruded straight out from the tree trunk these laterals were sawn close to the trunk and cut to length. When we had the required amount we would sit on a fallen tree trunk then shave, point and chamfer every peg until we had a bag full. There was no cleaning up to do as this was all left on the woodland floor just a nice bag of clean pegs to take home to drill and twine them and hang them up in the shed until further use.

These larch pegs turned as hard as iron, in fact there is one or two still in my shed over 30 yr old. As I have already mentioned there was a minor problem with them which occurs when snaring out in wet stubbles what happens is this. The snared rabbit runs around in a circle and as it repeats this process the round peg starts to widen the top of the peg hole until it is around 2" to 3" diameter. The hole become like a cone shape and if the rabbit starts jumping upwards then it will pop the peg and escape. This is particularly likely when the trapper is checking his line in the morning and some of the rabbits start leaping around. When I encountered this I walked quickly down the line stepping on the pegs and dispatching the rabbits immediately. This problem can be solved by using a longer peg or an 8 inch broad flat peg like elderberry. There is another method that can be used to good effect using normal pegs should you encounter soft ground not just wet stubbles - it's called the tapping stick method.

Using a Tapping stick

This is a method shown to me by another old mentor of mine many years ago, the illustration below depicts a snare peg in a hole. This trick is used anywhere soft ground is encountered in fields or along hedge rows. Should the reader encounter a scenario such as this, where the ground feels a bit soft, I take my boot and firmly and gently push the ground downwards at the side of the run, next to a single beat to make it more firm and compact. Just to remind the reader, when I am setting out pegged snares once the peg has been inserted into the ground so far by the heel of the hand it is hammered into the ground so that the twine lies straight between the tealer and securing peg. But not over taught as to put strain on the tealer to pull it backwards from its vertical position. When the snare is set like this the whole system is tensioned from the noose to the tealer to the twine and the peg. The minute a rabbits head enters the noose the strain is taken immediately as there is no play or slack in the system. This is one of the secrets to making a high catch rate using pegged snares.

Now getting back to setting the soft ground the pegged snare is set in the exact opposite way. What you do before you insert the tealer into the ground is you must pull the twine right down to the very base of the tealer pin. Then you take hold of the securing peg and instead of pulling it out and away from the tealer pin you now insert the securing peg right next to the tealer then hammer the peg down to ground level. You now apply the tapping stick which can be round or square shaped to suit the trapper's personal need. The tapping stick is ¾" diameter or square so that it sits square and firmly on the top of the securing peg. Then hold the stick firmly and tap the securing peg right down into the hole, twine and all, until the twine feels slightly taught between the base of the tealer pin and the securing peg as shown in the illustration. Now well below ground level when a catch is made the twine helps take the strain from the peg due to it being pulled against the top edge of the hole.

My old mentor just used to hold the hammer head in his hand and knock the securing peg into the ground with the end of the hammer shaft. When I used this method to insert the securing pegs I found that it chipped the end of the hammer shaft, the hammer shaft also became very muddy and slippery, and your hands become dirty wet and cold. This is when I came up with the tapping stick method to eliminate the latter problems. The stick is made long enough to knock the securing peg right in to the ground to keep your hands clean.

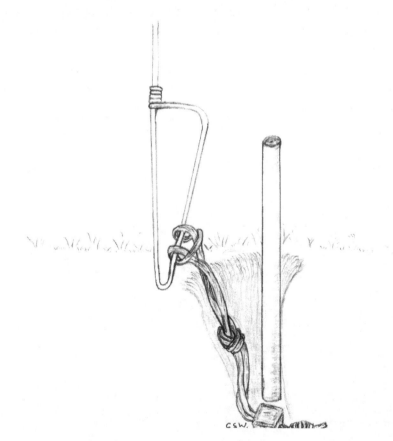

The Square Rabbit Peg

What you see below is an 8 inch long, square, tapered rabbit snare peg with baling twine attached. I have heard people stating that the twine between the tealer and the securing peg should be 12 inches long. This is pure nonsense and I often wonder to myself how much snaring have these people really done? First of all to twine an 8 inch peg as seen, you must cut your twines 24 inches long, then double them and tie a knot with the two loose ends. Then feed the loop through a 2.5mm hole, drilled 1.25 inches down from the top of the peg. Pull the twine all the way through until the knot stops at the back of the peg as shown.

Now go three quarters of the way along the twine <u>from</u> the peg and make a second knot in the twine leaving a larger opening between the twines to slip either your hammer shaft or a 4 inch wooden toggle, half an inch in diameter, through behind the knot so that you can pull your securing peg more easily from the ground. Now that you have made two knots in the baling twine you will notice that the looped end of the twine is hanging an inch below the peg. This is all that is required. You now slip the looped end of the twine between the base of the double wire tealer (or through the central loop of the single tealer), feed the peg back through the loop in the twine and pull tight. This leaves enough length in the twine to pop the peg through the bottom of the snare loop for easy carrying and eliminating any entanglement of the pegs.

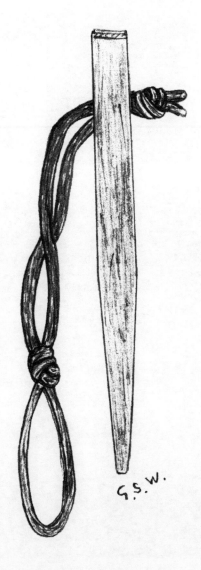

Ash pegs with baler twine. Although orange is more common the black has many benefits. It is harder to see, is less effected by the UV rays of the sun and rabbits never seem to chew it.
Melted ends of the knots stops the twine from fraying, keeps them nice and tidy so that they don't fill with mud and dirt.

Snare Twine

The twine also plays an important part in the construction of a fully made up pegged snare, to hold the snare together between the securing peg and the wire tealer pin. Many people still view a snare in the image of the old traditional method with the wooden hazel tealer, old rough hairy binder twine and a big cumbersome type tent peg, which some carried as parts separately and assembled them in the field. Could you really imagine trying to set a few hundred snares in a day, working like this? There are still a few of these old romantics who live in the past and still can't see past their antiquated methods. Anyway traditional snares like the latter have had their day. But like the old enemy father time we must move on and advance, therefore we must use modern materials that are available which are far more suitable for the job instead of old twine which rotted and shrank.

We now use modern baling twine which is very easily acquired, for free, it's very strong and also waterproof and stands up to the elements very well and can last for years. The best baling twine ever used was the black coloured twine, McMaster used this stuff on all of his snares and it was he who gave it to me. The beauty about this twine was its colour and thickness as it became soiled and weathered it was hard to see, making it ideal for snaring as it blended into the surroundings very well and non-attractive to prowlers. Another great advantage the black twine had was that it was unaffected by the ultraviolet rays of the sun, there was no killing off the stuff except for an occasionally fraying through continual use. Alas like any good product they never seem to last on the market, when my old friend died I inherited a half bag full of the coveted twine. I travelled around many farms in my quest for more of the stuff, they either had none or had gathered it up and burned it, all that were available were the red and blue colours. Another great feature about the black twine was that the rabbits never seemed to chew it, it seems the latter twine can be purchased practically in any colour except black and dark green or brown. Phil Lloyd my good friend from Hayling Island managed to pick up a couple of part rolls of black for me one day at an outdoor market. Another English friend called Alan Salmon sent me a couple of part rolls that he also purchased from a similar market down south, but as the saying goes all good things come to an end sooner or later.

Now I have no option but to use the red baling twine which a farmer friend gave me two brand new balls which contains miles of twine. Although it is a nice 3mm thickness and strong and also waterproof it's not as good as the black coloured twine, especially against the sun and seems to bleach a lighter colour. Also the rabbits appear to be attracted to the red colour and will sit and chew it, sometimes one strand of double twine is nipped clean through, although the rabbit is still held. On occasions they chomp clean through the two strand and escape, other times the two strands are partly chewed and on approaching the captured rabbit it gives a last lunge and breaks the twine and is free. To help avoid this happening I take each twine and rub a handful of dirt up and down it to darken it and it seems to work. It also helps to camouflage it as red coloured twine is more readily seen than the black colour. I totally hate the blue coloured twine which would have to be a last resort I'm afraid.

When assembling hundreds of twines for attachment to snares I do not sit around and measure each one individually as this would be a most laborious task and time consuming work for any self respecting trapper. To make the twines quickly I have a length of wooden strapping fourteen inches long, ¾" thick and 2" broad with two 4" nails protruding from the wooden strap 12" apart. Each nail is hammered through 1" from each end and I marked one end with an X.

I then tie a loose single knot and slip it over the nail at point X which is held in my left hand and then with my right hand I then proceed to wind the twine in a clockwise fashion around the two nails until they are full. Counting each full turn at the same time to give you the correct number required, always finish at the nail marked X where you first started. After this process is finished you then take a large pair of scissors and cut through the snare twine at the end of each loop <u>at point X</u> three or four at a time. This process only takes a few minutes and once the loops of twine have all been cut through at one end you will find their total length will be two feet long. To complete the process take a hold of each end of a single length of twine and put the two ends together the tie them into a secure knot do the same with every twine until the task is complete.

The next step is to select a snare peg which has already been shaped dried and drilled with a $^3/_{16}$" hole one inch from the top end. You now take hold of the twine and insert it through the peg hole and pull it through until the end knot in the twine is tight against the peg. Once this has been done, make another knot in the twine three quarter way along <u>from</u> the peg so that there is a smaller sized loop in the end of the twine. Once every peg has received a length of twine and completed in the latter fashion they can be hung up in bundles of twenty five until they are required. The reason for making the second knot in the twine three quarter way along from the peg, is that this gives the trapper a larger space to slip the shaft of his hammer into, or his little ash toggle whichever one he prefers to use when pulling his snare pegs from the ground. Long twines on a pegged snare look terrible and there is no need for this, assuming all your snare nooses, tealers, pegs and twines are all cut and made to the same length and size, as they should be, the snares have a real professional look. The twine length should only lie long enough to clear the point of the peg once it has been looped round the tealer pin slipped through the small end loop to complete the snare. The total length of the twine will now be around 8½" long between the tealer and peg.

I have watched people setting snares, even a professional, with 12" twines between tealer pin and peg which is far too long. They hammer their securing peg into the ground first then proceed to wind all the extra length around and around the tealer then set the snare, continually repeating this same stupid process until all of their snares were set. All they had to do was insert the tealer, setting the snare first, then pull the peg back and hammer into the ground. On showing these people the error of their ways they looked in amazement at their stupidity and would say *"I never thought about it that way"*. Why give yourself extra laborious work when it can be avoided with a little forethought. 12" long twines are not needed between tealer and peg, it's too long on normal 8"pegs. Should you have longer pegs at approx 11" to set in softer ground then the twine will have to be longer so that the longer peg can be slipped through the end of the twine when attaching it to the tealer pin.

Another silly thing to do is to take a length of twine and push one end through the peg then through the base of the tealer pin and tie a knot leaving just a circle loop holding them together, should a rabbit bite through the twine it's gone in a heartbeat, also it looks so amateurish, which it is in my opinion.

Adding a swivel either homemade or a 4-0 fishing swivel in conjunction with the double knot gives good freedom of movement in the whole system and takes the strain of the noose. Although the double knot system is a very efficient swivelling system I keep a few snares with extra swivels attached. In the old Scottish double wire tealer pin where the snare noose was attached permanently to the tealer pin, McMaster taught me how to make small simple swivels to the attach to the double base of these tealers which helped to extend the life of the snare noose due to it being permanently attached it was simple but effective.

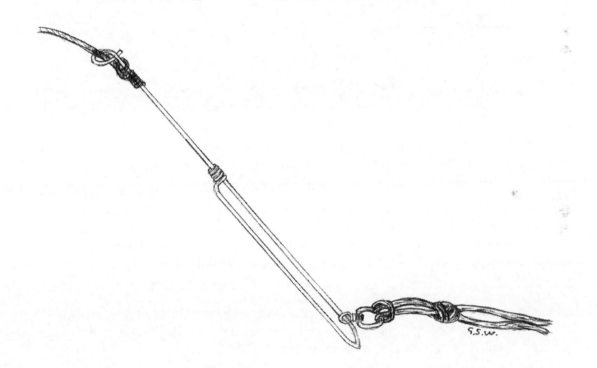

Rabbit Snaring Without A Peg

In this method the tealer is held in position with a double wire tealer attached to an oval quick clip ring and a large fishing swivel, held fast with a narrow wire hoop.

The hoops consist of a 16" length of galvanised 4mm fence wire, bent into a tight U shape, 8" long. This simple system is excellent for the person who only wants to set out a dozen or so snares to catch a few rabbits. It saves cutting wooden pegs. A dozen tealers with nooses attached can be slipped into a inside pocket or small bag and the wire hoops placed in a separate pocket with shaped tops upwards for an easy withdraw from ones pocket.

Just insert tealer into the ground, so that the big noose sits over the middle of the small beat, then slip a wire leg of hoop through swivel eye and push it into the ground so far. Then use the heel of your boot to push it right down to secure the whole system, this type of snare is good in grass fields. The narrow hoops can be made a bit longer if required. I have used the wire hoops system to secure the mink traps on many occasions over many years. It's extremely simple and effective, the swivel allows a 360 degree rotation, they can be set quickly and lifted quickly by slipping a small snare toggle through the tealer under the thumb grip and extracted in seconds.

Chapter 6 - Peg Snare Variations

The New Breakaway Rabbit Snare

The Breakaway rabbit snare was devised by me, (G.S Waters), to stop woodland deer losing a foot when accidently foot snared. This could happen whilst a trapper is controlling rabbits that are causing damage to young trees in woodlands and plantations where deer are prone to be present. Another factor that was taken into consideration was accidental snaring of domestic pets such as small house dogs and prowling cats. Therefore I had to find a breakaway that would hold all of the rabbits and release larger animals from domestic cats upwards.

Whilst discussing this system with my friend Woodga we took into consideration the numbers and the weights of wild rabbits. The average adult weighs three and a half pounds, but in some areas big winter rabbits go to six pounds in weight. I once snared 140 winter rabbits from woodland and they weighed from 4.5lbs to 5.5lbs. I have taken them at the six pound mark and Woodga has certain locations on his ground where he has taken them on the six pound mark also. Another crucial point considered was that this type of pegged rabbit snare system with the double knot that acts as a swivel can account for up to thirty rabbits before the noose needs to be replaced. This depends on the beating and abuse that the noose has taken, such as occasional kinking and an odd broken strand. The snare loop must be replaced with a new noose should this fault occur.

All these factors had to be considered when testing this breakaway system, therefore the breakaway system had to withstand the pulling power and shock of each and every rabbit and still remain strong enough to hold every rabbit caught and only release heavier non target species, from domestic cats upwards.

The first breakaway system I made was of galvanized wire 1.65 mil, it was thin but just too strong. There was also the problem of oxidisation between the galvanized wire and the ends of the brass wire loops. Next a thinner copper wire 1.35 mil was tried but was just too thin and Woodga, who was doing the test, phoned to say that the adult rabbits were just hitting the end of the snare and were gone, not even a mark left on the grass. The next size I used was 1.75 mil copper S hook. This was the business; it held rabbits but <u>released</u> five fox cubs and one adult. These cubs were out hunting for themselves and a good size. A smaller diameter copper type wire that Woodga purchased and that worked well also, the beauty of the copper is that it dulls to a nice dark brown, blends in well with the weathered brass snares, and does not cause oxidisation to the brass snare wire, they are very compatible.

In the end copper was found not to be consistent therefore I now use 1.6mm galvanised wire. I make a few hundred at a time then boil them for half an hour with tea bags and allow to cool naturally.

The permanent fix stop added to the snare loop is only a simple brass snare eyelet spun into the snare cable this prevents full closure of the snare loop. This stop system was taught to me almost 40 years ago by one of my old mentors "Willie McMaster" or "Willie Mac" as he was known to everyone. The stop eyelet is attached to the snare cable 5" long from the end eyelet of the snare. The latter measurement is taken from the outside of each eyelet, the stop eyelet is just inserted between the strands of snare wire, three on either side of them spun up into a nice firm cable.

There is a point I would like you to note, when using a brass eyelet as a stop, check the type of eyelet that you have purchased as some of them have an even smooth eye on either side, these are fine but if your going to use the ones that have larger dished face on one side and the smaller smooth face on the other side, make sure that the SMALLER and smoother face lies in the middle of the noose as it lies more flush and level with the cable and has more flush level feel to it and more animal friendly. Always keep the larger rim of the stop eyelet to the outside of the cable, this stop system eliminates any trauma around the head of the rabbit, and allows any birds to be released, should they accidentally get caught.

I have now adopted a copper stop in place of the 'stop' eyelet which is more easily applied to the snare than the 'spun in' eyelet.

The simple wire snare is a very cost effective device, used to control predators and rabbits, therefore to retain this system in the future we must lose our complacency and become more humane in our methods of control. That is why I devised the breakaway fox snare and the breakaway rabbit snaring system. We must have this vision to look ahead and safeguard our methods for the future fieldsports generations to come.

The 5 inch stop loop on the rabbit snares with the breakaway system is not recommended as it is too small and causes rubbing on large rabbits at 5lb plus in weight. I reported this to the Scottish government. A 6 inch loop is better and keeps hares alive - a hare will activate the breakaway and free themselves but in 6 inch stopped non-breakaway snares your hare is alive and well.

Remember :

> "*The wise man's eyes are in his head, while the fool walketh in the darkness*"

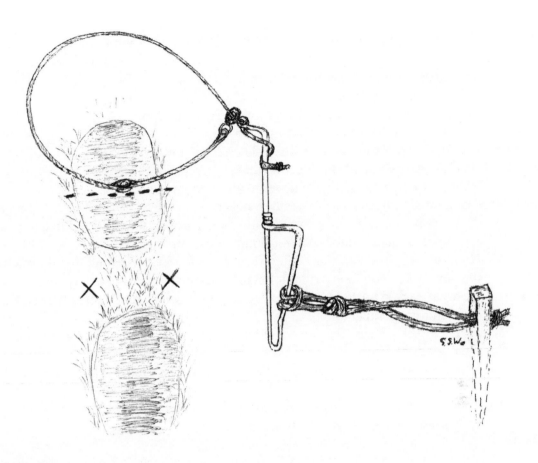

Snare Illustration

1. Shows professional snare system with the added components i.e. fixed stop also breakaway S hook. No slack in twine between tealer and peg.

2. Shows snare loop set in proper position over middle of small beat, dotted line shows exact position, set snare loop 6 1/2" high to the bottom of the noose.

3. X shows space in between beats, NEVER set snares at this location.

4. Many authors and fieldsports scribes also say to set extra snares to compensate for misses, which is unnecessary.

The New Improved G.S. Waters Breakaway Rabbit Snare

1. The most advanced humane rabbit snare in the UK.
2. It vastly increases animal welfare.
3. The new 6 inch stop length allows for a larger stop loop.
4. Full closure of the snare loop is now prevented.
5. Prevents any restriction of snare cable on the animal's neck.
6. PVC sleeve gives added protection and is more animal friendly.
7. Rabbits are now held alive and well with freedom to eat.
8. The animal's stress factor is vastly reduced.
9. The new larger stop loop prevents any trauma around the head and neck.
10. Any oedema and swelling is now eliminated completely
11. Non -target species such as adult roe deer and muntjac can now free themselves from the new larger stop loop, without having to activate the Breakaway link.
12. Necrosis caused by accidental foot snaring of the roe deer due to a broken snare has been totally eliminated.
13. Heavier deer such as Red, Sika and Fallow will activate the Breakaway link to free themselves in seconds.
14. Livestock which accidentally get their foot snared will also activate the Breakaway link.
15. The new 1.6mm Galvanised Breakaway link is much more consistent than the original copper link and is also much stronger.

In recent test completed by M. Pritchard himself where 400 rabbits were snared, 20 adult rabbits activated the copper breakaway link and escaped. All adult rabbits in snares fitted with the new galvanised breakaway link were held alive and well, with no escapes. On completion of the overall field testing of the G.S.W. Breakaway snare system it was found that the 1.75mm copper breakaway link was not consistent and it was therefore changed to new type 1.6mm galvanised wire which was consistent and worked extremely well. Over 2500 rabbits were caught in total in this test. The four snaremen who participated in the test were:

Colin Woodhall, Martin Pritchard, Lee Moore and Nick Williams, all from England.

*Note
The end eyelet that runs along the snare cable should have the larger dished face to the front to give a nice smooth running action, while in the stop eyelet it should lie on the underside of the snare cable (Not on the inside of the noose).

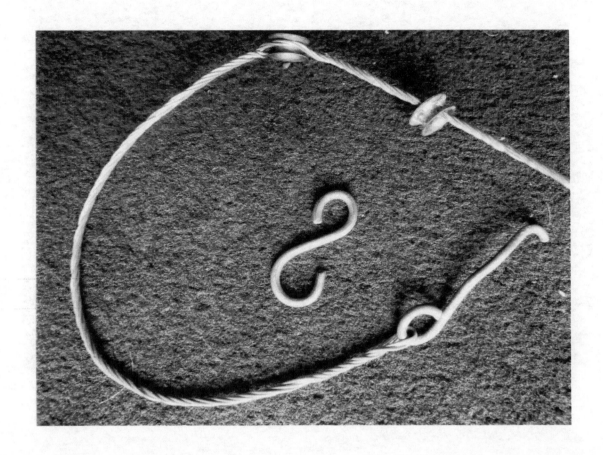

The breakaway on this snare was activated by a hare, which freed itself. Replacement 'S' hook ready to be attached.

C

lose up of the break-away system in action. Two fingers in the space between the neck of a 6lb rabbit's neck and the 6" stopped loop. The rabbit's head is free from trauma, (no swollen head or bulging eyes), which is common in unstopped snares. A 5 inch stopped loop can cause rubbing on some large rabbits' necks.

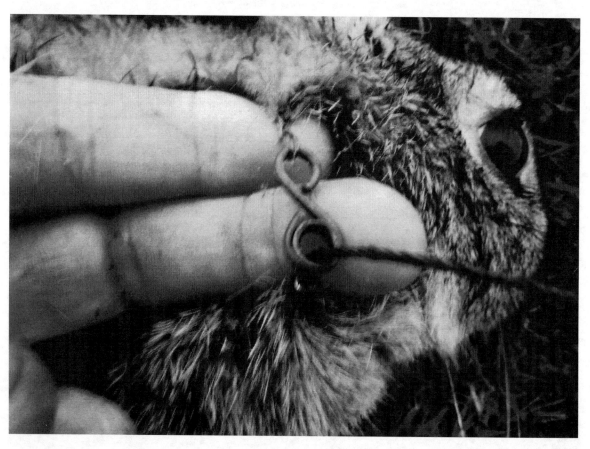

Benefits to deer and changes to Scottish Legislation.

If a deer is accidently foot snared in an un-stopped, pegged rabbit snare, the snare will tighten around the deer's foot before snapping. The tightened snare would remain around the deer's foot, cutting off the blood supply and therefore causing necrosis, which would eventually lead to the withering of the foot and it dropping off.

In March 2010 the Scottish government made it law that all snares must be fitted with a stop at a distance of 13cm (5 inches) from the running eyelet. The 5 inch stop loop in my opinion is too small, my stops are fitted at 6 inches on all my snares, for the simple fact that the wild rabbit has become much larger now where many years ago they averages at 3 ½ lb weight. It is not uncommon now in certain locations for rabbits to be caught at weights from 4 ½ lb up to 5 ½ lbs or 6lb. Not just odd ones, but every rabbit is weighing in at these latter weights. Everyone who wishes to set snares now in Scotland must go on a snaring course run by the main field sports organisations. (i.e. Scottish Gamekeeping Association, GWCT, BASC and Scottish Association of Countryside Sports).

At the end of the course a snaring exam must be sat. After passing the exam a snaring certificate is granted. You must take your snaring certificate to the local police office along with identification to become registered with the police and pay the sum of £20 to do so. You will be allocated a police tag number a few weeks later which must be stamped on tags to be attached to every single rabbit, fox or hare snare. All the tags fitted to each snare must contain the first letter of the target animal along with the snarer's allocated number. For example, if a snarer's ID was 007:.

R-007   Rabbit
F-007   Fox
BH-007   Brown Hare

It is illegal to snare White Hare (Mountain Hare) in Scotland.

Illustration of Roe Deer's Foot in a Breakaway Rabbit Snare

A. This illustration opposite shows the foot of a roe deer in the new breakaway rabbit snare system and how it works. The eyelet runs along the cable and meets the permanent spun in eyelet stop which prevents full closure of the snare loop around the animal's foot, eliminating any permanent damage to the animal itself. It shows how the loop of the galvanized S hook around the end eyelet opens up, due to the increased pulling pressure from a deer which has been accidentally caught by the foot.

B. The permanent fixed stop eyelet bears the pressure instead of the leg itself; the closed loop is approximately 1 ¾ by 2 inches in diameter. Even testing this size loop on a large roe deer's foot from a dressed carcase of 50 pounds, there is a gap of 3/8 of an inch between the leg and the wire loop. Should the very worst scenario take place such as the snare breaking no harm will befall the deer as the loop will never ever tighten to cause a necrosis, and the broken snare loop will eventually slide off itself. In the event of the deer itself pulling the breakaway system open, then the snare loop just falls freely to the ground therefore causing absolutely no injury whatsoever. The end snare eyelet can't get lost as this is prevented due to the permanent stop. All that now is required to slip another galvanized S hook around the eyelet and squeeze it closed. Then slip the ends of the cable loops onto the bottom eye of the S hook and close it, then re-tension, shape and set the snare again. It's only a two second job to a fit a replacement breakaway S hook. Even the smallest woodland deer will free itself from the rabbit snare system in a matter of a few seconds.

C. Shows the double eye of the tealer pin being pulled horizontally as it's designed to do, once an animal (i.e. rabbit) is caught. Baling twine is attached to the wire tealers double base and an ash peg which secures the whole system into the ground.

D. The double knot in the end of the six strand brass snare cable acts as a very simple and ingenious swivel system, which allows snare cable to rotate to prevent twisting and kinking. This simple action helps take the strain of the cable by being able to spin freely in a 360 degree turn.

When snaring predators (e.g. fox) an added S hook breaks away at the bottom eye of the hook. But I designed this galvanized S hook attached to a rabbit snare to pull away at the top loop around the eyelet by making the bottom loop smaller than the top loop. This is to prevent any damage to wire loops at the end of the snare cable in the event of being pulled over the cut edge of the galvanized S hook, as any scarring which may occur to the brass wire end loops leads to weakening and eventual breakage. By making the bottom eye loop smaller than the bigger loop around the eyelet this increases the strength of the bottom eye loop to allow the top loop to open more readily in the event of an accidental catch of a non target species.

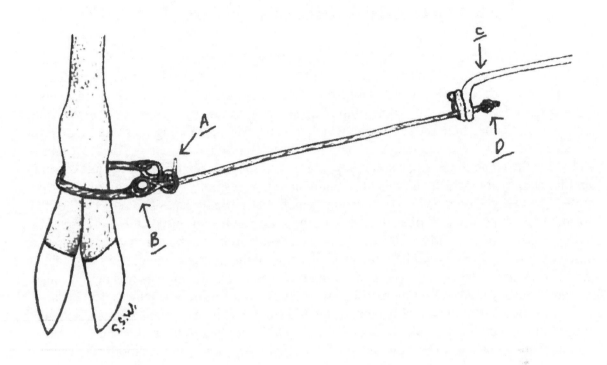

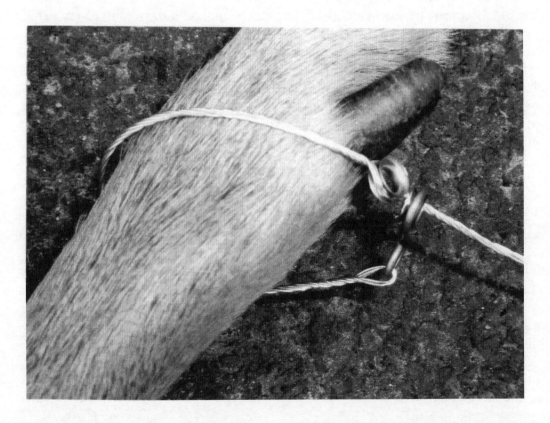

A clear gap between this Roe deer leg and a 6 inch stop loop. This is why I devised the breakaway rabbit snare system with the larger stop loop. This system has completely eliminated woodland deer losing a foot due to necrosis from a broken, unstopped snare.

The Humane Collared Rabbit Snare

This illustration depicts a variation of the new breakaway rabbit snare I devised a few years ago. The large loop shows a brass snare eyelet spun firmly between the brass wire strands which acts as a deer stop six inches along the cable from the end eyelet of the snare. This was the recognised system used by some of the trappers many years ago when the stop was at a distance of 5 inches from the end eyelet which I found causing rubbing on some of the large winter rabbits that I was catching weighing in the region of the 6 lb mark. Therefore animal welfare is the name of the game so I made all my stop loops at 6 inches with a quicker and simpler stop system which consists of nothing more than a small ¼ inch length of copper brake pipe the type used on everyday motor vehicles. A little tip here is to buy a roll of the normal brake pipe which is of a softer consistency and can be cut into small ¼ inch lengths most quickly and efficiently with a mini pipe cutter, hundreds can be cut in a short period of time and fitted quickly by slipping the little piece of tubing over the end of the snare cable and then crimping it into place. Avoid purchasing brake pipe called bundy as it is more robust and good quality it takes a bit more effort in cutting with the mini pipe cutter. The normal brake pipe will suffice as it's only being used as a simple stop. The brass snare eyelet and the copper stop are both good but six copper stops could be applied in the time it takes to fit an eyelet evenly between the brass wire strands then spin them into a nice smooth cable.

This illustration shows a thin sleeve green in colour placed over the cable between the breakaway system and the deer stop to form a soft collar around the rabbit's neck. This same appliance was tested on fox snares also. I tested the rabbit snares and my friend Martin in England tested the fox snares. The tests were similar. The rabbits appeared to avoid them in short pastures. Some catches were made in higher grass due to the cover. Martin sat and watched one fox joining an actual fox run where he had placed three trail snares approximately thirty yards apart. The fox approached the run between two of the snares, and turned to the right at a point where the grass was slightly shorter. As it walked toward the collared snare it stopped momentarily a few feet back from the snare noose, it cut off the run walked further the trail and straight into the third snare. Once again avoidance in more open ground.

What I really wanted to use for the snare collar was a material called shrink tubing but could not seem to be able to purchase it in small diameter rolls in a suitable colour. I am sure this would have worked as heating the shrink tubing onto the steel snare cable would have made it slightly thinner and less visible to the eye. I may pursue this idea later, but up until now there is absolutely no problem with the plain simple wire loop's catching ability. "It works for me".

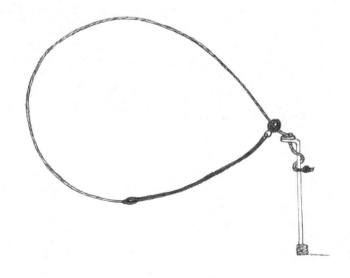

The Hare Snare

This illustration shows a figure 4 tealer system for hares. This tealer is eleven inches long with a double eye loop where the wire coils have been wound around a 2 mil masonry nail giving a narrow circular hole inside the eye loop. You will notice how the snare noose is attached to the tealer pin, the end of the snare cable has been inserted down through the tealer eye loop from the top, then a double knot has been formed at the end of the snare noose. The end of the noose has been attached to the tealer wire with one tight turn as shown to hold the snare loop firmly in place when being set.

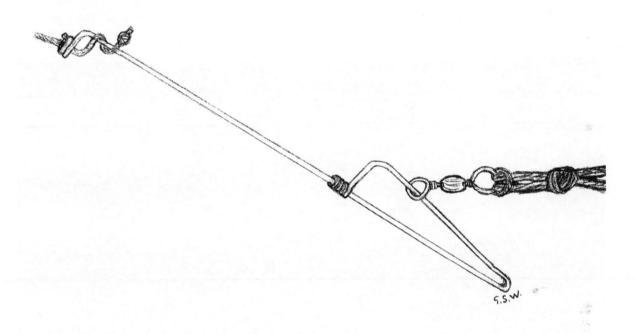

The base of the wire tealer pin has a 4/0 size stainless steel fishing swivel of 650 lbs breaking strain with a double swivelling action. The reason for using a strong swivel is to retain full strength of the whole unit. It would be futile to use a smaller weaker swivel which could jeopardise the strength of the whole system which would be unacceptable due to the fact that it could be the cause of an animal escaping with part of the system attached to it. When using breakaway links attached to snares, the snare should always be made to hold heavier animals than the target species so that the complete system is strong enough to take the strain and only break at the designated point once the breakaway link has been activated to free the non target species. The swivel is added before the final completion of the tealer pin during manufacture. The twine loop is inserted through the opposite eye of the swivel the securing peg is then dropped through the loop and pulled tight to complete the job in hand.

The length of the snare cable is approximately 26½" to form a large noose at the end of the 11" tealer pin to give the proper height and larger kill area. This is to allow the all round clearance for the hare's head to enter the noose of 9" x 7" loop which correlates with the characteristics of the hare's head. Although the six inch stop loop on rabbit snares keeps hares alive, I make my stop loop 7" long on all of my hare snares.

I will only snare two or three hares in the season (from Oct 1ˢᵗ to last day 31ˢᵗ Jan) to eat. The hares can free themselves from the breakaway rabbit snares with relative ease. Hare numbers have fallen over the years compared to yester years. Therefore I only take a couple for the pot now and again in season which does no harm to their numbers at all, having a few hares on the ground to make runs throughout heavy growth and crops allows game bird chicks to use these passageways helping to keep them dry in wet weather. The same goes on grouse moors.

This snare system has a triple swivelling effect taking any snare loop and the whole system in general allowing for all round freedom of movement for the target animal as the 7" stop takes the strain from the neck therefore eliminating any trauma around the head and neck increasing the welfare of the animal.

The catch from two mornings snaring - 220 Rabbits.

The Ruby Snare and Other Variations

The ruby snare was devised and used by the old Scottish rabbit trappers some of whom were my old mentors. The normal brass rabbit snare wire consisted of six stands of brass wire either .455 or .457 diameter with a brass eyelet fitted at one end. These six strands were spun up into a tight cable with a little shirt collar effect just below the eye. The cable was not over spun due to the fact that the wire would become hard and brittle with a harsh rough feeling about it, leaving practically no play or pliability in the cable making it hard for the trapper to incorporate tension and shaping of the snare noose. It was also prone to snapping due to being over wound. The brass snare wire itself which was soft and pliable consisted of a mixture of 70% copper and 30% zinc. The old rabbit trappers would make up their six strand rabbit snares consisting of one double strand of bronze wire and two double strands of normal brass wire. The bronze wire could possibly be of the same consistency and similar mix of the brass containing 62% copper and 38% bronze (instead of 30% zinc) as in the brass wire.

My old mentors said that by adding the double strand of bronze (which in itself was malleable) to the two double strands of brass wire, it made the snare cable more robust and firm on forming, tensioning and shaping the finished snare noose. The bronze wire is coloured similar to rose coloured gold. (This reddish hue led to the snares being called the ruby snares and the bronze wire referred to as ruby wire). Many years ago I acquired a drum of this bronze wire. I actually made all my 22 ½" snare nooses with six strands of this ruby wire itself which formed a nice firm pliable noose easy to work, tension and shape. These snares served me very well over many years of successful snaring operations.

The Seven Strand Snare

The standard rabbit snare comprises of six strands of brass wire spun carefully into a nice pliable cable with a brass eyelet at one end. In the bible it states that the complete number is seven. Many years ago it set me thinking about snares and I set about making snares consisting of seven strands instead of the standard six strands.

To make these seven strand snares first of all attach the snare wire to an eyelet, then place the eyelet over a nail on your winding board. Then proceed to wind the snare wire around the bottom nail bringing it back up and around the groove in the outside of the eyelet on the top nail. Complete three full turns finishing at the bottom nail, snip the wire strand, then take hold of the eyelet and give it two or three twists in an anti-clockwise fashion. Hold the eyelet and run your left hand down the wire strands straightening and smoothing them out. Now hook the eyelet onto the hook attached to your seven pound weight, or onto your hand winder then spin the wire strands into a nice firm cable. The seven strands when spun all fit into each other to form a beautiful perfectly smooth snare cable. Once again do not over spin making the cable hard and brittle to the feel and touch.

The problem is you can only make one of these seven strand snares one at a time, but the finished product is worth it. The snare noose is stronger and forms a lovely firm shaped noose with a smooth perfect running action. All my seven strand snares are fitted with 650 lb breaking strain stainless sea swivels attached to the tealer pins before completion which makes an exceptionally strong working pegged snaring system capable of many years of hard work.

Pure Copper Snares

A good many years ago a friend of mine who deals in scrap and non ferrous metals gave me a 100 metre roll of copper wire. When the protective covering was stripped off the copper cable consisted of seven strands of wire. The wire itself was the same diameter as a seven strand brass wire snare cable. I cut the copper cable into 24" lengths attached it to an eyelet and twisted it tightly around on itself three times. Looking carefully at this cable I noticed that due to it being machine spun, and me being right handed, I had to hold the cable with the pliers in my right hand instead of my left hand. I gave the already formed seven strand cable a spin in the opposite direction just to give the seven strands a little tightening up, to firm up the cable a little more. Due to years of experience I felt the seven strands were just not tight enough hence the latter procedure.

This copper cable weathered well out in the inclement weather and blended in the surrounding pastures when set. The wire was pliable, easy to tension, form and shape the snare loops. It was also very smooth running due to it being formed from seven strands the complete number. This copper cable performed extremely well over a number of years accounting for many hundreds of rabbits and hares. In fact it was as every bit as good as the brass wire. The beauty about this copper cable was that the strands were already formed into a seven strand cable which saved me from spinning up each and every individual snare into a formed cable. All that was required was to adjust the cable with a very slight tightening to firm it up a little, attach an eyelet, form a noose, then run each and every new snare closed with your thumb. Always run every new snare closed then open the nooses, then shape and tension the loops otherwise a new snare loop will not run closed until the latter procedure is carried out.

Corlene Snares

These snares were manufactured over 30 years ago they were made from what appeared to be a thin double strand of orange fishing corlene and two double strands of brass wire attached to a brass eyelet. There were of good length pliable and also very strong. I used these latter type snares for hangers setting along fencelines. Before setting I would gather a handful of wet dirt and rub it into the cables to dull the orange colour of the corlene in order to camouflage them from prowling eyes.

They worked okay for a while catching many hares and rabbits over a couple of years the colour bleached and they eventually frayed due to age and constant use out in inclement weather. I got some green corlene and made some up myself same procedure with the dirt and used only of fencelines. Just another phase in life and trying out another market product over the many years. The estate owner had purchased these corlene snares for me to try out. They were okay for a casual snarer but not for professional use.

Section 2 - Using The Professional Pegged Snare

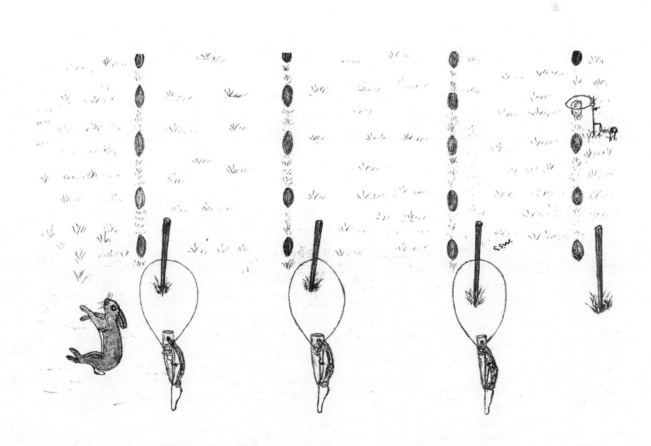

Professional Rabbit Snaring

Chapter 7 - Setting the Pegged Snare.

Proper Snare Placement

As has already been explained, set your snares with the large snare loop sitting over the middle of a small beat. The striking curve should be sitting in the middle of the bottom wire of the snare loop ready to take a rabbit under the chin when it travels along the run. This illustration shows two example rabbits runs A and B.

A - Let us start with run A. The first large beat is an X showing rabbit droppings covering it. Avoid these large beats at all times for the simple fact is you can't set them properly as the rabbits sit on them and sniff around. The second X shown is between two beats. This is called on the jump, never set here either. The problem with this setting position has been explained previously. The dotted line shows the proper placement of the snare loop over the middle of the beat, pick three or four beats in a straight line and set one in the middle of them because the rabbit will hit these beats most accurately all the time as he travels along the run.

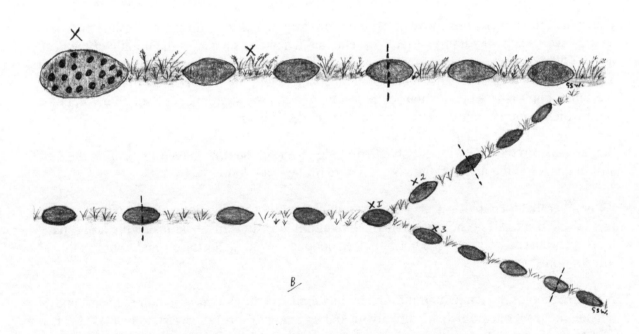

Run B - Once again dotted line over middle of the beat on straight part of the run is the location to set. As we move along the run we come to three beats X1-X2-X3. Do not set any of these beats because the rabbit strikes these beats at an angle when travelling outwards and coming back inwards along the run. Therefore once again set beats with dotted lines showing, make sure that one is set further along the fork from the other so that once a catch is made the captured rabbit can't knock the other set snare loop.

How a Rabbit Runs

Understanding how rabbits move along the run is key to understanding how this method of snaring works and why it is so effective. The rabbit snare is set across the middle of the beat as the dotted line shows. This is where you get the true height of the rabbit's head. The large 7 ½ x 5 ½ inch loop covers the run, properly set at a height of 6 ½ inches from the bottom of the snare loop to the ground when set in pasture grass. The snare must be set higher in taller flora which is pure common sense and covered in detail later.

Set the tealer to the side with only the large loop covering the run, shaped to position the striking curve in the middle of the bottom wire of the snare loop

Remember that the rabbit is travelling through the small beats and not stopping. The front feet hit the front half of the beat first which naturally positions his head inside the large snare loop. The striking curve at the bottom of the loop is tucked under the animal's chin as the illustration shows.

As the motion of the jump continues the rabbits hind feet are drawn in to come up past and outside the front ones which are already tucked up ready to spring forward to the next beat. The body weight of the rabbit on its forward line of travel springs the noose which closes around its neck and holds the captured rabbit securely until the trapper arrives to check the snares the following morning.

Large Squatting Beats

These illustrations shows a large beat with droppings present. These larger beats can be up to 10 inches plus long and are usually called 'squats' as the rabbits stop and sit on them to defecate or urinate, scratch and sniff around generally doing what rabbits do. Some people set snares on these squatting beats but they are best left alone as misses occur and sprung snares are usually the order of the day. Therefore it is best to forget about them and set the smaller beats where you will attain a higher success rate and catch ratio.

Misalignment on the run

This illustration shows a large snare loop set properly on a rabbit run. The dotted line shows a common mistake in which the large noose is set to far over on the opposite side of the run this will cause misses due to much play in the snare loop. The desired effect is for the rabbit to strike the bottom curve of the loop under its chin.

You will notice there is no play in the twine between the vertical double tealer and the securing peg and therefore the whole system is geared for the immediate strike force of the rabbit as the whole system is tensioned from the loop, to the tealer, to the twine, to the peg. Setting pegged snares like this with no play in the system ensures high catches as the snare closes on impact immediately on being struck by the rabbit. These are the little tricks that can make you or break you.

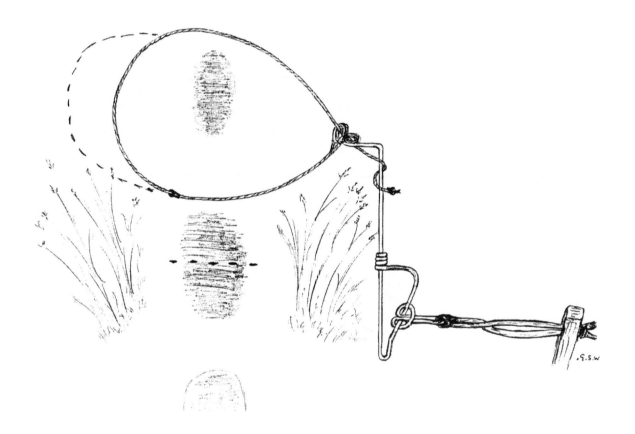

Pegged rabbit snare with 'teardrop' indication.

What you see here in this illustration is a professional pegged rabbit snare set over the middle of a beat on a rabbit run. This is the proper placement of the snare set on a rabbit run with the striking curve sitting dead centre over the beat to take the rabbit under the chin as he bounds along the run. This is the point where you get the true height of its head, not between the beats on the jump where a lot of amateurs advocate to set. You will also notice a bead or teardrop of water hanging directly from under the centre of the snare loop - on damp, dewy and wet mornings you will see this scene in the mornings. This indicates that the big snare loop is sitting perfectly over the run awaiting a catch.

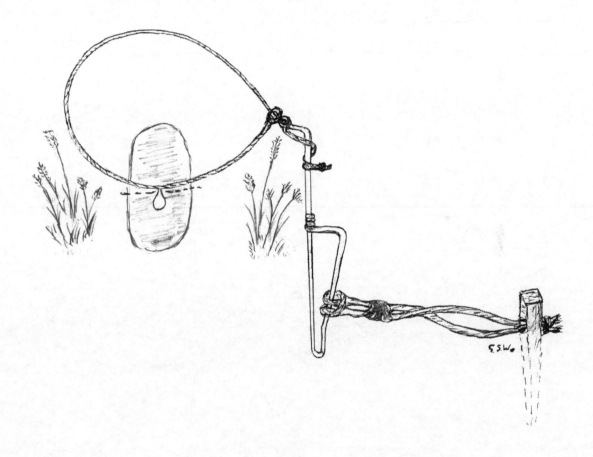

The Right Height

The height of your snares is critical and this illustration shows the height to set out at on pasture grass. A picture is worth a thousand words they say and this drawing will help amateurs and also new beginners to set their snares properly. With the nonsense that's been written about rabbit snaring over the years, advocating silly small nooses set low to the ground, it's no wonder that many adults and youngsters became frustrated and totally gave up.

It's the kids I feel sorry for, getting themselves all excited in the morning anticipating a nice catch when checking their snares, only to find nothing but tripped snares and no rabbits. Or maybe one rabbit that has happened to get caught by sheer luck rather than good snaring.

The bottom of your snare loop should be 6 ½ inches from the ground, when snaring in normal pasture grass.

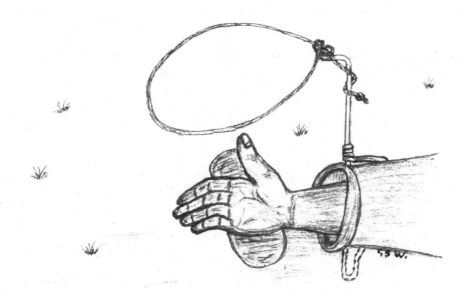

Basics of Snare Height and Placement

This series of illustrations opposite show how the height of the vegetation effects the height at which rabbits jump and therefore the height your snares should be.

(A) This illustration shows a rabbit run in higher grass. The arrow markers shown indicate the rabbit's forward line of travel along the run. The dotted line across the middle of the beat shows the proper placement of the snare noose directly over and above the middle of the beat. This is the point that you get the proper height of the rabbit's head as it lands and takes off on its journey along the run. The X marks the spot between the beats, this is called the jump. Many authors and scribes over the last century have advocated to set at this point on the rabbit run this is totally wrong, to prove my point think about this, how are you going to set a silly little 4 inch snare loop three or four fingers high in between the beats when the grass could lie 12" high plus. Waken up you boys it's not going to happen ! Ask yourself this why are these flattened patches called beats are only showing every 14 inches-18 inches and 2 feet apart at times. This is because the rabbits are jumping up high to get up and over this high standing flora from beat to beat. When setting in high grass as shown in illustration (A). Make and keep a couple of hundred pegged snares with longer tealer pins 10½" plus to compensate for the height of the high grass. When setting such locations the longer tealer helps attain the proper height of the snare which must be set **9½" high** plus at times to catch the rabbits as they spring high to get over the higher flora from beat to beat. I know professional snarers who would forsake these locations because they did not know how to set them. Nobody ever taught me how to snare in high grass, weeds, clover, buttercups, etc. I figured this out by myself and perfected it over the years until I became really good at it, now I am showing the reader how to become successful in snaring high grass.

Illustration (B) shows the same type rabbit run only it is in normal pasture grass. Again the arrows indicate the rabbit's forward line of travel along its run, dotted line across middle of the beat indicates the proper placement of snare noose over the middle above beat, where you get the true height of the rabbit head. X indicates the jump between the beats do not set here. Never, set your snares at 6½" high to the bottom of the snare loop, when conditions are wet or dewy raise them to 7" as the rabbits don't like their bellies getting wet and they rise a bit higher . You will attain good catches with very few misses. No author or field sports scribe ever stated to set snares at this height until I put illustrations and snare heights up on the Hunting Life website a number of years ago around 2005, except one old rabbit trapper called Albert Spring, he stated that the snare must be set up to correlate with the height of the grass.

(C) shows a line of beats along part of a rabbit run, the only problem they are not in line with each other they are all offset should you come cross a situation like this, you can move further along the run to find three or four beat in a straight line and set one in the middle of them as the rabbit hits them more accurately and straight on not at an angle. What I do is very simple. I take my foot and stamp the run straight along the top of these offset beats then I remake the beats with the ball of my foot along this section of the run and place a snare on one of the beats I've made, I have done this hundreds of times over the years and catch rabbits all the time never complicating things. Keep it simple.

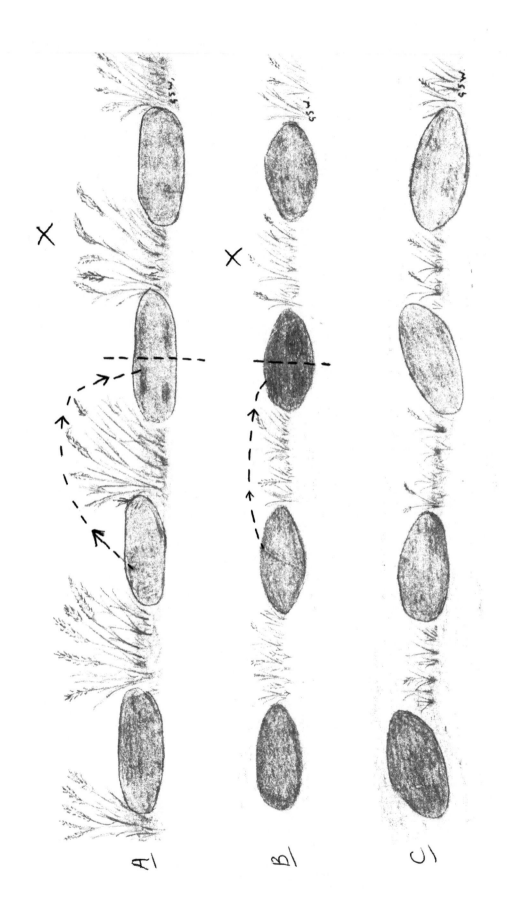

Easy Snare Height reminder for Beginners

This illustration shows a simple method for beginners to acquire the proper height to set their snares if they are unsure. What to do is measure 6 ½ inches along the hammer length from the underside base of the hammer head then wind a couple of turns of electrical tape with red or yellow around the hammer shaft at the desired length then stand the hammer in a vertical position and tweak the snare loop either up or down until level with the tape which should be 6 ½" to the bottom of the snare loop out in the pasture grass. The coloured piece of tape around hammer shaft is eye-catching therefore it will help so that you don't leave your hammer lying on the ground and walk away without it.

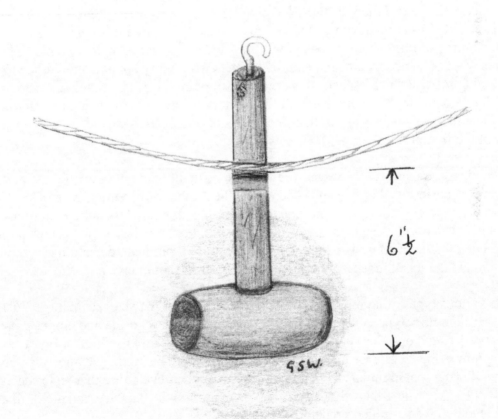

Snaring in High Vegetation

Setting snares out in grazing fields void of any livestock where the grass is short and the rabbit runs are more visible and well defined makes snaring a lot easier. Even for the amateur with limited experience and knowledge, the rabbit's presence is more evident to see on well travelled runs. The rabbit's continual nightly forays leaving well defined beats being very prominent and visible to the naked eye. It must also be remembered that the activities and movements of animals, even that of rabbits, are very much influenced by the type of weather conditions and the differences in certain types of terrain available at various locations. Therefore the trapper must use his powers of observation as the seasons change and across the many varying circumstances and surroundings, so as to acquaint himself accordingly with them to suit his line of work. This at times can be made more difficult for him depending on the location and the type and height of crop or vegetation in which the operation is to be carried out.

This is where the professional overcomes as he can relate and draw from that vast wealth of knowledge and experience he has accumulated over the many years of his lifetime of being on the job. Snaring short grass is easier and a more favourable option to many. When circumstances change to a more difficult location with high verdure present the idea of snaring is quickly abandoned with all the various excuses put forward, such as it's too difficult, rabbits can't be snared in high grass, they don't run well in high grass etc. The latter statements were not made by amateurs but by keepers who in my opinion should be more capable and familiar with all aspects of snaring and trapping. But alas times are changing and shooting has become more favourable with frequent use of the .22 rifle being a preferred option. Obviously this is because of their inexperience and being incapable of setting snares properly in the first place.

Snaring in high grass, crops and weeds etc is a more difficult than out in open grassland, but practice makes perfect as they say and necessity is the mother of invention when faced with certain problems to overcome. Rabbit runs in rough high grass are less defined at times as in open ground. The normal sequence of events facing the trapper when viewing such a location are just a line of ill-defined beats - some faint, some more prominent, depending on the type of vegetation at the location where snaring operations are to commence.

There are various types of high growth that I have snared over the years, sometimes just plain high grass, rough tufty type grass, clover, buttercups and grass set aside and amongst carpets of weeds bordering cropfields such as wild forget-me-nots etc, all knee high at times. But it's surprising how effective snares are in these latter locations. The high vegetation also gives good cover for the snared rabbits to sit and hide in and under, even ones that have succumbed quickly to the snare where the wire has also wrapped around the back leg and are dead are less visible to aerial and ground predators.

A longer tealer pin is the order of the day when snaring in these conditions. This is a must to get the snares up to the required height to neck snare the rabbits as they are rising high when jumping through such high growth. This is where the big loop becomes very effective once again, as it always allows for a margin of error. Always remember to pull any stalks of grass or weed away from the front and back of the snare loop so that allows for a clear passage for the rabbit's head to enter, forgetting to do this could cause a miss due to any firm stalk of stiff grass obstructing the front of the loop, especially the Timothy cocksfoot and the Italian rye grass.

The former is thick and quite strong so it's most advisable to clear the front of all snare loops no matter what type of vegetation you're working in at all times, once the snaring operation commences.

The distance between the beats in certain locations, where the latter type of grass abounds in large acreages sometimes wellington boot high, usually averages from fourteen up to eighteen inches apart at times. When setting these locations I don't set far out from the edge as there is no real need for it. Also I do not want to be leaving a lot of tracks in the grass alongside the true runs themselves, at times the beats can be quite visible to the eye, on other occasions in thick rough grass the beats are not so well defined and only a small indentation appears to be seen, many of the old timers frowned upon the standing on a run whilst setting wires.

Although I don't actually stand or walk on a run, on occasions I will take my foot and stamp down directly and exactly on top of one of these ill-defined beats, why I do this is to make a good landing and takeoff point for the rabbit, then set my snare directly over the middle of this beat which I have now created. This latter practice has never put the rabbits off at any time and I have snared thousands of them over the years on these beats, after a catch I do exactly the same and reset the snare exactly over the middle of these same beats and take rabbit after rabbit. I carry out the same procedure out in shorter grazing fields only I just use the toe of my boot on small beats only if they need remade after a catch and it works every time.

I used marker pins for every snare. This is imperative in long vegetation never mind just in short grazing fields. Remember the heat of the day and the dew at night with touches of rain in between at times and the grass is growing every day makes it hard to see weathered snares and dyed tealer pins even to the professional's well practised eye. To see the marker pins more clearly I just create a small flat circle in the grass about a foot from the side of the run and then insert the wire marker, with a blue flag, into the ground at a sixty degree angle. This makes it far more visible when walking forward to check the snares in the morning.

The illustration above shows the trapper standing alongside the run with high right leg and foot raised above a beat on a rabbit run in high grass, what the trapper is about to do is to place his foot just above the beat and give it a few quick downward stomps, what's been achieved with this simple action is to make a good landing and takeoff place for the rabbit as he bounds along the run.

When rabbits are springing through this high grass, up and over from beat to beat, the snares must be set higher to compensate for the immediate surroundings and the distance between the beats. I set my snares at 9 ½ inches plus high, sometimes they are set over 10 inches to the bottom of the loop. The biggest percentage of your rabbits will all be neck snared at this height but you will occasionally still catch odd ones around the middle. Even half grown rabbits will be taken in the snares at this height. Once again the big loop it a must as it catches rabbits either on their outward journey or when they are incoming. I use a 10 ½ inch tealer pin to gain extra height.

On occasions where the ground may be a little soft along the side of a run I will give it a quick stamp with the heel of my boot to help firm the ground up a little. If this is not sufficient, at times I will reduce the loop size slightly and extend the inch or so of the spare snare cable in a vertical position upwards from the double eye of the tealer. This gives added height and still retains a respectable sized catching loop (see the illustration how to adjust the snare loop). It's amazing how high rabbits jump in longer vegetation, more so when conditions are wet therefore it is only commonsense to elevate the snares to the proper level to compensate for the height of the surrounding vegetation and different weather conditions. The half and three-quarter grown ones are lighter in bodyweight and are more lithe of body than the full grown heavier adults and spring forwards more speedily through the long grasses more so than the adults. .

To gain extra height use a 24"
noose and a 10 ½ " tealer. Make
the noose the same as shown as this
gives an extra inch of height above
the tealer eye.

Another little trick I'll divulge to obtain extra height when the ground may be a little soft, or when snaring in longer grass, take your knife and cut a small square of turf, then bed it stable on the ground to the side of the run then insert your tealer pin into the turf and knock your securing peg into the ground. White showed me this little trick a number of years back and it works well as I have used it on a few occasions to gain extra height.

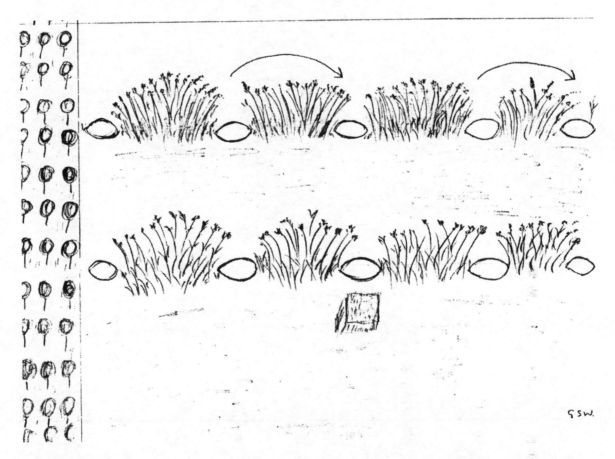

It is generally found when snaring in long vegetation that an odd hare may be taken in a snare. If they are alive I release them but on occasions, although they are always neck snared, the snare cable also becomes wound around one of the back legs which usually results in a quick demise for the creature in question.

Wet weather makes snaring in long vegetation even more difficult because your hands become wet and rabbit fur not only sticks to the snare wire it also sticks to your hands making operations uncomfortable. When despatching numbers of rabbits, smoothing out, reshaping and incorporating tension into snare after snare forcing the trapper to rub his hands together or wipe them down his arms trying to remove wet rabbit fur and drying his fingers at the same time, any wet fur stuck to the snare wire must be removed also at the eye of the tealer pin and around the double knot as this may impede the smooth fast closing action and swivelling ability of the snare resulting in slipped and empty snares.

RABBIT SPRINGING
UP AND OVER HIGH FLORA
FROM BEAT TO BE AT

Professional Rabbit Snaring

I was asked by the head gamekeeper one day to inspect a field of young crop bordering woodland as he noticed rabbits going to and fro between the woodland and the crop field. After viewing the location I noticed there were very few noticeable runs entering the field although there were a fair number of rabbits present in the crop which was about seven or eight inches high. As I walked the field edge bordering the woodland examining and scrutinising the ground very carefully looking for beats, lines of droppings going out into the crop, also dirty coloured stems and leaves of the plants caused by the dirt from the bottom of the rabbits' feet, all of a sudden a good idea flashed into my mind again to go into the field in the early morning while the dew was still present before sunrise as the rabbit runs would be more prominent and visible to my eye.

On arrival the following morning lo and behold it was just as the thought and the vision I was shown the previous day the dewy tracks were very visible. I had no snares present with me at the time only a bag of hazel marker pins. I walked quickly along the field edge inserting a marker pin at the side of every visible track going out into the dew covered crop. On completion of this simple task I then started to kick my boot along each visible run for a length of a few feet then stamp out beats with the ball of my foot on every run. The marker pins were left in place. This process was repeated the following morning to mark other fresh runs that were not visible the previous morning. I left the runs for a few days while still snaring other locations. On returning to the crop field days later there were droppings on every run, dirt on beats from the rabbits' feet showing regular rabbit traffic.

Remember when setting in high grass, crops, weeds, set-aside clover stubbles, buttercups, silage grass, anywhere the flora is high standing get the snares set up high as I have already mentioned and use the simple tricks I have shown. Have you ever read or seen any articles in other books or magazines showing how to set high flora ? Never, because the authors didn't have the experience or the skill to do it.

Another tip I will give you is to make your own runs at locations where there is none and an example of this springs to mind. On a large crop field of barley there was not one visible run in a three hundred yard by fifty yard wide bare field edge which was totally devastated by rabbits. Eaten down to ground level all that remained present was dry bare soil and small stones right out to the high standing crop which was about a month away from being cut - the farmer was not a happy chappy. After visiting and surveying the location I certainly was not going to ruin my old army boots kicking out runs the whole length of this devastated field edge. I came back that afternoon with a garden hoe I had borrowed, looked where all the droppings and activity was present then scraped a line of runs about a couple of yards long the full three hundred yard length which was eaten all along the field edge.

After carrying out this process, if you check these runs the following morning you will find droppings along many of them. I usually leave them four or five days then snare every run. From this latter field I caught approximately 200 rabbits much to the farmer's delight of course, although he said "*I wish you were called in months earlier*". I have told a number of friends over the years how to do this of which they too had good success.

Another major problem with setting in longer grass is when it rains, due to the fact the longer stalks of grass or weeds will become bent over the snare noose in heavy wet showery conditions, sometimes making the snare nooses inoperable. Therefore the higher grasses surrounding the beat must be held firmly and pulled off to prevent this happening. As always it pays to be aware of the daily weather conditions when snaring which helps in avoiding later problems on the snareline.

A problem which will definitely arise daily while snaring in all types of high growth is the kill marks which appear after every catch is made. This is the unsightly large flattened circular area you will see along every run where a rabbit has been snared at each location. To counter this problem is quite a simple matter, to save yourself a lot of work by having to uplift each and every snare that makes a catch and move it to a more forward position along the run. This definitely adds a lot of extra labour and hard work to the trapper.

All that's required is to reshape and tension the snare loop, pull the tealer and twine clear to the side of the run, then take your foot and kick the run straight through the catch circle to join it up on the opposite side, reforming the run. On completion of this task take the ball of your foot and restamp new beats along the newly formed length of the run. Then open your hands into a claw like shape and start to pull the flattened grass at the sides and fluff it upwards. Then set our snare across the new formed beats that you have made roughly over the top of the original beats that will still be partly visible. Should the grass be lower and flatter the snare need not be set quite as high off the ground. A good dose of old fashioned commonsense is usually all that's required but sadly in this day and age it does not seem to be common I'm afraid.

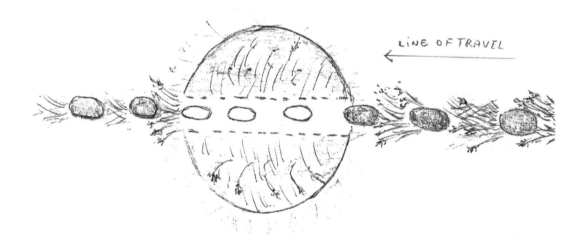

LINE OF TRAVEL

Holding and safety procedure when setting a pegged snare

Like any business that supplies and keeps tools to use on a daily basis there are certain procedures to be carried out such as safety, way of holding, and how to apply them properly in a working capacity. Snares are the tools of the rabbit trapper which are applied in a similar manner to suit each and every job at various locations. Let us first of all cover the safety aspects of the wire tealer one of the main components of the snare unit that is handled in the setting of each and every snare being applied daily throughout each and every snaring operation.

There are two main points which I will bring your attention. Firstly on the wire coils of the eye of the tealer, the top coil is cut off so that it lies slightly back from the centre of the top of the middle coil. The purpose for this is to stop the larger lip of the brass snare eyelet snagging on the cut end, which it would do should it have been cut further forwards. Remember to always file the sharp cut end as it can cut your thumb tip, it could also scar the brass wire strands of the snare, leading to breakages and lost catches. This is due to the rotation of the snare wire within the coils of the tealers' eye loop, this swivelling action being enabled by the double end knot at the end of the snare noose.

Now the second point to be aware of is that, once again, the last turn of the coils at the tealer grip should be filed smoothly as the sharp end will cut your thumb with continual insertion of each and every tealer placed in the ground. Once the last coil is cut and filed smoothly, tap it neatly into place with the hammer. On completion of this process lay tealer flat and give the wire coils three sharp taps with the hammer to set the coils tightly. Then hit the wire to bevel the grip for good.

Always make sure that the snare strands are always kept wound firmly and taught for an inch or so in front of the double end knot to take the strain and swivelling action at this main point.

Care should also be taken when handling snares out in the field due to the fact that large catches constantly being made eventually leads to fatigue in the snare loop. This is due to the constant play and pressure exerted every time a catch is made and the continual process of smoothing out the snare cable before retensioning it and the shaping of the noose. I continually used my hand for this latter procedure and would occasionally pay the price for my regular and continual action by having my fingers pierced with the occasional broken fatigued strand or two. On occasions a finger would bleed profusely on being punctured quite deeply with a broken strand of snare wire. So it is most advisable to use a small wooden toggle or the shaft of your hammer when carrying out this regular procedure to every snare that has captured a rabbit.

Another little tip is to carry a small roll of electrical tape in your pocket which helps cover these latter problems as well as cuts and other run of the mill minor emergencies should they arise when out in the snaring field. When cutting your snare pegs be careful with the hand axe, or table saw depending on your preference of manufacturing the pegs. Should the pegs be hand cut with the axe always smooth them down for safe handling and be careful when carrying out the hole drilling procedure.

Looking at the illustration below you will see how to hold the snare properly before the setting procedure. The thumb is bedded well into the bevelled edge holding the tealer firmly between the middle and fore finger. Your three bottom fingers curl around the top part of the peg holding it firmly in the hand, ready to insert into the ground at the side of the run. Position with the large loop over the middle of the beat with the dotted line showing exact position of the snare noose.

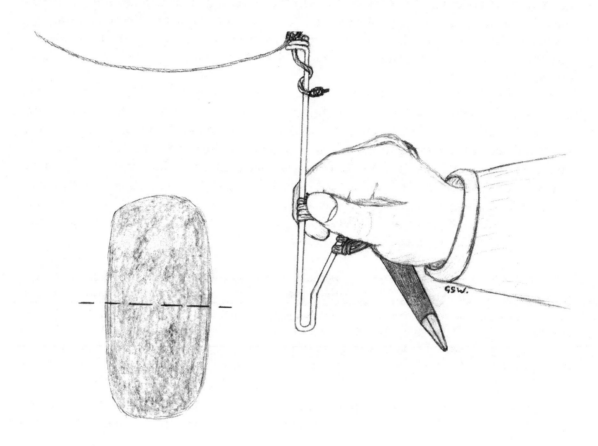

How Not to Set Rabbit Snares

A number of years back while reading a field sports magazine, a scribe had penned an article about rabbit snaring. Throughout the text he proceeded to enlighten the readers about tealers, small snare loops and the setting procedure of the snares. Lo and behold he had the snares set with the loops hanging in a downward position similar to a pear hanging from the branch of a tree. (A). It was most obvious the writer was very limited in experience when it came to snaring, making and the setting of them. Do not set rabbit snares in this manner at any time either with smaller loops which will be knocked and tripped or larger loops set too low rabbits will slip through them or they will be hip snared due to the way the noose hangs in a downward position.

Look at Illustration (B), which shows the same snare side on. It plainly shows the problem - the animal once caught in the snare has to travel approx 8 inches forward as shown before the noose even starts to close. As I said the animal will either slip clean through the noose or be hip snared. It amazes me the amount of people who set their fox snares in this same way using the commercial snares hanging from a thick wooden tealer that would do justice to a gate post. As this is a rabbit snaring manual I won't go into intricate detail as it would take a page to explain the problem of this system to snare foxes. As far as setting rabbit snares using the method shown in this illustration is a no-no. I certainly would not use this method ever to set snares for either rabbit or fox.

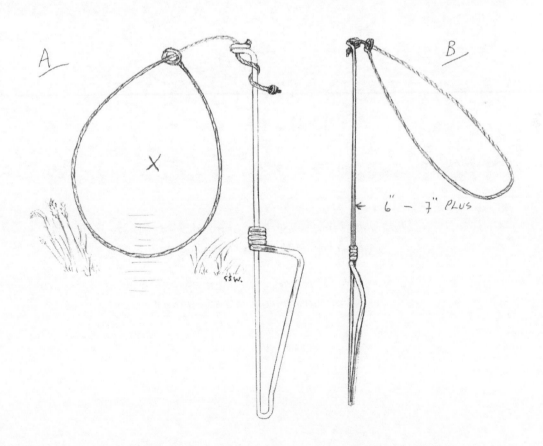

Rabbit control in a young tree plantation at Smiddy Hill
which was suffering extreme damage.

This is a typical situation where skill snaring in high vegetation was required and over 50
rabbits taken from this small area.

Professional Rabbit Snaring

Marker Pins

Using Marker Pins

It is imperative that marker pins are used when setting snares, as it is only sheer laziness not to use them. The effect of not using them is only too common at times, where ignorant and inexperienced snarers have left a few snares behind, which capture its quarry who is left to suffer and die bringing undue publicity upon the field sports fraternity. This is a common occurrence all over the country I'm afraid. When snaring out in grazing fields forgotten snares could have serious consequences, especially should a prime steer be caught by the tongue. The professional on the other hand knows of the danger and the suffering that can be caused by snares that have been overlooked and left behind. Therefore he does not set his snares indiscriminately but sets them in either a straight line or a half circle, circle, or L-shape depending on the location either open ground, woodland, or rough growing areas with brambles, gorse, whin, etc. All snares receive a marker pin or similar identification marker of some shape or size and material.

The problem arises when working with well weathered wires as they blend into the grassy surroundings extremely well at times, particularly when setting in higher type grasses. This is especially true when setting out snares in summertime, carrying out rabbit control in young crops and in silage grass. You must remember that with the dew in the evenings and the warm summer days the grass is growing an inch or so every day, making it even harder to see weathered snares. Therefore it is imperative to use a marker pin to every snare and that the snares should be counted before being set out and counted in when they are being uplifted to ensure there are none left behind in the field.

It is a very simple process to place a marker pin alongside every run then set your snare a couple of yards out from it. Snares can virtually be set anywhere but the best place is to set them well out into the field for the most fruitful results. It is also harder to detect snares set well out from the perimeter edge. The trapper must also always be aware of prowlers, in certain areas he may be operating in. When I set my hazel markers or crow feathers I set them at a low angle almost flat to the ground, therefore anyone with nefarious activities in mind will not see them if walking along an edge looking out into the field due to the low setting angle. Also a well weathered snare is also very hard to detect but to the trapper who is looking right along the field from an end elevation sees all the low lying markers quite easily. The crow feather is also set edge on and can't be seen easily, but is easily viewed from the side as you are then looking at the broad face of the black feather which stands out very well against the green grass making it a simple process to uplift the snares.

When lifting the snare it is a simple process to lift each snare and place the loop over each marker pin all the way along the field. Should any rabbits be caught the same morning, just place them also beside the marker pins alongside the snares. When you come to the last snare just walk back along the line lifting each snare and marker pin plus the rabbits and any maker pin without a snare loop placed over it, you know to look along the run and then uplift it. This saves you carrying snares all the way along the line and carrying them back again.

Many of the old timers used a shard of pottery or the heel mark of a boot to mark every tenth snare. This method would be sufficient out in short grass but I'm afraid the latter methods would be insufficient to me when snaring in high thick grass or vegetation. When snaring in the latter type of locations I take my boot and stand in the grass at the side of each and every run and twist my foot left and right a couple of times like the movement of a vehicle window wiper. This flattens a small patch to place my marker on so that it is more visible to my eye as it is so easy to overlook a snare and then you must waste time having to backtrack looking for it.

Once you get used to using markers it becomes habit, a second nature if you like, and takes only but a few seconds to insert one into the ground. It use is most effective in recovering each and every snare set. Always strive to be a true professional in every way and have respect for the animals your trap and snare, so count your snares every time before you set them and re-count them when the operation is over. Always use marker pins as they save you time and lost snares and peace of mind. It also ensures your good name and professionalism for future reference in being recommended to other landowners who may require your services at a later date.

I'll add a good tip here when setting snares in higher vegetation and crops up to a foot high where the rabbits are bounding up and over from beat to beat where they are approximately 18" apart and you can see the slight depressions in the long grass. Take your boot and place it directly over the top of the beat and stamp your foot down a couple of times. This gives the rabbit a good landing and takeoff place with plenty of room. Set your snare in the middle of the now larger beat and it works every time. Many of the old timers say not to stand on the run which I do not do except on occasions to remake a beat with my foot and I do it all the time and as Hunter the TV cop says "it works for me". If it were not successful I most certainly would not do it.

There are three types of marker pins that I use. One is dried hazel wands $^3/_8$" of an inch thick twelve inches long and pointed at one end for penetrating the ground. Hazel is scare in the vicinity where I live so Phil Day brings me a couple of hundred every so often when he comes up to visit from England. I also use crow feathers with a wire 'spike', which are lightweight and many can be carried at any one time as they are not bulky. Once the wire end is inserted into the ground they take a firm grip and will stand well in a howling wind, the black colour is most visible to your eye out in the shorter grass fields. I devised this simple method over twenty years ago and it works every well.

The third type of marker is constructed from an 18" length of 2 mil galvanized wire with a small loop formed at the top where a short length of blue baling twine is knotted to the loop. Andy Whyte devised this type of marker for use in clear cut ground and various other types of locations. It is most visible, light to carry and it is very easy to insert into the ground; it is a very reliable and weatherproof marker.

The following illustration shows three different types of marker pin.

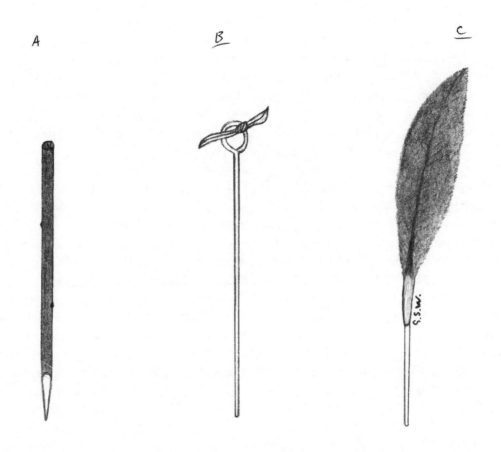

(A) Represents a simple hazel tealer cut a foot long and approximately ½" in diameter pointed at one end just insert the tealer pin into the ground at a 45° angle about 4 inches away from the side of the rabbit run so that it points along the run towards the set snare.

(B) Shows an 18 inch long length of wire with a formed half inch loop at the top you will see with careful observation that a length of blue cord is attached to the loop. These type of tealers are very easy to see especially when snaring in high stuff such as long white grasses along the sides of steep motorway bankings, silage grass, weeds, woodlands, set-aside high stubble crop fields etc. The blue tag is very eye catching in these latter locations and you don't miss any snares using this type of marker. There are no hard and fast rules to the length of this type of marker pin, they can be made shorter to suit pasture grass and many other locations. They can be easily made with 1½ mil fence line wire just bend the loop around a length of ½" bar held in the vice. This type of marker pin was devised by A Whyte.

While shopping in Pound World one day with my wife I noticed packs of steel kebab skewers for sale, each pack held one dozen items so I just purchased ten packs. They are 14 inches long with a nice little neat loop at the end. It was a bargain because I had 120 readymade marker pins available just to attach the twine and they are already pointed and work very well as they are quite strong making for easy insertion into the ground.

(C) Is an idea I came up with a few decades ago using the primary feathers from crows' wings. First of all snip the tip of the quill then insert a length of 2 mil galvanised right up into the quill as far it will go, then snip the wire off leaving 2½" of wire protruding so that it can be inserted quickly and easily into the ground. This gives the feather a good stable grip in the ground and ensures the feathers don't blow away in strong windy conditions. The secret to using the feather marker pin is when using them out in the snaring field insert the wire end into the ground at a 45° angle position with the feather pointing along the run, edge on. The reasons being anyone looking out into the field from the edge will not be able to see the marker feather easily or the well weathered wires set well out in the fields. The snares being set out in a straight line right across the field where it may be a hundred or two hundred or more each will have its own feather marking every pegged snare.

Therefore when checking the snares in the morning the feather will be easily seen as you start to walk the snareline for the simple fact that you will be looking at the broad face of the feathers all the way along the whole snareline instead of looking at the feather edge. This type of marker pin is so simple to make and assemble. We will assume you have a hundred feathers to start with, now cut only the tip of the quill and have a little tube or tub of glue dip one end of the wire into the glue then insert the wire into the quill and then push the wire all the way along the quill into the feather end until it comes to a stop then snip the extra small length of wire of, leaving 2½" of wire now protruding from the end of the quill. Job done. The feather markers will also have a few gull or even pigeon feathers amongst them so that the brighter coloured marker pin will be used to mark the 25th and last snare on every batch as my snares are carried in bundles of 25 therefore every 25th snare will be marked with a light coloured feather making it a very simple process when it comes to lifting the snares after the work has been completed. This type of marker pin is very light to carry and hundreds can be carried at one time in bundles of 25. 24 crow feathers and one light coloured one.

Chapter 8 - The Peg Snaring Sequence

Setting Out Your Snares

Before the setting of any snare it is advisable to view the snaring location in question beforehand to get a general idea of the land, to survey the ground for rabbit runs, and to identify the ones in regular use which will bear the most fruitful results. The best time to set out your snares is in the morning especially in the later months of the year after harvest time as in the overcast winter days darkness descends quickly in the later afternoon. An early departure from the snaring field is advised before 2 pm at the latest as this allows the snares to air out and human scent to dissipate from snares in the damp winter air. All is then ready for the onset of darkness as the rabbits become active leaving the security of their burrows for to head out for the feeding grounds.

It is most important that your snares are handled with extreme care and must be kept away from any abnormal odours. Don't just sling them into the car boot alongside petrol cans or diesel/oil soaked rags, always wash your hands or rub them with grass or dock leaves, avoid scented soaps and aftershaves as the rabbit has a very keen sense of smell. It is imperative that the latter odours are avoided if large catches are to be obtained.

Snares must not be set indiscriminately over the chosen area. This is where the professional differs vastly from the amateur. The professional has mentally viewed and planned the exercise to be carried out with extreme precision to save him from any unnecessary effort and time to achieve the high degree of success of the professional. It is critically and most important when snaring to learn the proper setting locations and exact placement to lay each and every snare.

For instance if the rabbits are in residence in a thick hedgerow or in woodland the professional knows that the premium site to set, where the highest catch is to be obtained, will be further out around 50 yds from the edge of the field. The snares will be set accordingly. This also helps to ensure that only the target species will be taken, thus avoiding game birds being accidentally captured as they creep along and throughout the length of the woodland edges. They are a valuable shooting commodity to the modern sporting estate worth over approximately thirty pounds per bird on let days of shooting.

As dusk approaches the emerging rabbits will exit their burrows and sit along the edge of the field viewing their surroundings, watching, listening and sniffing the air for any sign of immediate danger, before moving out slowly and cautiously and picking up speed as they move further afield out to their feeding ground. It is said to avoid placing snares along the edges of fields and cover. One scribe wrote only amateurs set snares along these latter edge features well you can call me an amateur along with all the professionals who taught me because I've snared thousands of rabbits along with my mentors all along field and woodland edges. Once again it all boils down to practical experience, type of snares and time of the year. It is most obvious the latter scribe in my opinion has not the depth of knowledge portrayed as high catches can be made along these latter locations which certain methods will be revealed later.

With reduced ground cover at the back end of the year, runs that are being used on a regular basis are fairly easy to detect. On careful examination even an amateur will see clearly visible beats which are the well worn flat patches of ground. These beats are caused by the quarry bounding frequently along the runs, taking off and landing and flattening the ground. Closer scrutiny of these beats will reveal that they are of varying size. The large ones (about ten inches or so long) are known as squats, which usually have droppings on them, denotes a stopping place where the rabbits sit on them and have a sniff about especially buck rabbits as they smell the presence of any does which have passed along the run. These latter oversize beats are not worth setting as too many misses and sprung snares occur. Also you must remember that a few of the rabbits travel out into the field using one run and come back home using another. This can be verified by the placement of the snare loop on the rabbit's neck on removing the despatched animal from the snare the eyelet is on the opposite side of the neck this is a regular occurrence which any professional trapper will verify. This is where the true value of the big loop comes into play.

There are medium sized beats which can be set but the beats which are of most interest to the professional are the tiny ones which are at times just a slight depression in the grass about the size of a rabbit's hind feet. These small beats are caused by the rabbit moving quickly along the runs merely touching the ground almost with all four feet at once in a split second movement. These tiny beats are the ones to place your snare loop on directly over the top of and in the centre of the beat, on a straight section of the run. As the rabbit moves at speed along the run he strikes these tiny beats with extreme accuracy every time he moves along the run under the cover of darkness. Having selected the correct beat, then the snare must be placed so that the loop sites directly across the middle of the beat, as this is the spot where you can anticipate the true height of the rabbit's chin from the ground as it lands and takes off. For snaring to be successful the height of the snare's loop is the crucial factor along with a large snare loop size, the bottom edge of the snare loop must be at least six inches from the ground, this may appear extremely high to a lot of people but this is a very effective killing height. A large snare loop of $7^1/_2$" x $5^1/_2$" covers a beat perfectly and allows for any margin of error - regardless which way the rabbit goes along the run, the large snare loop still covers the run even in the strongest of winds on the wildest of nights.

The main factors to remember when snaring rabbits are the proper height of the snare, large noose over small beat and the coverage of the run. I can't stress the importance of this enough. Another crucial factor is to look at each run carefully and set it accordingly to varying conditions, look at the height of the grass, the time of year, distance between the beats, and the weather on that day. Everyone who sees my snares say to me and to many of the people I have taught, that the loops are far too big and the rabbits will slip through them. These same statements are also made by some gamekeepers. It's most obvious that they lack practical experience and knowledge. To these latter individuals shooting appears to be the easiest method of control. The rabbit will only slip through the loop if it's set too low, hip catches are also the result of the snare being set low. When are they going to waken up and realise that the snares needs to be set higher ? Age is no substitute for wisdom as there are a hell of a lot of stupid old men and very few clever ones.

1 Surveying the Ground

Before the setting of any snares the trapper must first of all survey the area he is going to set as each and every location is different from one another. It could be pasture grass, stubble, crop, tussocky grass, long grass, weeds, set-aside, scrub, clover, hedges, grassy fence lines, woodland or plantations just to name a few. The time of year must be taken into consideration, the height of the growth, distance of the beats, weather conditions, dry, wet, windy and so forth. Look carefully at the runs; are they prominent and fresh looking with regular rabbit traffic ? Well padded beats ?

When surveying a location let's assume it's in a tree plantation. You don't see any burrows or any rabbits, any dead carcasses lying around. How would you know if the rabbits in this location were healthy or if they had myxomatosis, the answer lies at your feet in the form of the rabbit's droppings. When there is a healthy population of rabbits in any given area the droppings appear to be round and full and saucer shaped as shown in diagram (A) in the illustration there is a healthy bloom to them when you look closely and examine them in fine detail, on the other hand if the rabbits are sick e.g. with myxomatosis their droppings are long thin and wet slightly pear shaped and don't have a healthy look about them as you would see in the droppings of healthy animals were present in the location. As the old Red Indian saying goes, walk little and look much. Unhealthy type dropping shown diagram (B).

While doing reconnaissance of an area before you commence setting out the snares you are looking the ground over for rabbit signs such as scrapings, flecks of fur, droppings, tree damage in plantations, bark eaten off fallen branches, crop damage in fields, polished stones and scratch marks going up and down and over drystone walls, polished entrances made by rabbits hiding in the walls. Similar signs going under gates, between the spars of gates etc. The list is endless.

Other sign to look for is new growth appearing on the beats on looking carefully you will see tiny little fresh newly formed shoots pushing up through the ground which indicates there is no rabbit activity on these runs. You will also notice the same new growth and small tiny Speedwell leaves growing inside the rabbit scrapes also on the little excavated soil heaps in front of the scrapes and diggings you will also see this new growth forming indicating the lack of rabbit activity and any presence of healthy animals in that location.

When surveying the snaring location the trapper must also look carefully for the sign of any predators working the ground; droppings, smell, runs, hair, which denotes any presence of these animals such as fox, cat or badger. Should the snaring ground border a river or stream otters living in rabbit burrows along steam banks can also be a nuisance at times. The pointed droppings containing hair and bones and a pungent musky odour indicates the presence of a fox, if the scat is black it's fresh, dry white weathered scat indicates that it's old. The prowling feral cat also has a distinct odour indicating its presence, its scat is similar to a fox only smaller and thinner sometimes it will be partly covered as the cat at times scrapes some leaves grass or small twigs over its droppings or partly covers a part eaten kill.

If there are trees present especially smooth barked young ash trees at times you will notice the prominent fresh claw marks as the cat stands up on its back legs and reaches up and claws the smooth bark of the trees. At times I have come across three trees within 75 yards of one another all ash with very visible deep gouges down the sides of the tree trunk between two and three feet up from the ground. The badger will scrape out a number of small shallow diggings and deposit its scat in them it also has a distinct smell around its presence.

The otters can damage quite a number of snared rabbits eating off the heads and necks down into the shoulders. A few weeks ago Colin arrived on the snareline at first light just in time to see an otter taking a half eaten rabbit from a snare and heading down the river to a sandbank. There it stood looking at him with disdain, then turned and swam across the river to the opposite bank to finish off his meal. They too like the badger are becoming a nuisance, doing serious damage to fish stocks at these fisheries.

Yes the trapper must develop good visual awareness over the years to read the ground and to know what is happening at each location before even setting a snare.

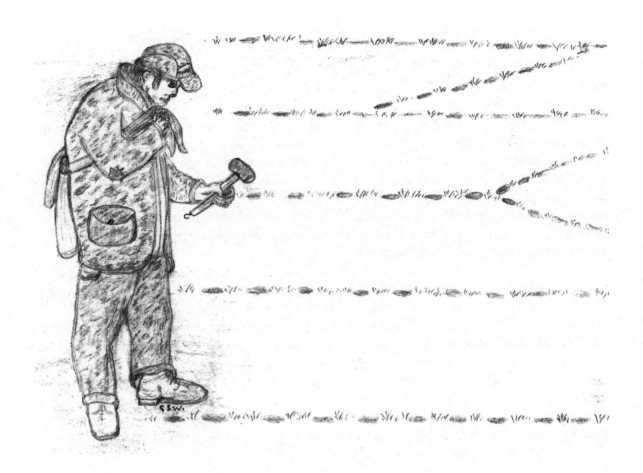

2 How to Set Pegged Snares

Before dealing with the practical aspect of rabbit snaring and going into precise detail which covers the snaring of rabbits, it is necessary for me to refer to some of the general rules which will apply in regard to the snares being used and the precise manner of setting them. I have provided for the most part illustrations of the snares and their proper use and placement. Without a shadow of a doubt the snare in experienced and skilful hands is one of the simplest and effective tools in use today for capturing and controlling of rabbits in UK. The occasions for its use are far more widely numerous than that of the modern day steel spring traps. Making your own snares in large numbers it is very cost effective as they can be applied very efficiently in the capture of large numbers of rabbits, over a very vast area of land under varying conditions of inclement weather.

For general field snaring there is nothing to compare with the modern pegged snare with the wire tealer and the big loop. To be successful in snaring you must use the best snares available made with modern materials which make them weatherproof in every aspect. Set with a light tension they will respond with quick and immediate closure. Then kept clean and checked over thoroughly for broken pegs and snare strands or twines after each snaring operation, they will always ensure a quick and positive closing action regardless of how long they are exposed to varying weather conditions. Neglect of snares and not being kept in proper working order is usually due to the handler's ignorance, inexperience and downright pure laziness which leads to broken snares and lost rabbits out in the field, causing unnecessary suffering and unwarranted cruelty.

Snares should also be counted before setting them out and a marker peg should be used for every snare to ensure that the correct numbers are collected after the operation is over. Idleness and ignorance on the part of a lot of trappers not using marker pegs and not counting their snares in causes untold suffering. Many snares left behind and uncollected over various parts of the countryside causes public hostility and much unwanted publicity to field sportsmen, so if you're too lazy to check them don't set them. It is the true professional who is dedicated to his work that is the least cruel as he respects his quarry and his good name and reputation. Therefore his equipment is of the best quality and kept in proper working order, as he knows through many years of experience that any neglect in his technique and equipment will lead to poor results throughout his daily outdoor work. All cruel people always meet a just end sooner or later.

Rabbit control can be carried out all year round using snares but the best time is in the autumn after the harvest when the rabbit population are mature well furred and full bodied. Grass fields and established mature grazing fields make the best snaring locations, although snares can be set in many different types of terrain. Where rabbits prevail in large numbers their runs are easy to see, which are their lines of travel from their secure residence out to the feeding areas. Well marked runs are most visible in fields to the amateur, but to the well practised eye of the professional newly made narrow and ill defined runs, which I call secondary runs are more productive than some of the old well defined ones.

In grass fields on occasions you will come across runs which are well defined but dull and dead looking where the droppings all along the runs are very dry and well faded and not worth setting. It is exactly the same on runs that show new growth of tiny blades of grass and small weed shoots appearing on the beats and scrapes untrampled tells you there is no rabbit traffic along these runs. The same new growth showing on rabbit runs over bare ground also indicates infrequent use of the runs and a non-productive setting.

Now that we have covered some of the general rules on snaring operations I will now go into precise details of the practical points on the setting of pegged snares. First of all let us assume that all of your snares have been checked over, properly tensioned and they are in perfect working order. There are a few important details to remember before the actual setting of a snare. The equipment must be kept clean and kept away from any abnormal odours which will linger on your hands, wires and clothes e.g. scented soaps, aftershave. Don't handle ferrets or oil, petrol, diesel, creosote or put your bag and snares in the car boot alongside any of these latter appliances which could contaminate your equipment.

Take into consideration the time of year. In summertime snares can be set out later in the daytime due to the long hours of daylight and drier warmer weather. In the later months of the year after the harvest when darkness descends in the later afternoon it is best to set out your snareline in the morning so that the snares will air out in the wind. Try and be off the snaring field before 2 o'clock as dampness descends in later afternoon, therefore you want the snares to be free from any human scent as quickly as possible which helps in obtaining high catch rates of rabbits from the snares, as rabbits possess superb olfactory senses. These are most important facts to always keep in mind. I keep my snares in neat bundles of twenty five which makes easy counting. Securing pegs must be slipped through the snare loops; this procedure keeps the snares neat and tidy and eliminates any entanglement which would happen if the pegs were allowed to dangle freely of their own accord. The snaring operation would be made extremely difficult due to the pegs and twines becoming twisted and hopelessly wrapped around each other, creating nothing more than a tangled mess and wasting valuable time having to separate them.

The proper way to carry pegged snares is to loop a bungle of 25 over the left arm, assuming that you are right handed of course. You will then proceed to the starting point out in the field where you will begin to place your snares, which will be set out 50 yds, or further, from the perimeter in a straight line parallel to the field edge all the way along the field. On selecting the first available rabbit run you will then withdraw a marker pin from your bag and insert it into the ground a few inches to the right hand side of the run, the peg will be angled at 45° pointing outwards towards the field. You will then walk a couple of yards forward and select a smaller sized beat. Then take the first snare from your left arm then slip the peg back through the snare loop, taking hold of the grip on the wire tealer firmly between middle knuckle of the forefinger and thumb of the right hand, with the remaining three fingers curled around the top of the securing peg. You now straddle the run with a foot on either side in a horse riding stance then lean forward and insert the base of the tealer pin securely into the ground to the required depth at the side of the run, either in a vertical position as I do myself or at a 45° angle depending on each individual's choice of setting. I personally feel that the vertical setting gives you greater stability as it's harder to pull out and will close a snare loop itself once a rabbit's head enters the loop due to its holding power in the ground in the vertical position.

Now that the tealer has been inserted the snare loop itself must sit over the middle of the selected small beat at the required height which is six and one half inches to the bottom of the loop in shorter grass and higher when setting in longer grass and vegetation where the beats are further apart. Each snare must be set accordingly to each and every run. The securing peg is now pushed into the ground with the heel of the hand and then hammered down vertically into the ground. In good holding conditions they can be inserted at a 45° angle if desired. The large loop itself should completely cover the whole of the run from one side to the other and there should be no loop in the twine between the tealer pin and the peg if possible as this allows extra play in the snare when struck by its quarry. Any slack in the twine should be eliminated if possible as the strain should be taken immediately on the rabbit's neck as its head enters into the loop. The big striking curve on the bottom of the snare wire catches up under the rabbit's chin and the end of the loop down round the side of the neck giving an immediate response and closure of the noose - the whole system is designed for this strike all the way down from the noose to the securing peg.

Some people set rabbit snares from the side of the run but personally I don't like setting snares in this manner at all. I like to straddle the run looking out towards the field in the same direction as the rabbit is travelling as I feel that you get a more accurate and truer placement of the snare across the run and the tealer pin sits partly off to the side of the beat and only the big loop itself covers the run properly. In daylight hours the dyed green tealer pin and the big weathered snare loop is practically invisible and high catches are taken in this type of snare especially out in short grassland where the old fashioned traditional method using thicker hazel pins are easily seen and avoided.

The wire tealer made from the 2.5 mil galvanised fenceline wire gives great stability and is far harder to see when sitting a little way to the side of the run causing no obstruction whatsoever and unable to come into contact with the rabbit's shoulder which happens when snaring with small loops which don't cover a run and the tealer is set too close to the side of the run itself.

Narrow Snare Loop

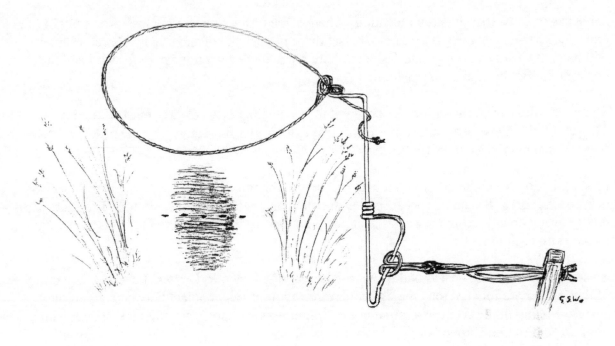

Although this pegged snare is set correctly the loop is too narrow, it has no depth to it resulting in sprung snares with the loop being tripped by the rabbit's head as it strikes the loop. Rabbits will be captured occasionally; more often they will be taken around the top of the head in front of and at the base of the ears and under the chin. This is due to the narrow loop restricting the entry of the head and the ears all at once. You must always take into consideration that rabbit runs with its ears up and in an erect position which measures six inches high from below the jaw at the side of the head to the tips of the ears on a mature adult rabbit.

Dotted line indicates middle of small beat, for exact position of snare loop. It's been said that rabbits snared around the top of the head are always dead, a large percentage will be but not every rabbit expires due to being caught in this latter manner.

Line Snaring

Line snaring means exactly what it says. Instead of snares being set in an indiscriminate manner all over the place they are set in a straight line right across the field at the required distance from the field edge, as far out as possible if the runs are still visible. First of all you insert a marker pin into the ground a few inches to the side of the run at a 45° angle pointing in an outward direction to the field, you then walk forward a couple of metres from the marker pin and place a snare over the run on the proper beat at the required height. This procedure is repeated in a parallel line to the field edge all the way across the field until every run is set with a snare. This is shown in the top illustration opposite.

An occasion may arise at certain locations where some of the runs are in close proximity of one another therefore the snares cannot be set directly opposite one another. Therefore they will have to be set in a staggering fashion where one will be set a few yards forward and the next one further back in a 'W' fashion

The lower illustration shows a forked run with three distinct beats clearly marked A, B, C. The reason that these beats are marked is to make the reader more aware of the problems that will be encountered should they be set.

First of all do not set the last straight beat (A) before the run forks and do not set the first two beats of the forks (B) and (C) because they are all at an angle from one another. Therefore ignore these three beats and always select a straight part of the run where the beats are straight in line with each other.

So set the snare *before* beat A and on a straight section of each fork *after* B and C. Set one of the forks more forward than the other therefore avoiding any contact between any of the snares. So that in the event of a rabbit being caught it won't knock the other snare over while jumping and running around.

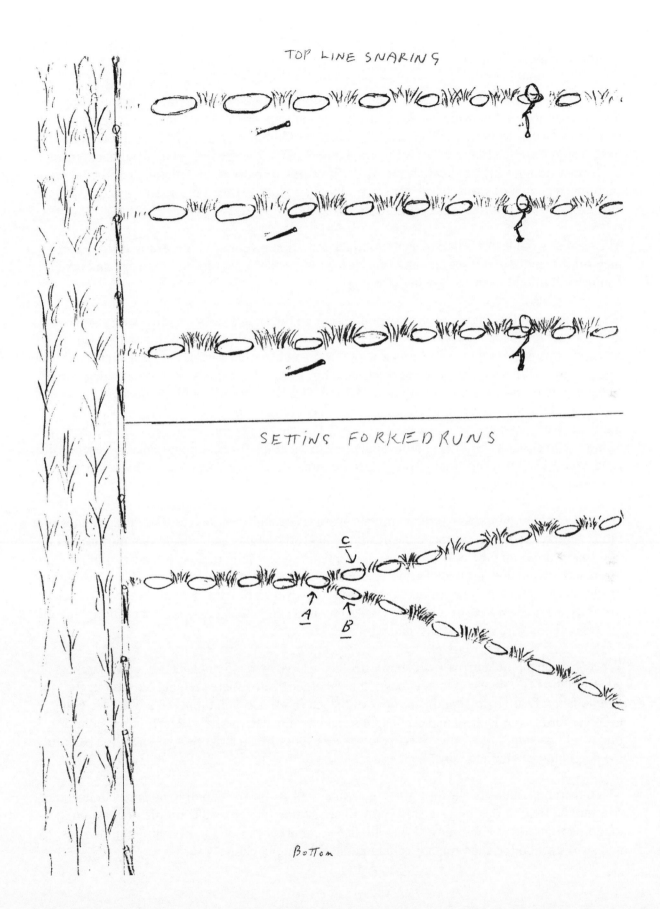

TOP LINE SNARING

SETTING FORKED RUNS

Bottom

Snaring Clean Ground

This is a term used by trappers referring to a method where rabbits are travelling out great distances at night to their feeding grounds, where the trapper would set snares up to a hundred yards and further from the field edge. The snares would be set in straight lines a few yards back from where the runs start to break up and fork out to the feeding area. The snares must be set in a straight line right across the field with a line of marker pins running parallel to the snareline a couple of yards apart. This is a simple and highly effecting snaring system. It's also a simple process to check the snare line each morning.

The trapper would set his line of snares and take the first morning's kill of rabbits, he would then lift his snares and reset around thirty or forty yards back <u>nearer</u> the field edge and take another kill of rabbits the following morning.

He would repeat this same process again by bringing the snares back a further thirty yards and take another third and final kill of rabbits from the snaring field and uplift his snares. In repeating this process he would be snaring a clean and different part of the field every night. The reason for lifting the snares and resetting them further back every day is that when rabbits strike the snares and are captured they squeal out. Therefore with many rabbits being captured on the very first night and their screams echoing in the darkness, others become more wary which halts their forward advances. The next night the remaining rabbits are afraid to travel out as far but are still caught due to the trapper resetting his snares closer to the field edge. The third and final setting takes the others that have become even more wary of travelling out far at all.

On really wild nights two to three mornings snaring is usually enough to take large catches of rabbits and reduce their numbers drastically. 140 -180 rabbits can be taken in a morning from 200 snares providing the conditions are right, good rough windy nights with a smirl of rain through the wind and no predator damage. Setting snares in grazing field at $6^1/_2$ inches high in shorter grass may seem excessively high but it is a very effective height. I personally set just over the $6^1/_2$" myself in wet or dewy weather and can take excessive catches of rabbits on the right nights when it's overcast and wild and windy.

When snaring a long narrow field approximately 100 yds wide do not set a line of snares 25 yds from the beginning of the field edge, then another line of snares around 80 yds out for the simple fact you are defeating the purpose of the exercise. Do you think the rabbits are going to travel further out with snared rabbits all squealing close to the field edge? In my opinion this would be stupidity ! Always start as far out as possible then work your snareline back to the beginning of the field edge.

The illustration opposite shows a grass fenceline with rabbit runs coming under the fenceline out into the field. Looking carefully you will see snares set across the middle of beats on the outgoing prominent rabbit runs. You will also see marker pins at the beginning of the runs and snares set on the edge runs travelling parallel to the fenceline.

3 Checking the Snareline

The illustration opposite is showing the trapper checking his snareline in the morning, standing out in the snaring field surveying the morning's catch of rabbits. As mentioned before the snares are set in as straight a line as possible right across the field, trying not to deviate too much. Of course I have been taught to use a marker pin to each and every snare set, therefore there will be one line of markers set at a low lying 45° angle. This is to retain a lower visibility to help secure the snares from any prowler's prying eyes helping to avert the possibility of any theft of the wires which is a despicable act at any time. A couple of yards in front of every marker pin there will be a snare placed upon every run making the checking procedure simple and highly efficient. The trapper walks along the line despatching the captured rabbits whilst retensioning, shaping and resetting every snare back on the beat and placing the rabbits next to the marker pins for collection on the return journey.

It's a great feeling checking the snareline in the early morning, breaking first light after a nice windy night, especially when the weather is just right and no predator interruption or damage to the morning's catch brings a sigh of relief to the trapper. There is nothing more frustrating than arriving on the snaring field and finding nothing but carnage, or twenty or thirty dead rabbits bitten across the back of the shoulders and their ribs all crushed in and flecks of fur lying scattered around every victim where the rabbit has been running and jumping about trying to avoid the fox's jaws. Also odd heads left in the snares, sometimes ripped body parts are strewn all over if more than one fox or a number of large cubs work the snareline - it's sheer devastation.

The same problem arises the following morning as the fox or foxes come back looking for the rabbits they have killed the previously only to find new, freshly snared rabbits awaiting them. I just lift all the snares and rabbits then set fox snares or get the keeper to come over with the night vision scope to shoot the culprits as they return looking for fresh new victims. Only this time their new diet is ingested lead from a 55 grain Winchester .222 which is an immediate cure to the problem. Such is life, these are just normal problems experienced on the trap line now and again. At times it is better to snare the foxes first if sign is found when surveying the ground in the first place, therefore eliminating the problem immediately before the snaring operation commences.

4 How to Approach Rabbits on the Snareline

Viewing the illustration below you see the trapper approaching the snared rabbit from the downward side of the snare peg and taking hold of the snare to restrict any further movement of the restrained rabbit lying in a squat position. This is the normal prone position the rabbits take once they are captured, they will tuck themselves readily into any surrounding tussocky grass which gives them instant cover from aerial and ground predators and shelter from the elements. If possible I always set the snares on the runs at certain locations where they pass through or next to slightly heavier cover so that they can hide and feel safe and warm and out of sight even from prowling human eyes.

I always approach restrained rabbits from the securing peg end, I don't give direct eye contact with the rabbit and walk to the side barely glancing at it from the corner of my eye. Then I step quickly upon the snare compressing it to the ground which restricts the rabbit's movement making it far easier to grip it over the lower back in front of the hips to despatch it quickly. Not every rabbit will lie still in this squat position as you approach it some start to run around and squeal - once again step on the snare to restrict its movement before despatching it.

5 Controlling a Snared Rabbit

When approaching a rabbit in a pegged snare as shown in this illustration, walk outwards from the peg. Don't make direct eye contact, look to the side and watch the animal from the corner of your eye and make as though you are going to walk past it. Then step on the snare wire to restrict its movement.

Then gently hold the rabbit over the saddle of its back. Lift it off the ground so that it has no purchase with its back feet then place your other hand over the front of the rabbits head in front of the ears curving your forefinger and thumb behind its jaw bones one on either side of the head. Then gently tilt its head back and with a quick downwards and forwards movement of about an inch the animal is despatched in an instant by dislocation of the neck. Too many people put their hand to far back over the head onto the neck then struggle to try and despatch the animal quickly.

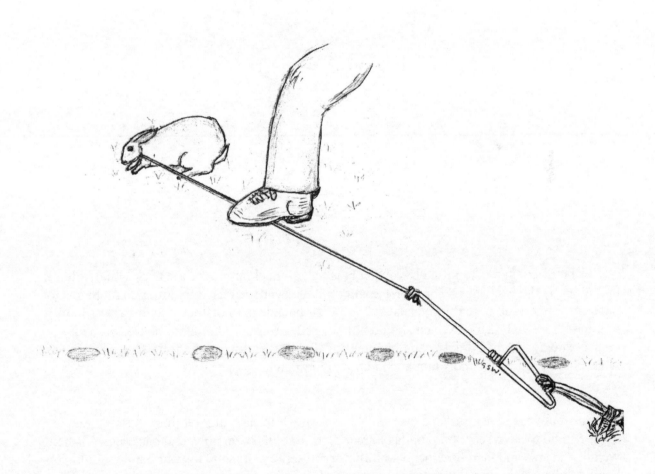

6 Dispatching Rabbits Humanely.

In this illustration it's showing the trapper holding a snared rabbit in his hands ready to despatch it. If you look carefully you will see that the creature is being held by the hind feet in the left hand, his right hand is placed over the rabbit's head this is the way a lot of people will hold rabbits to despatch them. The problem with holding a rabbit in this manner it that it can now gain leverage with its feet against the trapper's hand making it far more difficult to despatch due to its unrestricted violent movement of its body. This is why I never ever hold a rabbit by its hind feet while I'm in the process of despatching it.

The usual dispatch method used by amateurs is by karate chopping of the neck while holding the rabbit by the back legs. The worst method I have ever seen used to despatch rabbits is to put your foot on top of rabbits' heads and pull their back legs to dislocate their necks. In my opinion it's a cruel method which should not be used. Animals should all be treated with respect and despatched quickly and humanely. This illustration on the following page shows what I believe to be the most humane method of despatch.

You must always remember that care must be taken while carrying out this operation due to the fact rabbits have very sharp nails on their feet. Rabbits have powerful back legs for their weight and size and therefore they can inflict some serious damage to your hands should you handle them in the wrong way. I have witnessed these injuries on numerous occasions over the years of which I have been a victim myself.

Professional Rabbit Snaring

In my opinion after 60 years of practice, despatching thousands of rabbits over the years, the simplest and easiest method is to uplift the creature by holding it firmly across the lower back in front of the hips. When held in this position the animal cannot get any leverage with its feet due to being held across the back. I then take my right hand and place it gently and firmly over the front of its face and head at the base of its ears, my forefinger lies behind the jaw bone and my thumb around the opposite end. Then quickly and firmly tilt the head back slightly then with a quick and forward stroke of about 1 inch - the animal is killed instantly and humanely in a split second by dislocation of the neck which snaps the spinal cord.

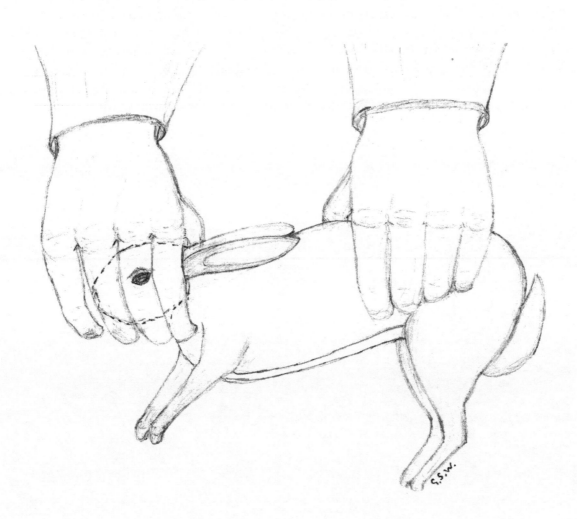

7 Removing Rabbits from Snares.

The trapper in this illustration has just despatched a rabbit in a pegged snare. As I have previously mentioned hold them over the back before despatching them quickly. By keeping a tight hold of them after they have been killed the snare noose can be loosened and removed with the opposite hand keeping you relatively safe from the powerful kicking action of the hind feet due to the violent incoordination of the muscles at the time of death.

Another simple method of removal is to hold the rabbit the way the trapper is showing in the illustration. After despatching the animal let it slide downwards as seen and by holding it around the top of the shoulders at the base of the neck, with its back to you and its feet facing to the front and away from you. This allows for the quick safe removal of the snare noose from the neck and over the head keeping you relatively free from any injury. Once when I was working with one of my old mentors up in the north one day, a momentary lapse of concentration for a few second, whilst in conversation with me, caused him to sustain quite a severe injury. A large buck rabbit's hind claws raked a line of deep long gashes down the back of one hand. Bleeding profusely he just calmly walked down the bank of a little stream to wash the blood from his hand, cracking a joke saying to me that these rabbits are not in the habit of wearing gum boots, therefore take care when removing rabbits from snares.

8 Snare Adjustment after Catch

Once the rabbit has been caught, despatched humanely and removed from the snare noose, there are a few basic procedures that must be carried out before the replacement of any snare back on the run. The first important thing you must do is to check the snare cable to see that there are no noticeable kinks or splayed strands visible in the snare cable - the whole length of wire must be carefully checked. Should any splayed or loose snare strands appear in the cable the simplest procedure required to fix this problem is to slip the snare noose over the hook on the end of the hammer shaft pulling it closed. Let the hammer hang down using its weight, then hold the end of the snare cable tightly at the eye of the tealer pin. Take your fingers and run them up and down the cable to ensure it's smooth with no breakages in the strands. After this procedure start and spin the hammer in a clockwise fashion until you are satisfied with the results that the snare cable is back in working order.

Splayed strands are a very common fault in shop bought snares and some homemade snares as they are only half spun not like the professional trapper's snare cable which is spun more tightly creating a nice tight smooth and stronger cable which beds well around the rabbit's neck and very rarely do you ever get splayed strands in the snare noose. The main problem with half spun snares is splaying strands being loose are prone to kinking, therefore instead of 6 strands taking the strain when a catch is made you now may have only three or four strands which are whole and perfect. The rest are kinked causing weakness in the cable which now becomes prone to breakages and lost catches which no self respecting trapper wants. We must be humane and consider the issue of animal welfare at all times. Kinks can also happen with snares fixed permanently to wire tealers. One of the worst problems with kinking in the snares is caused by smaller rabbits. These little culprits jump around, rolling turning and springing up and down causing severe kinking in the snare cable.

Now we come to the important part - what to do when you discover one or two actual kinks in the snare cable. It even happens occasionally in knotted snares that swivel, if the knot slips up and over the top of the tealer's right hand bend at the neck. On very rare occasions it can get jammed at the base of the double eye which prevents the swivelling action. This can be avoided when the spacing between the one and a half turns of the brass snare cable are kept at least ¼ of an inch apart and twisted firmly onto the shaft of the tealer at a 45 degree angle.

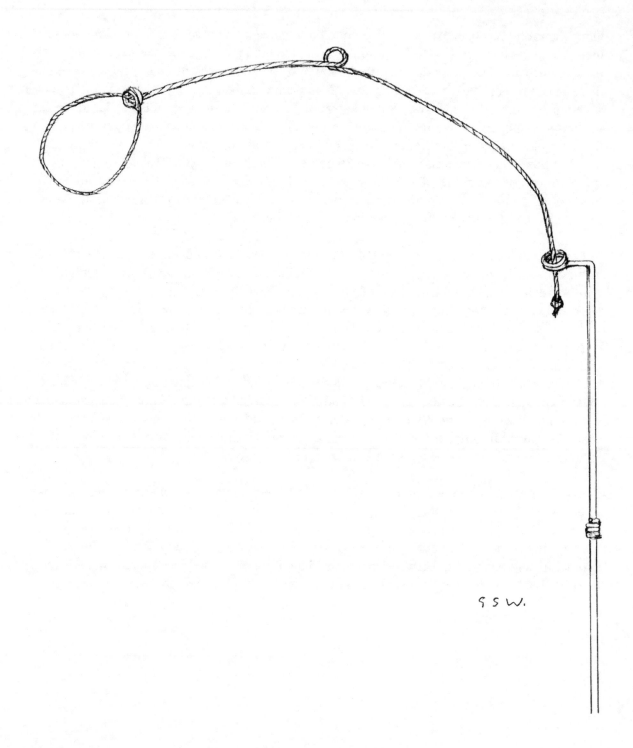

The illustration above shows a blatant kink in the snare cable.

To remove the kinks look closely at the distortion and then unfold the wire to free it from its twisted shape.

In the diagram below A shows a double kink in a snare. This would first be removed by 'unfolding' the twisted loops that you can see.   Once the kinks have been straightened out hold the snare wire tightly on either side of the kink mark, between the thumbs and the first bent knuckle of the forefinger as shown in B.   In practice the hands should be much closer to the kink - right beside it on either side. Rotate one hand firmly a couple of times, and then rotate the opposite hand - this action helps straighten up the snare strands.

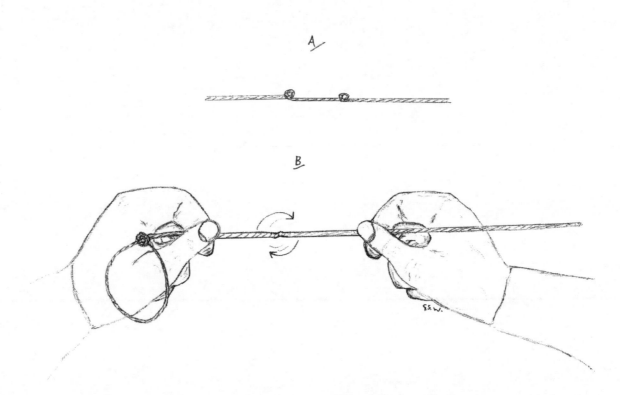

Next slip your forefinger into the snare noose and pull the wire taut as seen in the illustration opposite and proceed to rub your small hazel or ash toggle along the cable to smooth out and firm up the cable. It can then be retensioned or loaded then formed back into a nice big oval loop ready to reset upon the run.

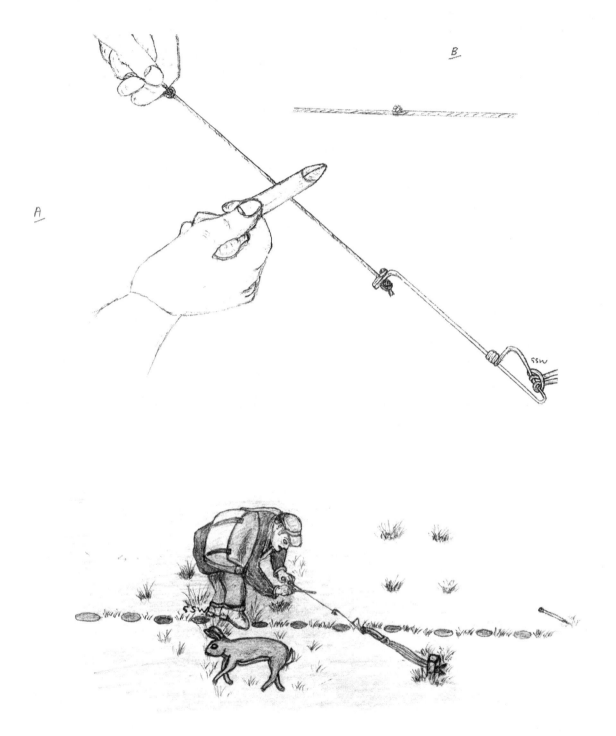

Remember and always carry spare twined pegs, nooses, spare S hooks when using breakaway snares, a small pair of snips and pliers come in very handy on the snareline for carrying out on the line repairs.

9 Setting and Uplifting the Snares

Before the snaring operation commences my snares are tied into bundles of twenty five to make it easier for counting and carrying. Four bundles is a hundred, eight bundles two hundred and so on. The snare location has been well surveyed beforehand checking out the terrain, the growth, roughly counting the number of active runs to correlate with the amount of bundles of pegged snares needed to cover all the runs. The snareman will then set about laying his snares by placing a snare on every run as he moves across the field in a relaxed methodical manner inserting the tealer firmly into the ground then pulling the peg to the side while partly inserting it in the ground with the heel of his hand then driving it home with his hammer leaving the twine lying in a straight manner with no play between the tealer and the peg the set snare is now sitting fully tensioned from the loop all the way along to the securing peg by setting each and every snare in this manner ensures a very high catch rate should the weather be fitting and no predator damage occurs.

Many authors and scribes have stated over the years to set extra snares to compensate for misses. If you set your snares the way I have shown in this text you will never be setting extra snares to compensate for misses, everyone gets misses, even I get them, but they are very few and far between due to the large loop system and setting higher. Should you be setting runs travelling uphill remember to angle the snare loop to the angle of the hill when setting out your snares the top of the snare loop should be tilted back towards you when looking uphill and tilted forward away from you looking downhill.

Once the snaring operation is over the snares and that morning's catch must be uplifted as efficiently as they were set, keeping the job as simple as possible. If you look carefully at the following illustration you will see how I work the snareline and then uplift the snares. It's imperative to use marker pins to every snare to eliminate the loss of any wires. You will notice that after every rabbit has been despatched and extracted from the snares. On the final morning each pegged snare is reshaped and placed neatly over each and every marker pin, with the snared rabbits lying beside each snare and marker all the way across the full length of the field. The rabbits are placed in piles of six or ten for easy counting and picking them up upon returning back along the line. You can see every marker pin which has been elevated to a higher more vertical position for easier viewing. Each and every snare along with the markers is carefully lifted, the markers placed in the bag with all the points facing in a forward manner for easier extraction and setting for the next outing. The snares are counted and tied into bundles of 25 and laid beside the rabbit piles. Should you approach a marker peg with no snare placed over it as seen in the illustration look along the run and the missing snare will be sitting a couple of yards along the run, still in the set position.

Once all the snares have been accounted for, uplift them and the rabbits and put them in the vehicle - job done. Looking at the other illustration of a fully made pegged snare neatly assembled this is how your professional snares should look once completed. If right handed the tealer grip should sit to the right and every peg should be slipped through the loop all from the same side to hang neatly as seen and tied into bundles of 25 at a time for easier carrying to eliminate any entanglement and easy counting.

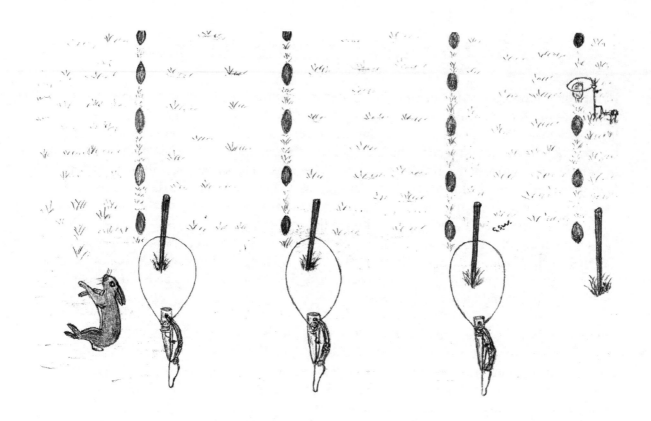

Remember this is the correct way to carry
snares to avoid entanglement

Professional Rabbit Snaring

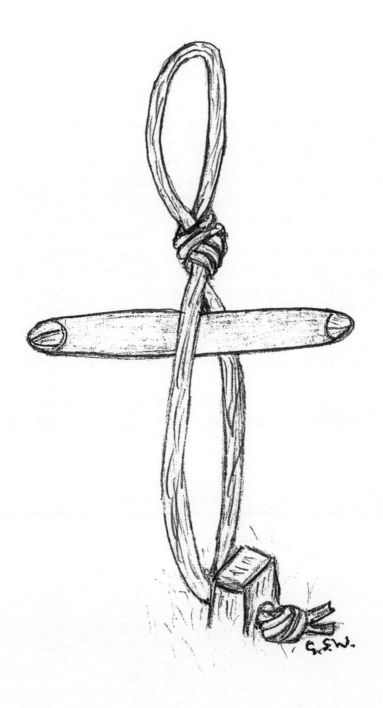

This illustration shows in clear detail how to extract a peg snare from the ground by either using a small 4" toggle as shown or the shaft of the hammer. Slip it through the larger loop in the twine between the peg and the knot. The little lightweight toggle is easier than carrying the heavy hammer.

Uplifting and Cleaning Snare Pegs

Around fifty years ago while out early one morning with old Willie Mac, checking his rabbit snareline, he was discussing various different procedures in connection with rabbit snaring. He would always explain the dos and don'ts connected to the operation in hand. Old Willie was very well versed to the snaring game, he was a fountain of knowledge on the subject as he practised it throughout his whole life in his daily employment. He had great visual awareness and nothing escaped his sharp beady eye. There was no transport then in his early keepering days he was one of the old school walked everywhere along all the field edges checking his traps and snares, a rare sight for modern keepers now as they travel in their 4 x 4 vehicles and quads compared to a bicycle in Willie's days.

Back to the snareline in question. That morning Willie had a good catch of rabbits, after they were despatched the snares emptied reshaped and tensioned. Helping Willie to uplift the snares that morning, he called me over and showed me this little trick as he pulled a snare peg from the ground with his small wooden toggle inserted between the snare twines behind the middle knot. He then took a hold of the snare peg in his right hand and the wire tealer in his left hand and then he proceeded to rotate the snare peg while running the wire tealer up and down the peg to remove any soil that was stuck to it after its extraction from the ground. This simple action ensures a nice clean securing peg ready to drop through the snare loop as the latter job only takes seconds to complete and also saves carrying the extra weight of damp soil along with each and every bundle of snares.

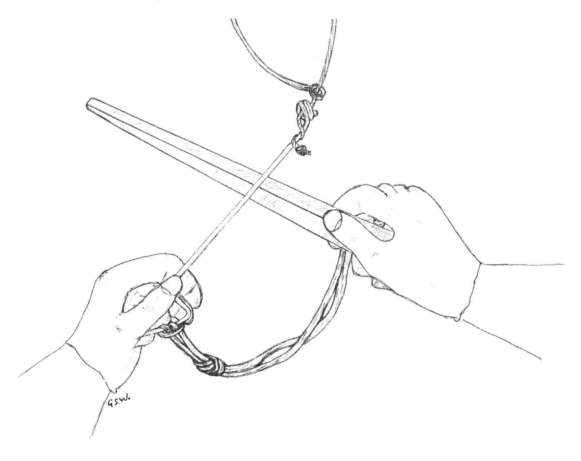

The Causes of Misshapen Nooses.

(A)   This is a classic shaped noose indicating that the rabbit has once again slipped clean through the snare loop without being caught. You will also encounter a similar shape when setting with a small loop set between the beats where the rabbit passes from the previous beat to the forward beat the small low set snare loop is now in a flat open position under the rabbit's belly the problem now arises as the rabbit's front feet land on the first half of the forward beat and as its back feet are being pulled in towards its front feet one of the back feet catch in the flat open noose pulling it partly closed hence the shape of the noose. To solve the problem of slipping through the normal big loop system is to set your snare higher. As for setting with small traditional loops between beats which is the totally wrong placement for the snare in the first place. Therefore this should be enough proof to enlighten any average intelligent person that the small loop system is non productive and start working with quality pegged snares with a large loop, setting higher across the middle of the beat, and certainly never between them.

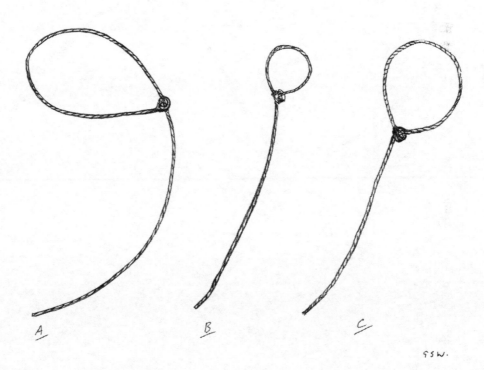

A   B   C

ᏚᏚᏔ.

(B)   Once again the snare loop has been set too low the rabbit has actually managed to slip through the large snare loop without being caught due to the fact the noose is very small as it almost caught the rabbit by a hind foot. Catching a rabbit by a hind foot as it slipped through a slightly lower set noose is now non-existent due to permanent fixed stops on snares.

(C)   The shape of this snare loop indicates the snare was set low and the rabbit has struck the underside of the top of the noose catching it around the nose in front of the eyes. After a few moments of struggling the rabbit has managed to fling the loop from its face hence the distinct shape of the snare, the small kinked loop the size of a two penny piece at the end of the taut snare cable. Once again do not set with small loops low to the ground they are practically non-productive.

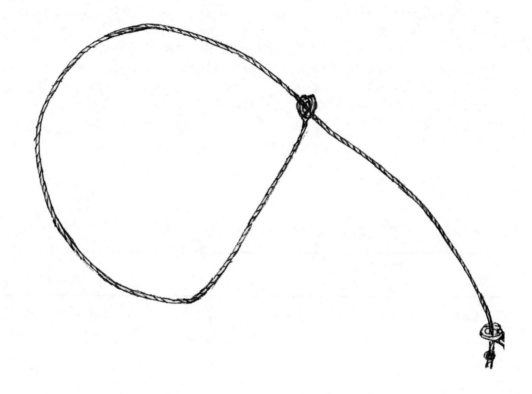

A snare loop found in this shape means that the snare has been placed directly in the middle of the beat, therefore the rabbit has jumped onto the bottom of the loop with its front feet, leaving a distinctive 'V' shape when the sprung noose is opened up. This can happen at times when setting less prominent runs on rough ground.

Chapter 9 - Advanced Tips

Making Rabbit Runs

To catch any animal in a snare you must set it on its line of travel, this is its run or trail which the creature uses on a nightly or daily basis to travel from its place of residence out to its feeding location. By placing a snare loop over the trail you are gaining an opportunity to take the animal by complete surprise while it's moving as it is unaware of the snare's presence. They are a creature of habit just like you and I as we ourselves follow roads and paths in a set pattern almost every day of our lives.

Imagine you were asked to control rabbits on a farm at a prescribed location - you are not permitted to shoot but you can set snares. I have been in situations like this many times over the years. On arriving at the said location many rabbits are visible and plenty of signs of their activity but that one vital aspect is missing, yes there are no runs available on which to set the snares. Well how do you go about catching these rabbits if there is nowhere to place your snares? This is where the experienced trapper prevails as he has many years of knowledge behind him.

There may be a perimeter fenceline but due to the noted presence of game birds no fenceline snares are permitted. Therefore only pegged snares or hoop snares must be used. Each and every location is different therefore various techniques must be applied to suit the crops, vegetation and ground conditions, so the mode of progression must differ at times. To partake in the art of snaring and to reach a high standard of excellence every trapper should make his acquaintance with and study every single aspect of the animal he wishes to capture. To capture rabbits in locations void of visible runs is actually quite simple once a little thought has been applied. First of all if it is young crops or grass that is the area in question the runs can be seen quite clearly at times by going round in the very early morning to view the location. The simple fact is that any rabbits that have ventured out into the field in the nocturnal hours to feed will leave tracks clearly visible to the naked eye in the early morning dew covered crops or grass. Therefore if you insert a marker peg at the side of each and every visible run then you can either scuff your boot for a few yards along each and every track seen in the dew or stamp a couple of beats so that they will be more clearly visible to the trapper when he comes to set his snares later in the morning. Another trick I have used on many occasions when checking out crop fields is to follow the rabbit droppings out and look for dirt on a couple of crop leaves which indicates the rabbit's presence, being left from the soil on its feet on real careful examination toenail holes can also be seen at times in an occasional trampled leaf.

This same practice is used in grass fields that have been overgrazed first by cattle all summer right up until the first of November, then followed by a month of sheep grazing. I usually leave these fields until January hoping for a mild spell of weather and a little growth to come forward, on occasions there may be one or two visible little runs present. The trick is to walk out about twenty five to thirty yards from the woodland edge and carefully walk along the field slowly, parallel to the woodland. Watch for fresh droppings, follow them and be looking most carefully you will at times see one small beat and nothing else. Just set a snare on each and every little beat found by doing this I have snared as many as thirty rabbits in a morning from extremely bare ground.

At times I will take the toe of my boot and make the beat more visible and then set it right in the middle of it. This compresses the verdure and makes it more compact and easier to reset once a catch has been made. At certain times of the day runs are more visible due to the light of the day whether sunny or overcast and sun angle. Another little trick I use is a pair of Polaroid glasses which cuts any glare and makes single beats and very faint runs stand out more clearly. Even runs running at a slight angle are easily picked up as they look more prominent in bare short grass to your eyes.

Other locations may be totally void of any grass altogether such as in young rape or peas where the rabbits have decimated the crop for many yards out, leaving only bare ground which may have a sandy soft type of soil especially in dry summer weather. Often droppings, scrape holes and flecks of fur are the only available signs denoting their immediate presence with the absence of runs once again. The perimeter of the field is often a hedge heavily overgrown and thick with aggressive stinging nettles and thick bramble bushes, an impregnable fortress of cover which holds the resident rabbit population. Again the answer is quite simple - just make false runs either by scuffing the sole of your boot in the soft bare soil a few yards out into the field from the perimeter edge or by using a garden hoe and scraping a straight line out from the edge exactly the same as using the sole of your boot. Do this right along the field leaving a space of six feet between the newly made runs which are prominent to the rabbits visibly, along with the smell of freshly scraped earth and attracts them readily into using them.

In dry soft sandy soil the use of pegged snares would be impossible which due to the latter conditions is self explanatory, I've found the best type of snare to use is the hoop snare. As covered later there is no hard and fast rules to the length or type of wire used to make them, the firmness and density of the ground conditions govern this itself. I normally cut my 3 mil thick fenceline wire approximately 44" in length (high tensile) and bend them into a nice hoop shape, the only reason for using the "high tensile wire" is that it is very strong and slightly harder to work with. Therefore 3 mil diameter wire of this texture would be a sufficient thickness to use and would make excellent hoops as they would never bend easily, cut into the required lengths they are ideal when inserted into the soft ground, leave the newly made runs about four or five days before returning to set them.

On arrival you will notice that all the new runs are covered in droppings all the way along them. On setting the hoops hold one wire leg in each hand, face outwards towards the field the way the rabbit is travelling (same when setting pegged snares), straddle the run by placing one foot on either side. Then bend over the insert and stagger the legs of the wire hoop forwards and back into the ground over the run, across the middle of the beat, same as a pegged snare. Then adjust the big snare loops which have already been attached to the hoops beforehand to the snaring operation, to the proper height.

Another trick that can be adopted is to use lengths of hazel or strong green dyed garden canes two feet long $^1/_2$" thick. Using pegged snares in the soft ground is not advisable so you just insert the tealer pin at the side of the run to hold the snare loop in place and either embed the snare peg with the heel of your boot or just leave it lying on the ground and insert the strong length of pliable cane in between the snare double twines and push it deep into the soft ground. This also holds well. Every problem has a solution, so just sit and think things over before applying yourself to each snaring operation. Would you walk through thick cover or over rough ground if there was a nice path available, think about it.

Working Soft Ground

This illustration shows a simple method I have used on many occasions when setting snares throughout woodland and strips of woodland along hedges, field edges etc. Everyone who has ever done a bit of snaring knows that every location is not perfect. Therefore a trapper must be innovative and quick thinking at times to come up with fresh ideas on how to overcome certain problems placed before us throughout our working days. We must consider weather and ground conditions and ask ourselves questions such as what can and cannot happen at this location. Constantly turning these thoughts over in our minds we try to come up with the right solution to solve a particular problem which arises now and again, trying to haunt us in some way. As I have mentioned before I'm from a psychic family, it comes through the family from my old great Irish gypsy grandmother from Sligo. Many times over my lifetime I have been shown visions of many things happening and voices telling me things and what to do to solve problems, something which has happened countless times over the years out on the snareline.

Getting back to the illustration - what you see is a pegged snare holding a rabbit which has wrapped the snare around a vertical branch protruding upwards from the ground. The ground density was slightly soft at this location and once the securing peg was inserted into the ground I didn't feel comfortable with the situation. Therefore I snapped off a length of sycamore branch as thick as my forefinger, pointed it at one end and then inserted it as deep as possible into the ground further along the run and off to one side.

This small branch did its job perfectly as it was designed for. Once the snared rabbit runs around creating a kill mark, as the catch circle is also known, it wraps around the stick a couple of times. This simple action takes most of the strain off the securing peg and holds the rabbits securely preventing possible escape. When snaring along field edges where there are no trees or hedges and you feel the ground slightly soft and where there is a possible suspected escape I take a slightly thicker hazel marker pin around $3/8^{th}$ of an inch diameter and insert it into the ground and this method has also worked well on occasions. The tapping stick method can also be used.

Avoiding Problems in Hard Dry Ground

When the ground conditions are hard and dry and no rain has fallen for weeks and a farmer calls and asks for your assistance to come and help to control rabbits that are devastating his silage grass or crop fields, how would you deal with this situation? Remember the ground is like iron therefore how do you get the securing pegs into the ground without damaging the snare pegs which can fracture and snap into two? It can also cause splaying of the points. The answer is quite simple. I carry a foot long half inch diameter steel spike to make a pilot hole before inserting the securing peg. Before I continue any further I want you to take note of what I am going to reveal. A peg inserted into a dry hole and hammered into the ground can on occasions be pulled out due to the arid conditions and by being pulled to and fro by the snared rabbit. I have had firsthand experience of this as it has happened to me. How can this problem be solved?

An old mentor of mine showed me a simple trick that you would not believe. He carried a couple of 500 ml plastic coke bottles filled with water which can be refilled from a stream or cattle trough or any watershed for that matter. He poured about an inch of water into the bottom of the pilot hole then inserted the peg and hammered it in. He said when the peg goes down into the bottom of the hole the water elevates up the sides of the peg or pegs and creates suction like you get in normal damp ground conditions and it's the bottom few inches of the peg that takes the grip due to the suction created by the water. This ensures a tremendous grip in very dry ground conditions preventing any rabbit and snare losses. The reason for using the small sized plastic 500 ml bottles is because they are not too large or heavy to carry. Also they are easy to handle and work with and take up little room in your large sized game bag. There are no hard and fast rules to the amount of containers you can carry in your vehicle should you have to set out a few hundred snares to complete your rabbit control work.

We have now solved only half of the problem. You may well ask yourself what other problem is to be solved. Well the securing pegs have been hammered in, now they have to be removed on completion of the work. For a few years I laboured laboriously doing a job I hated removing the pegs. I used a small roofers pick the type that is used to knock holes in slates and then nail them to the slats on the roof top. I have an old fashioned one which I acquired from a friend it's a work of art and performed well.

While sitting in my vehicle one morning having just arrived at the snaring field a thought came into my head out of the blue and being from a psychic family my spirit friends showed me a vision on how to extract the pegs from the ground without having to dig them out. I have had these visions all my l life, a voice in my ear so to speak showing me and telling how to do things in daily life even in the trapping and snaring game. My late father's voice spoke to me and said *"now that you have been shown go and try it out"*. I despatched the rabbits then I began the task of lifting the snares. Previously I started to use a steel spike to make a pilot hole to insert the securing pegs. Well the vision showed me to hammer the steel spike down into the ground next to the rabbit snare peg to the same depth as the 8" peg, then give the spike a couple of taps with the hammer on the sides to loosen it then pull it out of the ground. Next give the peg a light tap and Bob's your uncle as they say, then pull the baling twine to the empty hole side made by the spike and it just falls out no more laborious digging the job's done in seconds and the little pick is now redundant permanently.

Another tip I will impart to the reader is that it is imperative to pay attention to the weather forecast when setting in very dry conditions and keep your eye out for rain. This is due to the fact that if you set out snares in dry ground and a heavy downfall of rain comes down for a few hours throughout the night you will lose a few snares as the ground softens. At times your snares can be extracted easily and you will find a clod of porridge like dirt approx a couple of inches in diameter stuck to the snare pegs. To avoid this scenario keep your eye on the weather before setting your snares out. You can also wait until the weather breaks and set the snares a few days later after the rain has gone as there will be suction in the ground.

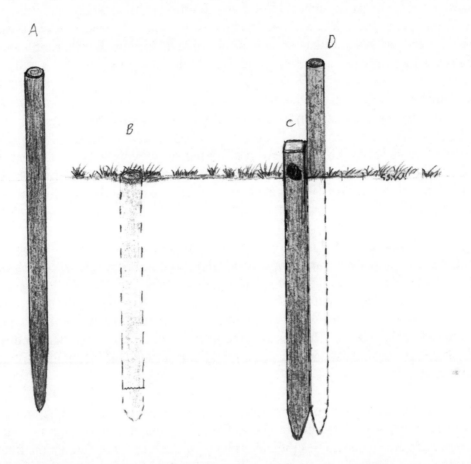

A - Steel spike 12" long.
B - Hole made by spike with 1" of water in the bottom.
C - Snare peg inserted into hole.
D - Steel spike hammered into the ground next to the peg to aid extraction.

Effective Snaring around Warrens

It's generally well known amongst snarers that the proper place to set snares is well out into the field away from the perimeter, where the rabbits are moving at speed as they travel out towards their feeding ground. Placing your snare loop so that it sits at the proper height over the middle of the small beats gives the most productive results as the bounding rabbit does not stop on the latter beats at all. In shorter grassland where the beats are closer together $6^1/_2$" is a most effective height to set the snares to obtain maximum results, where the grass is longer the beats further apart the snares will need to be raised higher especially in wet weather as the rabbits rise higher. Always be as observant as possible and remember that each and every run should be set accordingly to the present conditions at the time of setting the snares.

Over the years practically every scribe when penning manuals or articles usually states that it is of little use putting snares down near the actual burrows themselves as they are either brushed aside or knocked over and only amateurs set these said locations. I set the beats between the burrows but as the rabbits creep around there may be only 2 or 3 beats between the holes. When using pegged snares in this way caught rabbits will sometimes hide in the openings of holes in reach. Any well travelled runs leading out and away from the warren should also be set.

Ferreting usually is the accepted mode of practice to reduce the resident rabbit population but many of these old established warrens are very deep and on different levels of varying depth. They can be located in various types of ground such as chalk, clay, sandy type soils etc making digging a hard and sometimes impossibly tedious task when trying to retrieve a large ferret. On large warrens dozens of nets have to be set over the holes too enmesh the escaping rabbits as they flee the ferrets. There is also the problem of adverse weather conditions having to sit out at times frozen or wet waiting on dour rabbits that just won't bolt due to continual harassment.

Then there is the laborious method of trapping the rabbits in their burrows having to carry bundles of steel traps and sometimes buckets of dry soil, plus the tools, digging hammer, sifter, small spade etc. Then comes the disturbance of the burrows to adjust the holes to fit the traps which must be then covered with sifted soil to fool the rabbits of their hidden presence. All this tedious manual work that can really be avoided by a little forethought.

Once again this is where a simple snare can be applied with a little intelligent thought to capture a large warren's resident rabbit population, without having to go to all the bother of ferreting or trapping. All warrens are not textbook settings, but a large majority are and this is where the snare can be very effective at these locations. Once again the big loop plays a most important part when using either pegged snares or hoop snares. The tight smooth wound snare cable with a very little tension and no wind down closes very fast with very little resistance on the quarry's head entering the big noose, which is designed to correlate with the measurements of the rabbit's head and ears, and the distance of the sensors or whiskers of $7^1/_2$". A tiny loop set especially of the old traditional method is nothing more than an obstruction to a large full grown rabbit hopping slowly, which will just knock the snare over, unless by some unfortunate stroke of sheer luck more than a good skill or judgement may be caught by accident.

Like you and I the rabbit feels quite safe outside its home as it can make a quick exit to the safety of the immediate burrow. In the immediate vicinity around the warren the rabbits creep around slowly with their head held lower to the ground, unlike when out travelling along a more open run where the head is held higher.

Around the warren the snares must be set lower to the ground, (varying heights due to conditions), around 4 inches to accommodate the creeping rabbit's head. As the illustration shows set beats going over the top of the burrows which at times may be close together and as a few as only three beats may be visible. Also set the beats leading away from the holes and around the edges. Set the snares so that any captured rabbits can't knock other snares set nearby - the hoop snare restricts the distance of movement more so than the pegged snare which can be an advantage. Set out as many as you can and you will be surprised by the results taken in snares using the professional sized loop as the weathered wire poses no threat of any kind and the rabbit is looking right through it and the dyed wire tealer pin sits well to the side with only the big noose itself covering the whole run properly, just perfect across the middle of the beat. With the immediate large kill area of the noose allowing greatly for any margin of error, the silent sentry working 24 hours a day needs not food nor vet's bills, eliminates digging and waiting out in the cold, and works while you sleep. They only need to be emptied in the morning and reset, who says a snare in not effective.

On showing this method to a couple of snaring friends of mine down in England one lad took 73 rabbits in three days from a large warren. The other lad had 46 rabbits from a large warren in a field next to a market garden where the rabbits were doing extensive damage. **Set the snares according to conditions at the said location.**

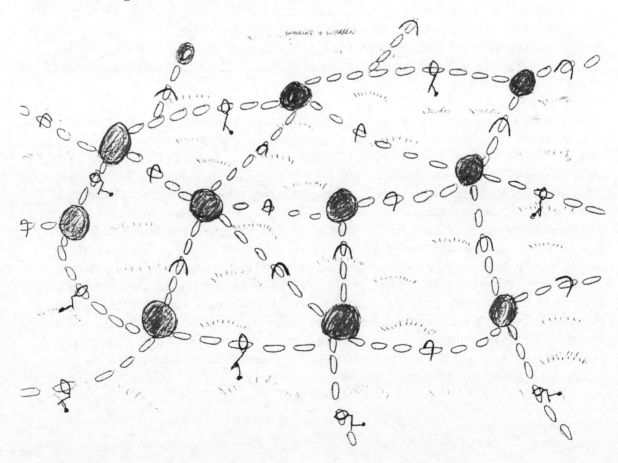

Snaring in Stubble Fields

After the summer when the crops are all cut is the best time of the year to set out your snares, a whole lot of different locations are opened up to the trapper expanding his range of habitat greatly. Carrying out rabbit control throughout spring and summer months protecting various types of crops, snaring operations are usually restricted along edge features; crop fields, hedges, fencelines, railway lines, motorway fencelines, bankings, woodlands, plantings, woodland strips in outlying areas away from rearing pens and fields. After harvest and the fields are all cleared, the trapper can now get some serious snaring done well out from the field edges in pasture grass and various different types of crop fields on dark and windy blustery nights, enabling him to attain good catches of rabbits.

It takes many years before a tradesman becomes efficient at his job. Over these years much experience will be gained to carry out many different aspects of his line of work enabling him to form solutions to work out various daily problems and how to overcome them. Well the experienced trapper has acquired the same level of skills over many years of working out on the trapline gaining much experience in his line of work also having to overcome daily problems he encounters each and every day, e.g. inclement weather conditions, predator damage, height of flora etc. Let us look at the snaring of stubble fields. Should the farmer require a lot of straw to bed his livestock throughout the winter months he will cut the stubble shorter. If he does not require a large amount of straw the stubbles are left longer. When it comes to setting this type of location I shall start with the short stubble growth first that averages 6 inches high. If you look carefully at these runs as they stretch out into the field you will notice they have beats similar to normal runs found in pasture grass. These runs in this short stubble I call 'corridor runs' due to the fact that they are usually well used with prominent beats showing, and they have a short 5" high wall of stubble bordering the full length of each run on either side, hence the name corridor run. Set these runs at normal height of 6½" /7" high to bottom of the loop.

When setting in high stubbles around 9"-10" high you don't have a short flatter normal type run. What you have here is totally different, the growth is higher therefore what you see is *high growth - a beat - high growth - a beat* etc all the way along the full length of the run. I know professionals who could not set them but it is not rocket science. It's just giving a little thought to solving the problem, such as making and using a longer tealer pin. Keeping a hundred or two hundred snares with the larger 7½" x 5½" loop and the longer tealers gives you the proper snare height and still helps retaining the "striking curve" in the middle of the bottom loop to take the rabbit up under the chin as it passes along the run. Set the snare to correlate with the height of the stubble around 10" high to the bottom of the loop, it's pure commonsense when the beats are further apart 14"-18"-2 ft apart and the growth is high between them. The rabbit has to leap up higher to get up and over the high standing flora to get to each and every beat as it travels along the run. Illustration (A) shows high standing stubble of ten inches, with dotted line showing proper snare placement over middle of the beat. (B) is the corridor run in six inch high stubble, dotted line shows proper snare placement over middle of a beat.

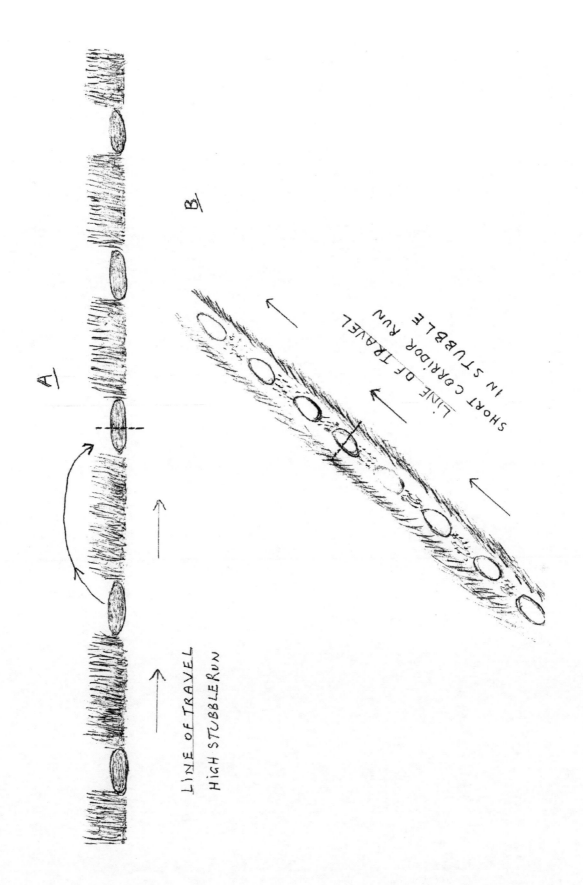

A

LINE OF TRAVEL
HIGH STUBBLE RUN

B

SHORT CORRIDOR RUN
IN STUBBLE

LINE OF TRAVEL

Professional Rabbit Snaring

Section 3 -

Exploiting Fences and Boundaries

Professional Rabbit Snaring

Chapter 10 - Fenceline Rabbit Snaring

The Snares (Scotland) Order 2010 effectively prohibits the practice of Fenceline Snaring in Scotland as it is an offence to set snares in places where captured animals are likely to become fully or partially suspended or drown.

In the rest of the UK there is no *legal* constraint on the placing of rabbit snares within fence-lines but the 2005 Defra Code of Good Practice on the use of Snares in Fox and Rabbit Fox Control states that '*snares must not be set in sites cluttered by obstacles such as saplings, hedges, walls, fences or gates, which increase the risk of injury. Sites that pose the risk of fatal entanglement should be avoided*'.

Setting snares on fencelines is also an art in itself, which can only be perfected by continual practice. To acquaint yourself intimately with this art you must be aware of the many different types of fencelines that separate the various grass and crop fields. Some consist of lengths of galvanised fence wire stapled to wooden posts inserted into the ground every six feet. The spacing between the wire strands can vary on fencelines, at different locations they can measure between 4" to 7" to 9" on the bottom half of the fenceline. The diameter of the steel galvanised wire normally used on the modern fencelines is 3 mil, on some of the older type fences especially along old railway embankments I have seen it 4 mil and thicker. Some of the old estate fences with the metal posts the wires looked really thick at least 5 mil. A lot of farms use Rylock fencing with the square mesh at the bottom approximately 4" working up to 6" squares at the top and is a metallic green in colour. Other similar galvanised fences start at 5" squares on the bottom all the way up to the top. There are also chain link and two inch square galvanised fencelines, the variety is endless but the latter mentioned are the most regular types encountered.

Before the setting of any snares on a fenceline you must look carefully and ask yourself one question; *What can and cannot happen at the said location?* First of all think of the dangers that may be involved; does it border near a public footpath? are there dwelling houses nearby? think of domestic pets such as cats and small dogs. Does the field hold any livestock within ? Is there any livestock in the next field that borders the perimeter fence? Is the fenceline new or it is of old standing with broken or cracked posts that are slack and shaky, due to previous damage sustained over the years by farm machinery working too close, or from heavy cattle leaning and rubbing and scratching on it. Do the wires on the fence look slack, loose or broken that the cattle can get their heads through between the damaged wires ? Or if they may be able to lean over it to graze on the other side?

One instance I was asked to snare a field where serious crop damage occurred which bordered on grazing field full of cattle. On viewing the location I noticed the headland on the crop field side of the wire perimeter fence, the grass was extremely closely cropped to the ground. I was puzzled for a moment or two as there was a single strand of barbed wire running parallel to the perimeter fenceline about four feet out in the grazing field side to prevent cattle from doing any damage to the fence. I also knew that it was not rabbits which had cropped the short grass as it was too neat and even and rabbits eat in uneven half circles. I followed the perimeter fenceline uphill and on reaching the brow of the hill I looked down across into the valley of the grazing field. Lo and behold there lying in the grass were young calves who could duck under the single strand of barbed wire and stick their heads through between the fenceline wire to crop the grass on the opposite side.

Do not under any circumstances set any fenceline with hanging snares or even set pegged snares in or near where livestock are present. Cattle have a long tongue which is rough and when they are grazing if you watch very closely you will notice the tongue will come out of the mouth from the left side then the right side and so on and wrap it around the grass pulling it into the mouth. They have no top front teeth only a pad, the same as sheep, except that sheep feed by a continual upward quick movement of the head. Horses have both upper and lower sets of front teeth and a long spatula shaped tongue. Do not set snares on fencelines bordering pheasant coverts or in the surrounding vicinity. I only ever set fencelines on far outlying areas void of game birds.

Always give extreme thought when setting snares of any kind and consider the danger to other wildlife and domestic pets. In experienced hands snares can be made almost 100% species specific and with a little careful thought many problems can be avoided. I cannot stress the importance of this enough. So always ask yourself what can and what cannot happen as the snare is one of the simplest and cost effective tools ever devised for the taking of rabbits in large numbers and we want to keep it legal in the UK so don't abuse it. Remember "one snare in the hands of a fool" can cause more problems than enough.

All commercially purchased snares usually come with a thin cheap cord attached to them which deteriorates quickly once exposed to the elements and the short length of snare wire is only suitable on occasions for certain types of fencelines. Professional snaremen never use cord on fenceline snares as it rots and is of no use in his line of work. Some people remove the cheap cord and replace it with stronger nylon cord which in my opinion is still a waste of time for the simple fact that it only serves to draw attention from all and sundry. People who use cord are usually limited in experience and have no real knowledge how to set snares in a proper professional manner. They usually secure the snare to the fenceline by tying a knot in the end of the cord and then looping the snare through between the twine, then winding the end of the brass snare cable around the fenceline wire. Others tie the twine to the fenceline in a knot. The favourite with a lot of amateurs when using commercial snares is to attach the snare cord to the fenceline then prop the snare up into position using a wooden tealer peg. Some of the settings that I have had the misfortune to view at times where snares were set along a fenceline like a row of drunk men, would have brought tears to a glass eye of any self respecting trapper. Setting snares in the latter manner is nonsense and only serves to give you more work that could be avoided with a little thought but some people just seem to struggle forward day after day without making life any easier for themselves.

Rabbits are wild creatures with their own little personalities and are guided by instinct. Look at the shape and characteristics of the rabbit, consider its environment, how it moves, runs and plays. Try to put yourself in its mind, every day of its life is fraught with danger, it is quite aware and very aloof, it is also lithe and agile and slips through between bushes and briars every day of its life and up and over and through drystone dykes or walls. Therefore to capture any animal you must remember that you have to overcome its senses which I call 5Ss scent, sound, sight and smell, sensitivity, or touch and feel. It's the same when snaring foxes, once you can fool all of the five senses of any wild creature you can catch it. When snaring you must keep these vital aspects in mind, whether pegged snaring or fenceline snaring or trapping for that matter.

Before setting out your fenceline snares they should all be counted exactly beforehand preceding the setting operation, good equipment should be maintained at all times and hanging snares treated like pegged snares and kept away from any abnormal odours, aftershave, scented soaps and any oil or diesel soaked rags, also make sure that your clothes are free from any of the latter odours and smells.

On commencing with the snaring operation the snares can be carried in your bag which has a natural rabbity smell anyway from carrying continual catches of rabbits. Don't be like some I have seen and carry them in your pockets and once they are withdrawn look like a bird's nest. Before they have been set always keep all types of snares neat and tidy whether pegged or hangers. Never ever be sloppy in this line of work, look after your equipment and it will look after you believe me. I have looked at many people's snares over the years and it's easy to pick out the ones who know their stuff from the ones who do all the talking about it. It's up to each individual trapper how many hanging snares he wishes to suspend from his left arm, ensuring that you're right handed of course and vice versa when left handed.

It is to be remembered that every fenceline is different in length and sometimes it takes a few hundred snares to cover the overall total distance of the fenceline. Keeping your snares in bundles of twenty five makes easy counting and working with, as each and every bundle is held neatly and securely by a twine slipped through all of the snare loops together. Each four bundles making a total of one hundred snares, therefore two bundles making fifty can be slipped over your arm with the twine removed from the first lot of twenty five to be removed in sequence from your arm. Once the first lot has been set along the fenceline a marker pin can then be inserted into the ground, continuing this practice until all of the snares have been set with a marker pin at every twenty-fifth snare. This makes counting far easier when the snaring operation is over, as you will then be aware that if any snares are missing it has to be between the marker pins. Every twenty five snares lifted should be recounted and carefully put into your bag so that you have exactly the same amount as you started with.

Attaching Snares to Fencelines - Double Hitch Method.

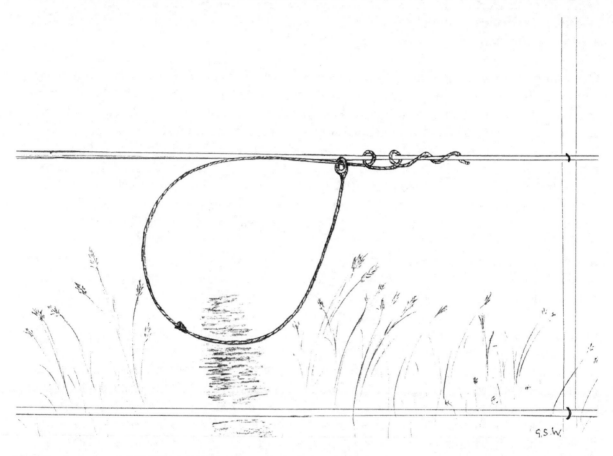

This is the way old Willie Mac taught me to attach snare nooses to a fenceline 47 years ago and it holds very well. The problem arises when a catch is made and the two hitches slide together forming a very tight knot - difficult to undo and with to potential to snap the snare. The illustrations opposite provide more detail.

A) Shows the double hitch method of attachment to wire fenceline strand it has been enlarged for the reader to see how it is attached more clearly.

(B) When a catch is made in the snare the weight of the animal (e.g. rabbit) pulls the two hitch loops tightly together. At times this makes the removal of the snare noose from wire strand slightly more difficult than with the more simpler 'trapping the second loop' system which eliminates this minor problem. In cold weather with numbing fingers one has to force the bottom loop at point (C) in a downward fashion with the thumbnail to allow a little play so that the right hand turn of the snare wire around fenceline strand can be pushed upwards, to help to loosen the snare cable from fenceline. In cold winter weather where an overnight frost may creep in during the early hours of the morning, and the double hitch wire coils around fenceline are pulled tightly together restricting any freedom of movement, the snare cable can break at point (D) resulting in a lost catch. I used this method of attaching hangers to fencelines for many years before I was introduced to the 'trapping the second loop' system by Whyte which was quick and fast for attaching and removal of the snare noose.

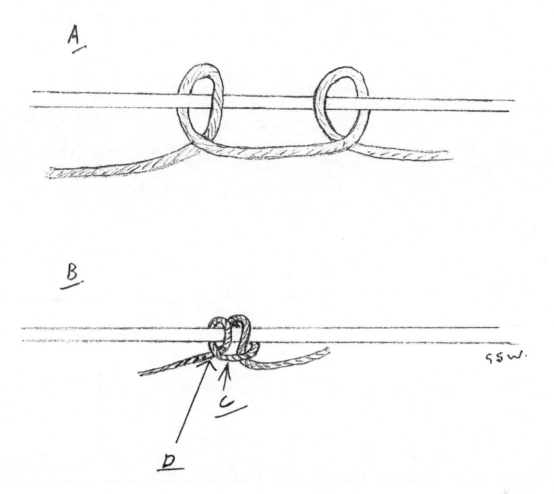

A.

B.

C

D

SSW.

The shape of this snare noose is also a problem which I discovered from firsthand experience many years ago - if I had not seen this happening by my own eyes I would not have believed it. What happens is the rabbits at times when approaching the snare set on the fenceline will clap down very flat to the ground they then somehow draw their body in making themselves narrower and flatter, they then spring with such speed and go straight through the round snare loop without even touching the sides. The rabbit has now landed in the field and the snare loop is still sitting in perfect position the exact way it had been set, the rabbit could see the whole circle of the loop which was an obstruction so it went straight through it. This same problem arises when snaring predators on crawl under or holes under fencelines such as foxes and coyotes. When they can see the whole of the loop circle they refuse to go under and walk away from it, especially on bare ground. Once again I learned this first hand out on the trap line.

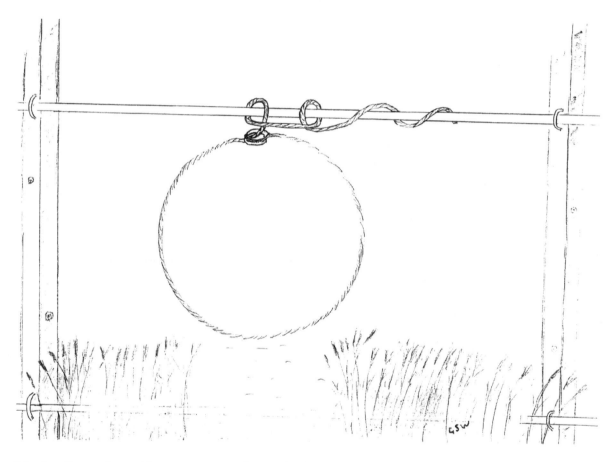

I had a discussion with a pro trapper from Montana who blamed the thicker diameter of snare cable for causing refusals by coyotes. I told him that I'm not saying you're wrong there is a possibility it can happen but that's not the main problem which I discovered first hand, they shy or refuse the snare set because they can see the whole circle of the snare loop which is an obstruction to them and should not be there. He must have thought to himself what does he know about snaring coyotes because he comes from Scotland a small country in the back of beyond. I told him I had snared lots of coyotes in Canada over the years with my friend and pro trapper Peter Alan from British Columbia. Then he started to listen. I also said to him he was setting his coyote snares with a long narrow loop too low to the ground as the coyotes were stepping through them. It always pays to listen as you can learn from anyone as they can look at a situation differently and have a better idea than you.

The way to avoid the latter problems with rabbits and coyotes is to always set with a good sized loop and break up the snare's outline by having the top part of the loop above the fenceline wire then you don't get refusals. Small loops cause many refusals especially with fox snares set on thick silly wooden tealers especially on ground void of any good cover.

It was a true saying among a few of my old mentors, "Amateurs just love making hard work for themselves", and boy have I seen it all over the years in the trapping and snaring game. The older some people get the more stupid they seem to become. All the wisdom seems to be leaving this world and snaring is the same. The amount of times I have witnessed people setting snares along fence lines and the methods used would actually bring tears to a glass eye.

One clown had set a number of snares along a fenceline and then wrapped white marking tape onto the fence wire above every snare. Another fool did exactly the same only he used bright red electrical tape. Snares tied with white string and blue clothes line rope were also used. Snares tied on the fence wire above the run then stretched upwards wound around the above fence wire, snares attached to sea fishing swivels with string. One of the best I came across was about 2 dozen brand new 4mm thick shiny snap links attached to the fence wire above the runs. The snare loops were not even attached to the fence line they were opened up to the usual amateur 4" loops and were placed in the grass and left sitting freely like drunk men and shaped like crinkle cut crisps. Honestly you couldn't make it up. Getting back to reality who in their right mind wants additional baggage like tape, swivels, string, rope and snap links attached to a rabbit snare noose when fence line snaring? You guessed it, only amateurs.

Trapping the Second Loop - The Preferred Way to Attach Snares to Fencelines.

This series of illustrations that I have drawn and shown here show the fastest simplest method of attaching and removing fence line snares. This method was taught to me many years ago by one of my old mentors Andy Whyte. First of all make a larger sized professional loop. If you are right handed tension and shape the noose next by putting the fingers of your left hand through the front of the loop to the underside of the loop. Compress the eyelet between thumb and fingers and hold firmly.

A   Place the eyelet next to the fence line wire then bend the tail of the wire over and under as shown.

B   Moving along 1/2" from loop A place the end part of the snare loop under the fence wire and bring it back over towards you This is your second loop

C   When you bring the third loop over you do not put it to the outside of loop B. The third loop is bought over tightly to the inside of the second loop B. Then wind the rest of the snare wire around the fence line . This method is called trapping the second loop. When using this method keep the tension on the snare wire and pull it firmly as you make the loops this hold the snare loop tight to the wire fence line. Once the snare is secured in position, the loop as shown with the top part of the snare loop above the fence line wire to break up the outline of the snare loop. With a little practise you will become more proficient and a lot quicker in setting as it really only takes seconds to attach a fence line snare using this method this method holds hares and even accidental fox cub catches.

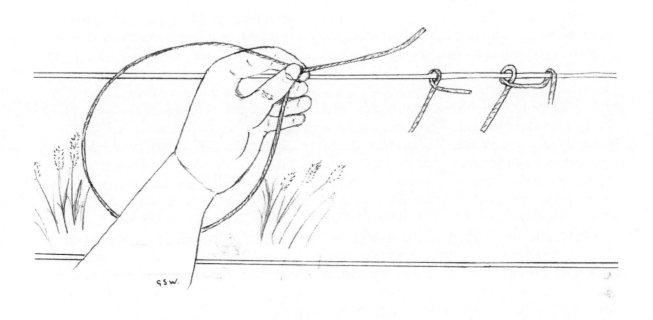

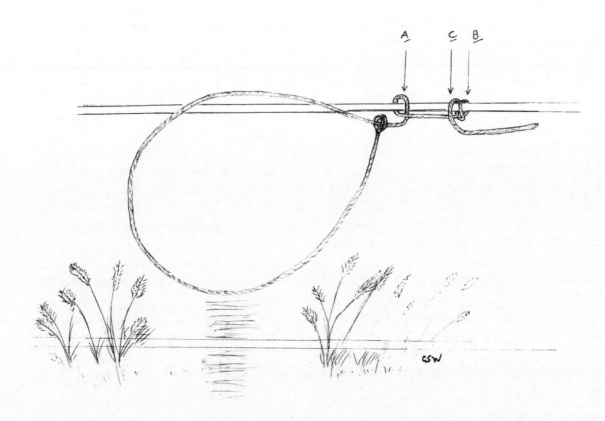

The two following illustrations denote rabbit snares set on a wire strand fenceline. This is how I set my snares on fenceline locations, with the larger loop system which shows the top of the noose protruding above the stand of galvanised fenceline wire to which the snare noose is attached temporary during the snaring operation. This method is used to break up the outline of the snare loop. As the rabbit's head enters the noose from the back of the fenceline the wire strand knocks the ears back. The rabbit's head slips through the noose and the striking curve on the bottom middle part of the snare loop catches the rabbit up under the chin on its forward movement as it passes between the wire strands of the fenceline.

Each and every location can be different depending on ground conditions and many different types of fencelines but it is imperative that there is some clearance between the bottom of the snare loop and the ground. This clearance beneath each and every noose can determine between success or failure. If set too low the rabbit can slip through with relative ease, especially the half and three quarter grown ones, as they are very lithe, stealthy and able to slip through an improperly set noose in a heartbeat. If set too high they can bump it with their forehead and turn the open noose upwards into a flat position on the wire strand as they pass underneath. This is more of a problem with tiny nooses and large rabbits but practice makes perfect as they say. If you read it carefully and pay attention to the detailed information gleaned from this book, it will cut out many years of trial and error for the reader, therefore bringing you up to a high acceptable standard of snaring ability in a short period of time. There is sixty years of snaring experience within the text of this manual therefore the readers will have to read slowly and digest the contents carefully.

Looking at both illustrations the top one (A) is a hanger or a fenceline snare set with 'trapping the second loop system' which is the fastest and simplest method of attaching a bare rabbit snare noose to a strand of fenceline wire and just as quick to move. Note the ½ " gap between the two loops round the fence wire.

The second illustration shows a problem common on older fences, the arrow at point (C) indicates undulation on an older fenceline wire. These beads of rust sometimes found on older thicker type wire fencelines, (e.g. on old railway embankments), can cause problems to people who are inexperienced in the proficient use of snares. Should these rusty strands be set just as they are your snares can be broken due to the fact the snare wire when attached to a wire strand in this condition gets bedded in between the undulated beads of rust restricting any movement in the noose itself. Therefore heavy winter rabbits pulling the brass wire to and fro at the one fixed point will cause friction and fraying of the wire strands on the noose, weakening them until they snap, leaving only a small tiny length of the noose protruding under the first turn of the bare wire where it was first attached to the strand of rusty wire. To compensate for this minor problem I carry a small flat piece of a broken safe edge file to rub the beads of rust from the fenceline wire, making it nice and smooth for a space of three to four inches in length taking only seconds. A small piece of very rough sandpaper will also suffice for the latter job but the little piece of file will last forever and it's very efficient for the job in hand. Once again as I have mentioned before about winding some soft grass tightly around the smooth galvanised stand of fenceline wire then attaching the snare tightly over the grass to give the most humane restraining devices in the world.

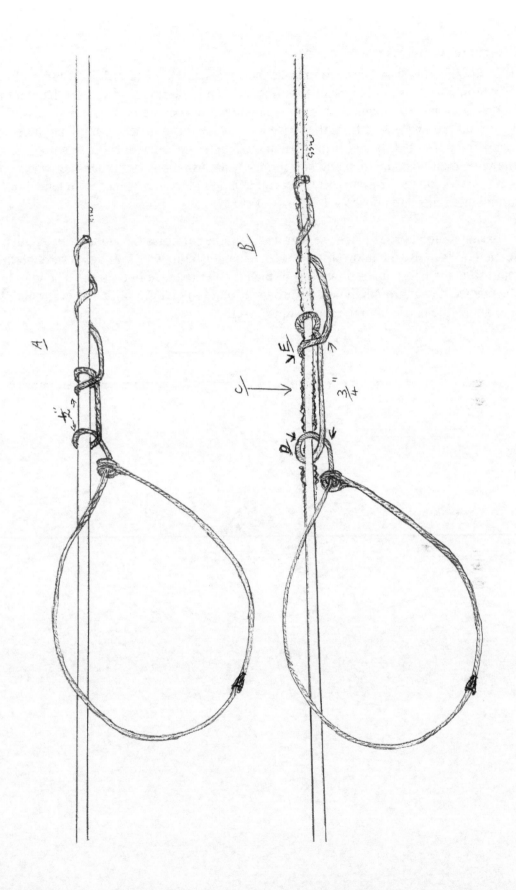

*Illustration A - ½ " gap between the turns on a **smooth** fenceline allows snare noose freedom of movement.*

*Illustration B - ¾ " gap between the turns on a **rusty** fenceline allows snare noose freedom of movement.*

How to remove the snare

The illustration below shows how to remove the snares quickly and efficiently from the fence line. First thing to do is to place your fore finger and middle finger of you left hand into the open loop on the fence line and pull it towards you while keeping it taught as shown. Then simply unwind the snare wire from the fence line. Once this has been completed take your right hand and pull it tightly and firmly down the length of the snare cable to straighten and firm the wire, then open the loop and slip it on to your arm along with the other snare nooses on your arm. Job done. This snare system can be applied to any type of wire fenceline, minimum length of snare noose 22.1/2".

When snaring a rabbit proof fenceline that has a number of holes throughout its length a simple method is to use the hoop snare system. Just push the wire legs down through the mesh and slide the noose up or down to suit the hole in the fence line mesh. The wire hoops must be pushed down through the mesh into the ground to give stability and is stronger than trying to attach the noose onto the rabbit mesh itself.

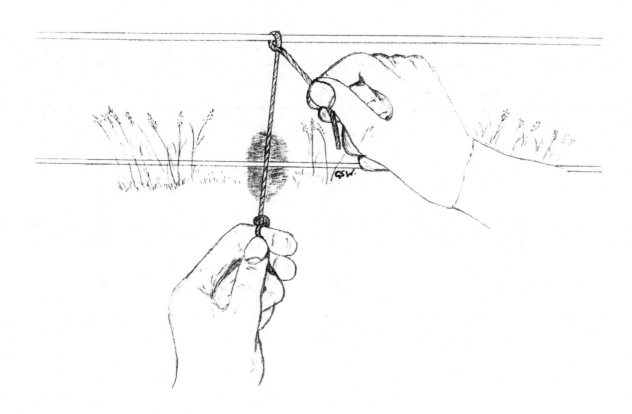

High Vegetation along Fencelines

When snaring where the flora is high (e.g. long white grass, silage grass, weeds, buttercups)along fencelines, field edges or anywhere you have to set snares in awkward locations out of the normal conditions, remember to pull any grasses or weeds away from the front and back of the snare loop keeping it free from any restriction at all times. When snaring dry weather this is fine. Always keep up to date with the regional weather forecasts to allow for the best snaring to help increase your catch rate.

There is one problem I will put you wise to that will reduce your catch rate greatly and that is setting the snares in high grass when heavy showers of rain and wind come in through the night what happens is this. The long grass and flora becomes soaked due to the driving rain which causes the longer grass to sag and hang over the tops of the snares covering the whole of the open loops making them sag lower also. What I do to avoid this problem is grab the long grass on either side of the snare tightly in my enclosed fist and rip if off down to a shorter level then bend the grass outwards away from the run to the front and back of the snare for a few feet to stop it bending and falling over the snare loops. Keep them free of any obstruction whatsoever. When faced with any problems on the snareline a little thought and commonsense can go a long way. Looking at the illustration the snare is set in high grass along a fenceline should heavy rain and wind arrive throughout the night this is when the latter problem will arise. I know through years of practical experience as this problem has happened to me.

Fenceline snaring mistakes and problems

Looking at this illustration and you will see an open snare loop lying in a flat position on top of the above fenceline strand of wire. This is a common result that amateurs will find on their snareline in a morning which is caused by setting with a small narrow loop. As a large rabbit approaches a crawl under, it pushes the smaller loop forward with the front of its head in an outward manner therefore the open loop swivels upwards around the fence wire. The rabbit passes freely underneath the open noose, which you see left in an open flat position. Once again always set with a large loop allowing for the rabbit's head to enter freely with plenty of all round clearance and space for his feet to pass under the bottom of the snare loop.

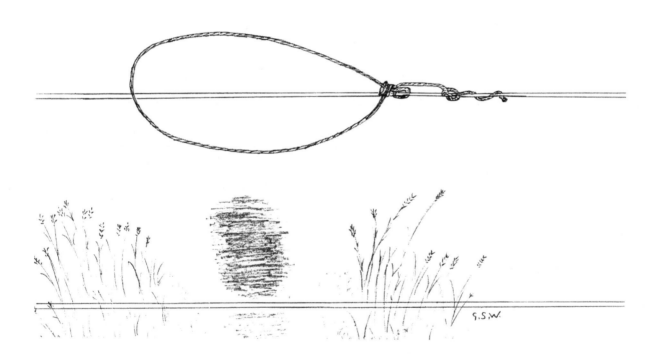

The Scottish legislation now states that an animal must not be suspended or partly suspended from any type of crossing over a ditch or stream, or suspended over the side of a steep bank, or any entanglement such as you see here in the illustration. Here a rabbit has been snared in a pegged snare but has pulled the wire through and over the fenceline and become partly suspended. A hoop snare would prevent this happening as the rabbit could not reach the fenceline.

Should you come upon a location like this go further out into the field and set the runs there. If the ground is bare with few runs showing, go along the edge of the bank and field and where you see beats extend the runs from the edge out into the field. Extend them by a couple of yards along the ground surface by scuffing the sole of your boot along the ground surface to make a more prominent fake run. Do this along the length of the fenceline you are snaring. I have carried out this practice for as long as I can remember and my old army boot lasted 26 years with no ill effects carrying out this latter practice should you be one of those people who don't want their boots marked use an old garden hoe.

There will be rabbit droppings along some of the runs the following morning after a few days all runs will be setting used by the rabbits. Meanwhile you can be snaring other locations then go back and set the fake runs and catch the rabbits. Look carefully and you will see an X next to the securing peg, look how close the peg is to the bank <u>face</u> where it drops into the field. Do not set a peg at this point, never, as it will pull out through the edge of the bank and your catch will be lost.

Always set your pegs further inward to avoid this problem.

Fenceline Snaring in Practice

This illustration opposite depicts a trapper removing his catch of rabbits from his snares along a plain wire strand (fenceline). This is the scenario which faces the trapper each morning on the snareline; rabbits lying dead, others hiding alive in the grass along the fenceline, some will be hung up over between the fence wires. All fencelines are different with different techniques to be used to catch the rabbits which pass to and fro through or underneath them. You get normal wire fencelines as seen in the illustration, rabbit proof fencelines, rylock fencelines, chain link, wooden strap fencelines as found along motorways etc. Some are clean and real easy to set while others can be a nightmare - overgrown with bramble briars, wild rose bushes, willow herb, stinging nettles, heavy thick long grass all usually entwined along hawthorn hedges - you name it I've snared it. A pair of little hand held secateurs are an ideal tool to carry with you in your jacket pocket to cut back jagged briars and thorn branches protruding through and over certain fenceline locations.

There are some that you just cannot set due to such heavy growth making it practically impossible, where heavy rhododendron bushes and wild privet completely engulf the whole fenceline. In these cases revert to the pegged snare setting further out from the overgrown edge on occasions having to make fake runs to complete the snaring operations.

Setting a nice clean grassy fenceline as seen in the illustration is extremely easy for an experienced trapper with an armful of hangers (nooses) hanging from his arm as he methodically works his way along the fenceline. Laying snare after snare setting a few hundred at a time, large catches can be obtained over a period of a few days thinning out the resident population to an acceptable level. The fastest and easiest method of attaching snare nooses to a fenceline is by the "trapping of the second loop" system which I have shown by illustration and by describing it in detail. Nothing but a simple snare noose with no added garbage such as any type of cordage whatsoever; no swivels, snap links or any fancy type extra added junk. Always work in a professional manner keep it simple at all times, why burden yourself with extra work as a simple noose can be applied to a fenceline in seconds it can also be removed in seconds. This is all that is required. Professionalism is pure simplicity remember that why give yourself extra work when it can be avoided at all times.

Another little tip to remember is when setting a fenceline with obstructions along its length such as odd patches of overhanging trees or briars that you may have to lean under to set a snare. Put your game bag down and kneel upon it, saving you from being jagged on the knees and legs.

Sometimes the rabbits come out under the bottom strand depending on the space between it and the ground level due to the contours of the ground. Alternatively the rabbits may slip through between the bottom two wires. If you look carefully you will usually see the galvanised wire is discoloured and dirty due to the continual rabbit traffic passing to and fro between the fenceline wires from their feet. You will also notice hairs attached to the underside of the top fenceline wire. The grass will also be padded on both sides of the fenceline, scratches and toenail holes will also be seen at certain locations along certain type of fenceline therefore it remains to be vigilant and sharp eyed when setting snares along these linear structures.

Optimising Fenceline Snares

This illustration is practically self explanatory showing a fenceline where the rabbits are squeezing under the bottom fenceline wire where the wires have been strung tightly along the whole fenceline. Chain link fences are also erected and fixed at a lower level near to the ground where the rabbits squeeze under the wire mesh fixture.

A trick I use when setting these type of locations is to take my boot and kick the run deeper into the ground, making these crawl unders easier for the rabbits to exit by creating more space between the ground and the bottom of the fenceline.

This greatly increases the capture rate for the trapper by allowing for larger sized loop with the top part of the snare noose positioned above the bottom of the fenceline, breaking up the outline of the noose. It allows plenty of room for the head to enter freely into the large loop and leave space under the bottom of the loop for the rabbit's feet to slip under, leaving the striking curve free to take the rabbit cleanly up under the chin. You can make a high catch rate from using this simple technique along tight fencelines.

Always remember after extending the depth of the gap to tap the ground flat with the ball of the foot by pushing it through under the fenceline. This leaves a nice deep and smooth exit and inlet hole making it easier for the rabbit's head to pass to and fro more easily.

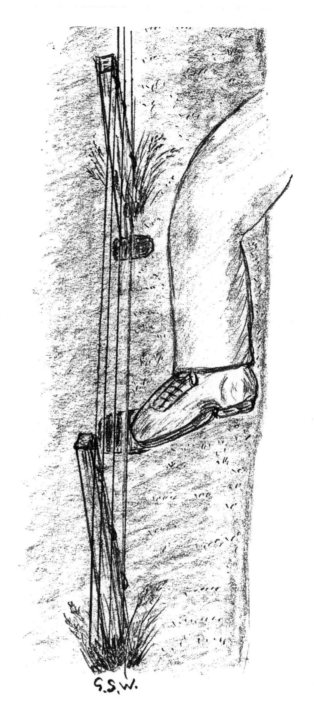

G.S.W.

Snaring Rylock Fences

This is one of the more awkward types of fenceline to set with snares. A number of years ago when summer snaring along these type of fencelines I used 4 strand snares constructed from four strands of 0.457 diameter wire spun into a nice firm cable. When set with a light tensioned loop these four strand snares were fast running catching half and three-quarter grown rabbits with relative ease as these young rabbits are lithe of body extremely agile on their feet and move very quickly. I stopped using these four strand snares at the back end of the season, coming in towards the winter months. Although many large heavier winter rabbits will be held and taken, losses will be sustained frequently through broken snares which no self respecting trapper wants.

Weather conditions must be taken into account especially in wet raw damp sleety weather conditions where you can get a heavy frost creeping in during the early hours of the morning. This will affect the components of the snare wire due to expansion and contraction with the wires being set in these very cold conditions. Therefore when a catch is made such as a large heavy winter rabbit the snare wire will then become heated due to the strain of the twisting and pulling action of the snared rabbit. This is especially the case if there is practically no gap between the first and second loop. Therefore when using this latter method when fixing a snare noose to a fenceline leave at least a half inch gap between the first and second loop to allow for play as I have mentioned before pluck some soft grass and wind it around fenceline before attaching the snare loop. This allows for play and has a cushioning effect on the snare noose it also helps stop the snare sliding along wire strands of normal fencelines, it will also help to protect the snare wire at the securing point from any frosty conditions throughout the hours of darkness.

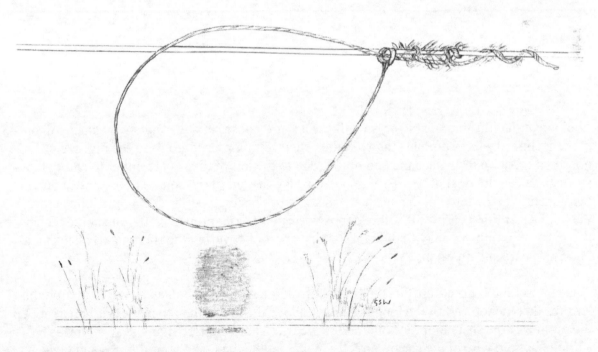

Once again remember to always have part of the snare noose set above the fenceline wire to break up the outline of the loop. When rabbits pass to and fro between this type of square wire fencelines the bottom squares appear to be around 4" deep and the further up the fence nearer to the top the wire squares are larger. Should the bottom squares that you have to set be only 4" deep a trick that I used with regularity is to put your foot into and onto the bottom of the wire square. Then insert your fingers into the square above your foot then push downwards with your foot and pull in an upward fashions with your hand. This helps to enlarge the square which allows easier access for the rabbit and increases the catching efficiency of the snare loop. Another trick I used was to set the bottom of the snare loop protruding slightly outwards away from the bottom strand of the fenceline square. The rabbit places his feet upon this bottom strand as it passes through the fenceline on its outward journey therefore by keeping the bottom of the snare noose slightly outwards and away from the bottom strand it prevents the loop from being knocked or partly sprung by the rabbit's feet. These little tips and tricks can help make you or break you in making a good catch of rabbits.

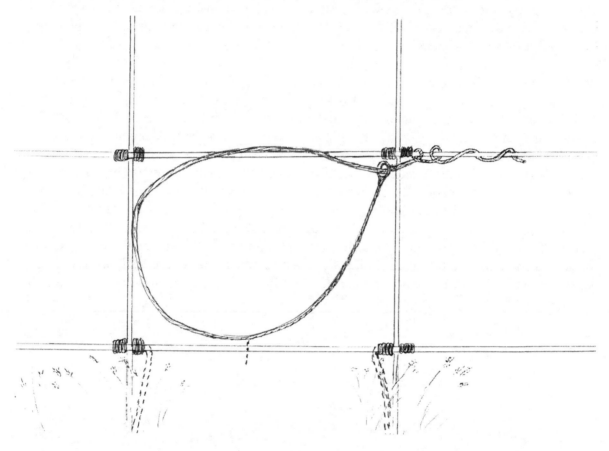

Looking at the illustration above you will see a snare noose set covering a wire square upon the fenceline. Before commencing with the actual setting procedure form the big size of noose you require then place the end of the loop to the left of the square either touching the vertical fence wire or slightly past it. You now take the tail of the square noose and attach it permanently to the top right hand square as shown. This method of placing the loop across the wire square <u>first</u> ensures that the loop is covering the run properly. If you should attach the snare loop first you may find that it's sitting short of covering the run properly causing a knocked snare and no catch.

Once the setting procedure is finished tweak the large sized noose in an upwards motion this ensures that the top part of the loop is slightly above the top of the fenceline wire breaking up the outline of the snare loop. Another effective trick that I devised many years ago was to snip the bottom wire of the square directly in the middle then take your thumbs and bend them straight downwards as shown in the illustration. This latter action gives the trapper a great advantage and large catches can be taken in a few days. On completion of the operation the wire legs can be pulled back up again into position. Always ask the farmer's permission before cutting these fenceline wires. Where rabbit damage is bad a lot of the farmers are only too willing once you show them what is required especially when they see the results with large catches of a few hundred rabbits taken in two or three days. It's not uncommon to set a few hundred hangers along a fenceline and check them in the evening about an hour before dark and take forty and fifty plus the rest and check the following morning and have well over a hundred more.

To help clarify this fenceline snaring procedure I have marked out and highlighted the various points in the illustration below to simplify it so that the reader can follow the instructions in a clear and precise manner.

(A) shows the gap to leave when setting the snare using the simple setting system this allows for play and free movement of the noose.
(B) you will notice a slight curve in the snare cable at this point, once I have attached the snare wire to the fenceline as seen I take the tip of my left forefinger and make this little outward curve in the wire. This is to allow for clearance of the snare eyelet so that its free running action is not impeded by the coils of wire on the fenceline as seen.
(C) showing the end of the snare loop touching the opposite side of the fenceline square giving full coverage of the run. The bottom of the snare loop should be touching the bottom strand of the wire square, do not set loop too low or it will result in misses and hip catches.
(D) showing the top of the snare loop above fenceline to break up outline of the noose.
(E) bottom strand of the wire square has been cut in the middle then the sides are pushed downwards with your thumbs making a larger gap and for more productive snaring.

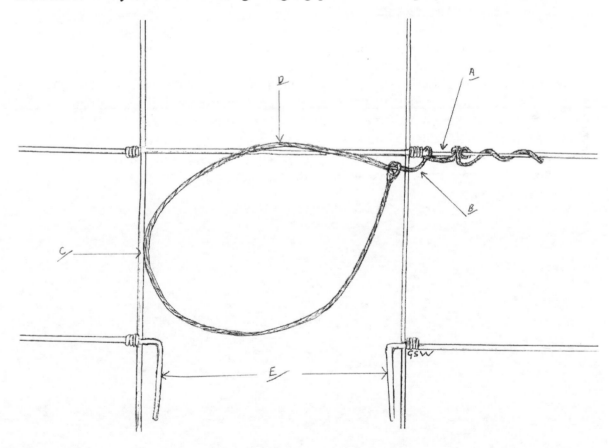

Fenceline Snaring for People with Impairment

As I have mentioned previously, professional trappers do not use cord on their fenceline snares or hangers as they are known by in the pro trapping ranks in Scotland. The simple fact is that professionals like all of my old mentors always liked to keep everything as simple and efficient as possible and cut out extra baggage at every opportunity. Carrying out fenceline snaring is an easy enough task to anyone who retains full dexterity of their hands and limbs. However we must take into account that not everyone possesses this ability, a person may be impaired due to severe arthritis or missing fingers due to an accident therefore having the addition of twine or cord on their snares would be an advantage in helping them to complete their snaring. It's a simple fact that the cordless noose would be more difficult for them to manoeuvre when trying to attach their snares to a wire fenceline due to the lack of normal dexterity in their hands and it could become a tedious and laborious exercise to accomplish.

To set a snare with cords is a simple enough task. First of all take the two loose ends of twine and form a double end knot to create a loop. To set the snare, open the loop you have just created by knotting the ends of the twine, place it over the top of fenceline wire then slip the snare loop through and pull - fixing the cord to the fence wire. Open up your snare noose, tension the loop and shape it to the appropriate size, then place loop against fenceline wire and wind the tail of the snare wire around the strand of wire a couple of times. This will stabilise the noose over the rabbit run to catch it on its outward journey. Look at the illustration to see the proper setting.

In survival situations carrying snares of good length such as ones made with soft proper brass wire for catching smaller ground game. (Picture wire is crap but will suffice for a very short space of time). Stronger steel snares will be good to catch larger game animals. Carrying a few good lengths of strong wine or para cord is also a good idea especially for spring snares to procure a meal for oneself and other either in jungle or Arctic environmental conditions. The simple snare could mean the difference of life or death. Always retain your survival skills because one day they may be needed. This is the type of situation where the trappers snarers and outdoor men will survive, whereas the animal rights fraternity with their Walt Disney mentality will die.

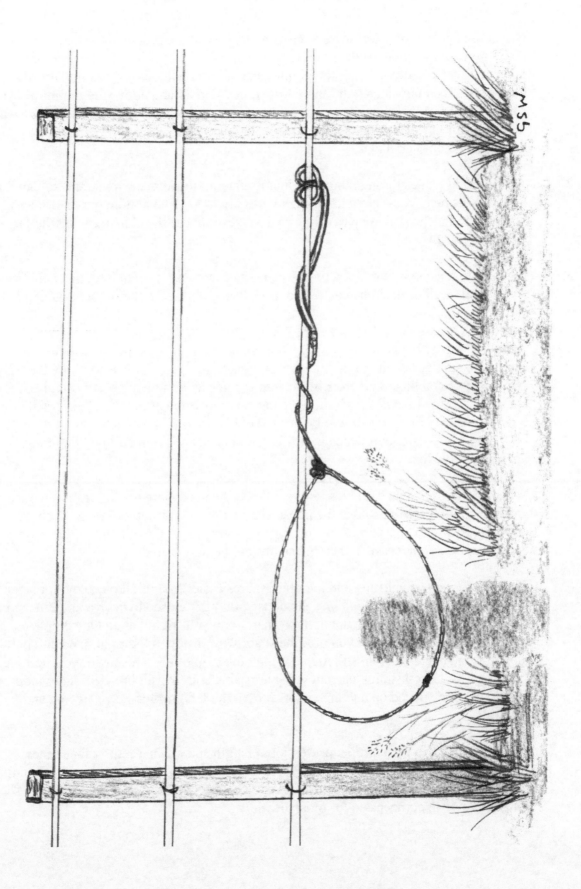

Fenceline Snaring Tips

1. On removing each hanging snare from your arm, form the proper sized loop to correlate with the width of the spacing between the wires of the specific type of fenceline you're setting. Then set a light tension into the loop, if it has not already been done. You now attach the snare loop to the wire strand above the rabbit run with part of the top of the snare noose above the strand of the fence wire which helps break up the outline shape of the noose while leaving clearance beneath the snare loop for the rabbit's feet to go under.

2. As the rabbit comes through the fenceline its ears hit the above wire strand so that they lie flat as its head goes into and through the snare loop. The bottom curve of the noose which is the striking part of the snare takes it under the chin allowing the feet to pass underneath.

3. It is best to tension a snare loop lightly as it sits exactly as it's required, nice and firmly and it holds well as it can be controlled more easily and set in the proper position in seconds.

4. Always snare with a good sized loop when fenceline snaring, especially at the back end of the summer coming into the later months of the year. This is to allow the fully grown mature rabbits to get their heads into the noose with plenty of all round clearance. If the loop is too small, which is a nationwide fault in the country with the biggest majority of snares, it will be pushed outwards and upwards by the outgoing rabbit until the snare loop which is still in the open set position will be lying in a flat horizontal position.

5. When fixing a tensioned rabbit snare to a fenceline make sure that it's tightly wound and hitched to the wire, so that the noose sits firmly and it's not loose. While in the catching position leave an inch or so slightly protruding at the tail end of the snare so that it can be gripped easily when the snares are being uplifted.

6. To make the job of uplifting and handling snares easier first of all place the fore and middle fingers of the left hand into the noose pulling it closed to keep a slight tension on the snare wire. You then unhitch the snare with your right hand. On complete removal from the fenceline, you grip the snare wire firmly in the right hand and pull it along the snare cable while still maintaining your grip of the noose with your left fingers. This action straightens out the snare cable and firms it up. The snare loop should now be opened up and then slipped onto the left arm for easy carrying and counting.

7. It is a good idea to use a proper professional length snare when setting fencelines, especially fences with five strands of wires as the depth of space can vary depending if the rabbit is slipping under the bottom strand or jumping through between them. The longer snare can compensate for most locations..

8.   Modern day fencing contractors when constructing a wire strand fence only insert the large holding staples halfway into the wooden posts, probably so that any future repairs can be carried out more easily if any breakages occur in the fenceline wires. With the staples driven only halfway into other posts this causes problems for the rabbit trapper on still nights due to play on the fence wires between the staples and posts. The fence wires twang and thump off the posts once any rabbits are snared, which coupled with the rabbit squeals when they encounter a snare, puts a lot of other rabbits off from coming through the fence as it frightens them and makes them very wary. To counteract the latter problem take a hammer and knock in every second staple along the fenceline along the main wire where the snares will be hung but a good overcast and windy night is best and does not affect the rabbit, therefore good catches can be made.

9.   A small sized round snare loop set between two fence wires at certain locations void of natural cover can be viewed as an obstruction at times throughout the daytime. I have watched rabbits from a concealed position stopping and sitting for a few minutes, then diving with extreme speed straight through the loop without even touching it, completely passing through it without even moving the loop. This also happens on occasions when setting a complete loop on a crawl under for foxes, they will walk away from it viewing it with suspicion.

10.   Fenceline snares, like pegged snares should be set out in the morning if possible to let the wires air out allowing any human odour to dissipate, more so at the back end of the year in the later months when darkness falls around 4.30 pm in the later afternoon. If there are a large number of snares to be set try and be off the snaring field at least by 2 pm as the dampness closes in therefore the longer time a snare is given to air out the better. Carrying out rabbit control throughout the summer months in the warmer weather and longer hours of daylight, snares can be set in the forenoon or afternoon but snares must be checked around three times a day. No less than twice a day because rabbits come out to feed and run around nearly all day in quiet secluded areas. Your first snare check would be between 5 am and 6 am in the morning, then around 2 pm in the early afternoon, then around seven in the evening as rabbits will be taken at every check. It's unfair to leave animals in hot weather, also greater losses will occur to aerial predators if the snares are unattended for long periods of time. The solution is very simple, if you are too lazy to go and check your snares, which is mandatory by law, then do not set them. The snares need only be checked in the morning throughout the winter months at daylight, around 8 am, as darkness is falling after 4 pm.

11.   Setting a nice big oval snare loop on a fenceline with the top part of the loop above the fence wire breaks up the outline of the noose.

12.   It allows the rabbit's ear to hit the fence wire so that they lie back flat as its head goes into the curved part of the lop, the striking part of the snare which sites below the fenceline wire.

13.   It is best to set a tensioned oval loop on a fenceline as the firmed wire noose can be controlled and set in the proper position in seconds.

14. All fencelines are not perfect as posts become broken and slack. The same goes for the wire strands due to farm machinery ploughing or backing up too close, also cattle leaning and scratching themselves on the posts loosens and breaks the wire strands. Also sometimes you will come across an old drystone dyke running parallel and to the back of the fenceline, some rabbits come over the top and others comes through holes and cracks midway and straight through the fenceline wire three and four strands up from the ground. Polished and also muddy fence wires give the game away, also the nail scratchings and polishing on the stones due to continual daily traffic by the resident rabbit population. Sometimes rabbits that exit from the dyke and fenceline midway up will come back and enter through the bottom fence wires and run up the face of the stone dyke back through their exit hole. You must be very observant when snaring, look for strands of hair along with the other latter signs mentioned.

15. Do not set pegged snares or fenceline snares along hedgerows and fencelines where livestock are grazing especially cattle. Should there happen to be loose posts or broken strands or wire or slack swaying parts of the fence cattle can lean over the graze along the backside or lean through the broken or loose strands to reach fresh grass on the opposite side. Always be observant and check each and every snare location and view the situation carefully and determine what can and what cannot happen as a little thought beforehand can save a lot of unnecessary problems later.

16. Rabbits will also run up the vertical face of rabbit proof fencing and up the support posts that lie at a 45° angle at end and corners of the fenceline. I nail a wire hoop over the support posts and set a snare on them and the rabbit is usually hanging down the side in the morning. If you look carefully you will see fur and mud between the top of the mesh and the top strand of wire, there they can also be snared. Andy White told me that if the top support strand of barbed wire along the mesh fence is exactly three inches high the rabbits that run up the vertical face of the mesh proofing are knocked off balance as they try to squeeze between them and fall back to the ground. This same tick will act as a deterrent to hares if the top support wire is exactly 4" above the mesh proof fence.

17. Professional trappers do not use cord on their snares when attaching them to the fenceline wires or mesh. There are two very simple methods for securing snares. The first method is by a couple of half hitches which are sometimes pulled tightly together once a rabbit is captured and presents a very slight difficulty on removal. The other method is to trap the second turn of the snare wire with the third turn of the snare wire. This latter method is very simple and presents no difficulty whatsoever and allows complete removal in a matter of seconds. These same securing methods allow for fast and easy setting and over a hundred an hour can be set most efficiently.

18. When setting out large numbers of fenceline snares try and pick the right weather, then set everything that looks like a run along the whole length of the fenceline which could be anywhere from one hundred to over three hundred snares. Setting them this way you can take a good kill in a couple of mornings them move on.

19.   Do not set fenceline snares near coverts which hold pheasants, also avoid public footpaths, near dwelling houses where domestic pets roam. If snaring on the estate at outlying areas near any cottages I notify the owner and tell them when and how long I will be snaring that area which is usually two to three days at the most, once I've finished snaring I notify the occupants. This ensures a good rapport and everybody is happy, a little courtesy goes a long way.

20.   Always count snares beforehand preceding the setting. Always count snares when lifting them to ensure the exact amount is collected and none are left behind. Always use a marker peg to every pegged snare this ensures that every single snare is accounted for when uplifting them. This is imperative in and around grazing fields where livestock will be released.

21.   And, finally if you're too lazy to look for snares don't set them at all as this creates a bad public image and unwanted publicity from the media. Always be professional in your work as we don't want to lose the use of snares by having them banned through sheer laziness and ignorance, the education in the proper use of snares is detrimental to their future legal use.

Chapter 11 - Snaring Drystone Walls

This first Illustration shows a drystone wall or dyke as it's called in Scotland. These type of field edge divisions are extremely common all over the British Isles and in Europe. Many mammals live within the confine of these walls e.g. rabbits, stoats, weasels, mice, rats, on occasions mink. They are a good source of shelter and security for the animals. They offer dry warm shelter from the inclement weather conditions here in Britain. At times even foxes and badgers will burrow down under these constructions. Some drystone walls are normal structures others as shown in the illustration have flat steel bars cemented between the coping stones every few yards along the top of the wall, with strands of fence line wire running through these metal supports. Where these dykes border along the side of woodland or strips of woodland or any rough ground or even pasture grass and crop fields you will always find signs of rabbits. As I said before, living inside the walls or passing through holes, gaps or jumping up and over them on a daily basis travelling to and fro from one location to the next.

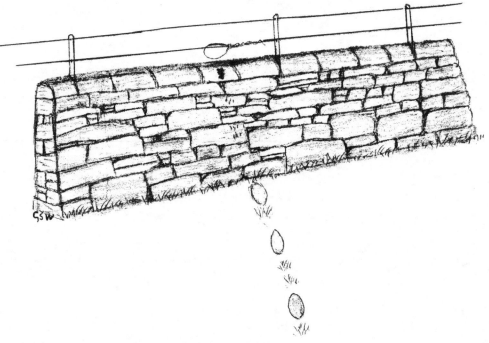

If you cast your eye along these walls carefully you will see toenail scratches and polishing of certain stones up the vertical face and on top of the coping stones as the rabbits travel up and over the walls. This is where I used to snare a lot of them over the years. This was the time before legislation came into force in Scotland March 2010 where stops on snares became mandatory. They also frowned upon fence line snaring of rabbits and foxes due to entanglement and part and full suspension of the animal from fence lines, log or pole crossings over streams and ditches or alongside these latter locations if there are steep sides running parallel to them. Such as life as they say.

These locations as shown in the illustration were deadly and in my opinion very humane and hundreds would agree with me. An old rabbit trapper I knew called "Sinclair Bruce" who has since passed on, once snared one hundred and nine rabbits along a fence line on top of a dyke as shown one morning. The rabbits travelled from a woodland across a field to feed upon young turnips on the opposite side of the walls they had been causing extreme damage to the crops before Sinclair was called upon to control the rabbits at this location.

In this second illustration, below, you see another drystone wall. Once again if you look carefully you will see toenail scratches and polishing of the stones on the vertical face and top of the wall. This time there is no fence line running along the top of the wall. Therefore in a situation like this I snared the rabbits in a hoop type snare by pushing the wire legs through the wall between the stones and bending them into hooks at the back to keep the structure stable. Then I would attach the snare loop to the wire hoop bent into a bow shape as seen.

On looking at the plan elevation (B) the big snare loop lay in a flat position an inch out from the wall. The rabbits do not get snared going outwards as they go down slightly and jump off to the ground. It is only on their inward journey that they get caught when they spring up the wall so far, then they flatten themselves close to the wall. As they grip the stones with their claws and crawl up vertically into the snare loop they get caught and they were all suspended along the length of the wall. Illustration B shows plan view of the snare set, these sets were used by trappers for decades before the law changed in 2010 now it's illegal in Scotland.

Chapter 14 covers the hoop snare in more detail.

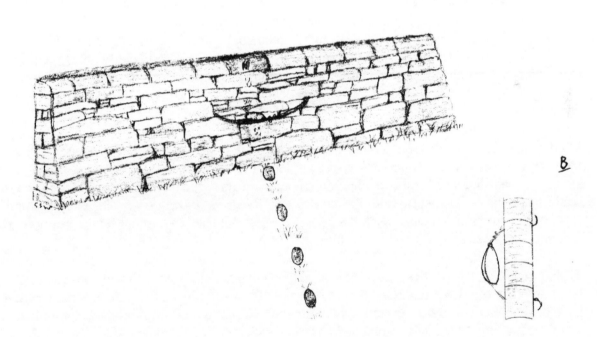

A

B

Chapter 12 - Snaring Hedges

Looking at the illustration opposite, every run has received a pegged snare along the full length of the hedge. If the hedge is bordered by good pasture grass or crop fields set both sides. Once the rabbits start to get caught along one side a couple of mornings the rabbits are not that stupid - they will start to feed out on the oppose side of the hedge.

Once when snaring a long thick hedge that bordered a busy country road the grass that I was snaring was around 8"-9" long. A wet spell of weather had arrived and I was catching rabbits but not the numbers I thought I would get. Slightly puzzled I walked along to a farm track that came all the way up from the east side of the field leading to an iron gate which allowed access from the farm to this country road through the hedge. I left my bag and rabbits at the farm road and climbed over the gate onto the broad grassy border of the roadside, lo and behind the council workers had cut the grassy verge a few days previously. At 9 o'clock that evening I drove along that road and there were quite a few rabbits sitting all along the road side nice and dry feeding on the short sweet grass.

Other times the rabbits will be in residence in holes under a thick broad hedge on one side of a road. Where there are horses or other livestock in that field they will cross the road through the opposite hedge and feed on young crop, due to the contamination of the grass by the livestock on their own side of the road. Good catches can be obtained as they cross over to feed on the sweet untainted grass and crops. Should a railway line pass through flat arable ground that you are snaring once again set both sides of the line. The same with long narrow woodland strips of trees, set both sides as the rabbits hear the squeals of others being caught a couple of mornings and they will start to feed on the opposite side to escape the unseen danger. Motorway bankings harbour great numbers of rabbits also especially the stretches of road that run along the top of the steep sided bankings. You only need to set along one side at a time good numbers can be taken from these locations and you are also doing the highways department a favour.

Many years ago I snared about a three-quarter mile stretch of fields bordering a main country road for a farmer friend of mine who had complained about the rabbits that were resident all along the roadside. His complaints had fallen on deaf ears. One day arriving in at the farm to see him and have a blether he said *Can you control those damn rabbits for me*? so I went and surveyed the ground and came back the next day. I set out each individual field bordering the road and snared over 1,200 rabbits for him.

The snare is one of the oldest and simplest methods that is deadly effective in controlling large numbers of rabbits in a short period of time. It is also very cost effective. That is why I have developed the breakaway snare system with the larger 6 inch stop loop which eliminates all of the main problems with rabbit snares therefore increasing animal welfare making the rabbit snare the most humane snare in the UK, in fact in the world along with my breakaway fox snaring system.

Chapter 13 - Snaring Field Edges

It's a common misconception amongst scribes and snaremen for that matter, who seem to think and often state that for snaring operations to be successful snares must be set well out into the fields ever time. It is true that excessive catches of rabbits can be taken on the correct nights when overcast and blustery, as the quarry does tend to travel far out to feed. The wind excites them and they feel secure under these nocturnal extreme weather conditions which also helps to dull their frightened screams on being captured every time one runs into a snare. Setting out 131 snares one day the following morning after a wild stormy night the results were 115 rabbits with only three of the remaining snares knocked, this was a considerable percentage of rabbits taken on a good night when conditions were just perfect.

It is also a common error by many to think that when snares are set nearer to hedgerows, field edges and burrows that respectable catches of rabbits cannot be taken as the rabbits are moving more slowly therefore the snares will all be tripped and sprung. I have even read where a scribe stated that only amateurs set along the edges. Well in my opinion the gentleman only proceeded in showing people what I already knew as to what little knowledge he really possessed about snaring. Most real professionals know that all locations are not textbook perfect and rabbits do not oblige us by just sticking to grazing fields. They are to be found in many inaccessible areas some which are more overgrown and practically impenetrable jungles of thorny hedges, briars, nettles and high weeds where rabbits abound in relative safety. The simple snare is all that is required to control the rabbits in this type of hostile environment. This is what makes you a good all round experienced snareman with many years of practice, working all different types of terrain gaining a vast knowledge of rabbits and their environment and how they live and move around in their everyday lives.

Once again it is the majority of snaremen who are at fault using poor quality snares and lack of experience. It is hard enough trying to snare rabbits with a tiny loop out on good runs in open grassland where rabbits are moving at speed, but to set tiny useless snare loops round edge features where rabbits are moving slowly is absolute utter nonsense, as the simple facts of the matter is that a small loop of any kind looks like an obstruction in an animal's path.

I wish I had a pound for every time I read a book or an article stating that rabbits can't be snared while moving slowly along an edge - not with a silly little 4" loop set at 3 or 4 fingers they can't !. I have already shown the two main faults when using small loops and low set snares.

Over the years I have taken thousands of rabbits along hedges, fencelines, crop edges etc using the large loop system, due to large loops being constructed to correlate with dimensions of the rabbit's head. As a rabbit always runs with its ears up the size of the large noose needs to allow the whole head, along with the whiskers or sensors across the face which measure 7 $^{1}/_{2}$". A small loop is an obstruction to an animal in its line of travel along a run <u>especially when travelling along slowly</u>. This is one of the biggest causes of avoidance when snaring foxes a silly small loop on a thick wooden tealer set low. Set higher when snaring foxes and rabbits - you want the animal looking through the loop not at it. If you don't take this information on board you are not going to become a successful snarer, but the problem is people are reluctant to change their old fashioned ideas.

The illustration below is of a field edge showing rabbit runs coming through a fenceline out into a field. Where edge runs are running parallel to the fenceline set them because these runs can also be very productive. Even runs that are prominent for only a few yards out into a field should also be set because you will still catch a lot of rabbits, especially when rabbits are crossing an established grazing field full of cattle where the grass becomes soiled and travelling up to two hundred yards to feed on a fresh clean grassy field edge around 25 yards broad. I have taken large catches from locations similar to this on many occasions.

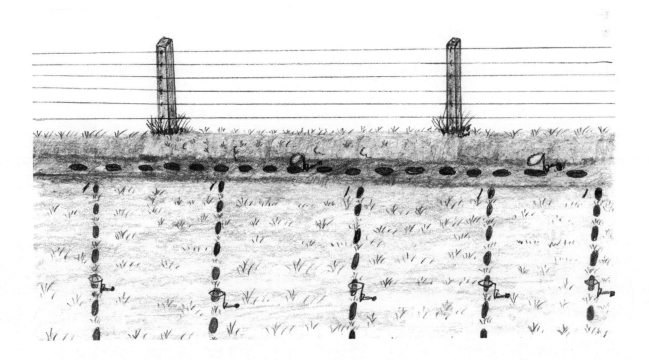

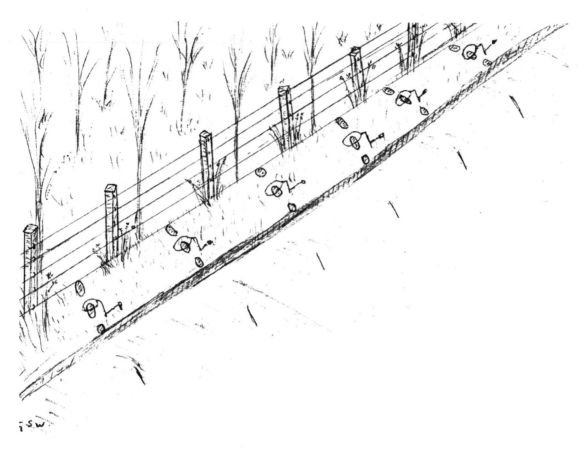

i.s.w.

SNARING FIELD EDGES

Let's take a look at this illustration of an edge feature, it shows the beats on the head ridge used by the rabbits as they exit the plantation and through the fenceline. Sometimes the beats are well defined and prominent to see with your eye, at times the grass is short, other times it may be longer, each and every location is different. When a rabbit exits the fenceline onto the first beat you will see them sit up with their head erect and move to the middle beat, then to the edge beat next to the field side and out into the field. At times the beats along the edge are more prominent and easier to set than the ones leading out into the field, all depending on the type of growth in the field itself. Of course on occasions it might be stubble which is flattened and in disarray due to the traffic of heavy farm machinery and no beats or runs are visible. Then again it could weeds and bare ground with short springy rack grass, again few beats or runs may be visible so the edge feature becomes the most viable proposition. Depending on the circumstances I'll usually set the middle beat but sometimes it's the small beat at front of the edge, next to the field side that's set. When setting the latter edge beat be most careful where the securing peg is inserted as it will be pulled free of the ground due to the vertical face of the field edge crumbling and breaking under the constant pressure and leverage exerted by a captured rabbit. This happens on occasions due to the securing peg being driven into the ground too near the edge of the vertical face itself, just the same as when snaring near to the edge of bank.

Another problem which will occur at these edge locations, one is that a large number of your rabbits will be able to reach the fenceline once they have been caught in the snares, which cause the problem of having to untangle many rabbits from between the strands of the fenceline wires therefore creating more work for the trapper.

When setting your snares along these edge features it is most obvious that you cannot face outwards towards the field, like you do when open field snaring as this gives you a true and more accurate placement of the snares. Therefore you must face inwards towards the fenceline as you have no other option available, unless access is possible alongside the back of the fenceline which on many occasions it is impossible due to the height of the tree growth and the surrounding vegetation.

Therefore I hope you will now understand the importance of the big loop system which covers the whole run properly and will take the rabbit's head coming each way with relative ease. A big loop tight wound snare cable, set with a very light tension in the noose so that the eyelets running in from the side and not up and over in a steep vertical climb, will take large catches of rabbits quite easily. The large noose does not create an obstruction and the tealer pin sits well to the side of the run. Therefore if a tiny loop cannot cover a run set the way the rabbit is travelling how will it be able to catch a rabbit coming in from the opposite direction moving slowly with a total head height of 6 inches and $7^{1}/_{2}$" broad whiskers, ask yourself this.

Snaring Gateways

This is a good gateway to snare showing quality, well padded beats indicating good rabbit traffic. At these types of locations set every run that is visible with a couple or even three snares as good catches can be obtained in a couple of mornings snaring.

My good friend Colin and young Phil have a good number of productive locations like this on their snaring ground. They are especially effective where rabbits come across moorland and down through these open gateways to feed in the pasture fields below. My two friends can snare hundreds of rabbits per season from these passageways with relative ease.

Section 4 -
Other Snaring
Methods

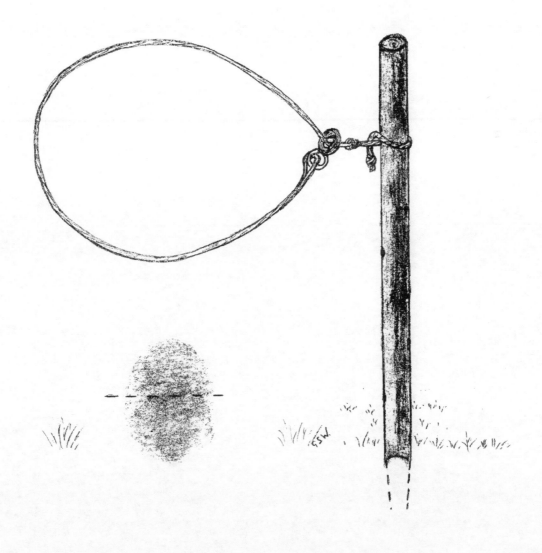

Professional Rabbit Snaring

Chapter 14 - The Hoop Snare or Bender

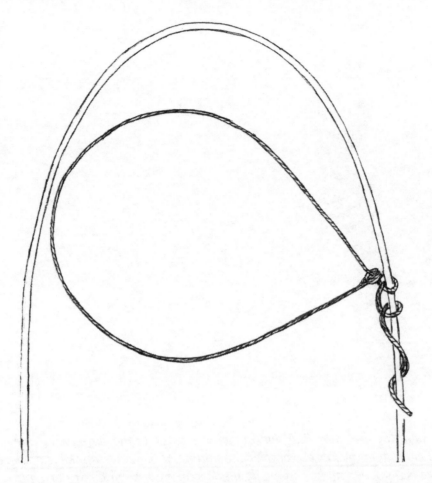

This snare is a simple but very effective snaring system to take rabbits and hares, no peg is needed and it's most effective in softer ground conditions. Straddle the rabbit-run with a foot on either side, take hold of a wire leg in each hand and push the legs down into the ground on either side of the rabbit or hare run. Then set your snare loop at the correct height across the middle of the beat. When the hare or rabbit is caught it pulls from the side and is usually entangled around the wire hoop. My hoops are made 44 inches long from 3mm high tensile wire. Double hitch the snare loop onto the wire hoop 22 ½ inches long snare noose for rabbits, and I use 26 inches long noose for pegged hare snares and hoops.

There are no hard and fast rules to the length of wire cut for hoops - cut them to suit your needs. In Scotland they don't want any entanglement of snared animals on fence lines or hoops but there is no restriction in England that I know of at this moment in time, but find out about what is legal and illegal before setting your snares. This hoop system was quite effective in preventing woodland deer from being foot snared while catching rabbits in plantations where extensive damage to young trees was being done. The invention of the Breakaway rabbit snare along with the six inch stop loop has now totally, 100% eliminated woodland deer or livestock losing a foot to a necrosis from a broken snare noose. This is a major step in animal welfare which we should always strive for.

This illustration shows a Roe deer standing out on pasture grass, to the right hand side of the deer you will see a couple of hoop snares set over the middle of the beats on these open rabbit runs. The hoop snare is a good, simple and easily made snaring system for softer type ground. It is also good at keeping Roe deer from being foot snared in various locations that they inhabit.

The hoop snare is simplicity itself - a length of fence line wire bent over your knee attached a snare noose and you're in business. A simple but deadly effective snare system, it can be used most effectively and can be set in multiple different types of locations to catch mammals or birds (although bird snaring is not legal in the UK). This system has been around for a lot of years - I do not know who devised this method but one of my old mentors Alex Chisholm introduced it to me around 40 years ago. Alex used it out on the Northern Scottish hills on grouse moors to control hares. I used to make my hoops from 4 mm galvanized fence line wire cut to 44" in length but remember there is no hard and fast rules to the length because all ground densities are different some softer than others. A good few years ago I changed my wire diameter to just over 3 mm. This wire was high tensile stronger and more robust than the softer 4 mm I had previously used. It also had a springy effect to it.

I also sprayed my hoops with grey primer which can be purchased very cheaply for £1 a spray tin from the pound stores. Be aware there are two different shades of colour one light and the other a darker grey, I prefer the dark colour. After spraying the hoops a dark grey, once they had dried I would coat them again with Vauxhall leaf green paint so that they would have a green grey camouflaged effect to break up the outline of the hoops. This is done to blend them into the surrounding background making them hard to see from the human eye. The

Professional Rabbit Snaring

length of the noose I used was 24" long the reason being once I had formed a 7.5 x 5.5 loop size it still allows a good tail length of the snare wire to attach it to the wire hoop leg. The method I use is the double hitch system shown in the illustration below but I prefer trapping the second loop system when fence line snaring. Some hoop shapes I have seen are 'M' shaped with the snare loop attached in the depression at the top. I don't like setting from the top because the snare loop travels too far before closing catching animals around the neck with a front leg through and even hip snares them. I prefer my noose to sit across the run in a similar position to a pegged snare loop. They are all neck snared.

The illustration shown shows a hoop snare with thin branches inserted down into the ground right beside the wire legs. This is a trick I used when hoop snaring in woodland where the ground is softer and it helps stabilise the hoop system, which I set with the legs staggered one forward and one back, the same system I used in the fields. Another trick I do is stamp the ground on either side of the run to compact the soil before inserted the staggered legs of the wire hoop. All these little tips and tricks the difference can help make you or break you.

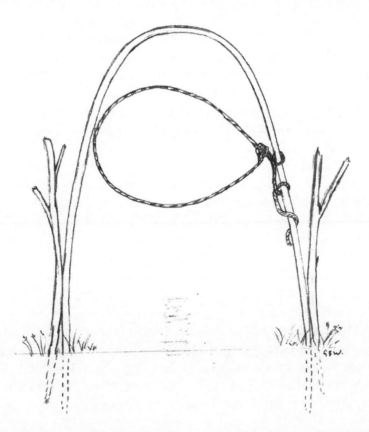

The total length of my hare snares are 26" long before being fashioned into a good big sized noose. All my snares are 6 strand spun up into a nice firm smooth cable. The hoop snare can be set on moorland, pasture grass, hedges, fenceline edges, on plough, woodland, crop fields and around rabbit warrens on runs leading to and fro between the burrows. When setting in this latter location set the snares low as they creep slowly around the warren areas and around woodland warrens. Another good location for hoop snares to be used is along rabbit proof fences if it is a brand new fence line just erected set rabbit snares every 25 yds all the way around the whole length of the fence to control rabbits trapped inside the enclosure. On an old fence line with open holes throughout its length, push the wire legs of the hoops down through between the mesh. The snare loop can then be slid up or down to suit the hole height.

How to set a Hoop Snare

The mere handling of a snare for a novice proves very awkward when using them for the first few times, in fact the same can be said of some who are supposed to be more experienced and accustomed to handling them. They more they are handled the more confident and proficient you become. People have a natural tendency to be afraid of them more so with steel traps as they fumble nervously with them frightened of getting their fingers caught and injuring themselves. Constant practice makes perfect as they say, therefore it is very easy to become adept in handling them.

To set a simple hoop snare the following instructions is the correct method. Hold the wire legs of the hoop half way down, one in each hand with the ends pointing away from you as you would hold the handles of a wheelbarrow. Then straddle the rabbit run looking outwards into the field the way the rabbit is travelling to its feeding grounds, then bend over and insert the wire legs down into the ground on either side of the run like an archway, directly over the middle of a small beat the same as you would do with a pegged snare noose. Once the wire legs have been inserted vertically into the ground to the required depth, staggering them one leg forward and one leg back, the tensioned snare loop 7.5 inch x 5.5 inch can be attached to the top side of the hoop using a simple double hitch. Then assuming you are right handed, slide the noose down the right hand side wire leg, (vice versa if left handed) and the large noose should now be adjusted to sit at the proper position and the required height to cover the run properly.

However before continuing I would like to say that I am thoroughly accustomed to the employment of these snares, therefore all of my snares are permanently fixed to the wire hoops. This saves valuable time out on the snaring field as it becomes just a simple matter of inserting the wire legs into the ground at the precise location and walking away. For easy handling of the hoop snares I keep them in bundles of twenty-five which also makes counting easier. I insert a length of old snare wire through the hoops and wind it over the top of the hoops a couple of times it's simple but very effective in keeping them together and prevents any tangling. To carry them just grasp the top of the hoops with your hand and insert fingers through the open snare hoops carrying them by your side as if holding the straps of a carrier bag. A simple method I have used on occasions is employing the use of an old belt, worn around the outside of your body. I cut two short lengths of 2.5 mm fence wire, fashioned them into an S hook shape before attaching them by inserting one end over the belt at the sides of my body. It was simple then to just hang a bundle of 25 on each wire hook which allows for complete freedom of the hands for the sole employment of setting the snares.

Constant and continual use of any implement day in and day out over the years will eventually expose faults in either the methods of setting or in the actual design of the system, which all professional trappers become aware of sooner or later. I will now endeavour to explain one or two faults which I personally found and will explain to you how to correct them. First of all I only use galvanised steel fence line wire (3 mm high tensile), I cut my hoops from old fence lines. I also acquire it from friends who are fencers. Why I use the latter type of wire is because it's well weathered strong and a dull greyish blue colour as it becomes less visible when set out in empty grazing pastures. To make the hoops even more difficult to see I spray them with Vauxhall leaf green auto paint which gives them a distinct olive colour, before painting degrease the hoops in boiling hot water with some liquid soap. I do exactly the same process with my steel fox snares. If you don't degrease them the paint won't take. Don't ever use household paint - the auto paint contains a fine cellulose flake and the smell dissipates quickly in a matter of days, more so if they are flung into an old barrel of rainwater and left, the cold water also hardens the paint. Although the auto paint dries in minutes I wait an hour and then submerge them in the water. The latter paint process camouflages their appearance making them less visible to humans and less prone to theft. In mature grazing pastures in proper conditions the hoops can be inserted well into the ground. When conditions are very dry in summer time and the ground is baked hard, they can't be used for obvious reasons. Using the hoop snare in crop fields and in stubble fields in wet weather when the ground conditions are softer I will stamp my feet down onto the ground on either side of the run to make the soil more compact then I will insert the wire legs if I am in any doubt about it stability I will insert the wire legs in a different position of one leg forward and one back so that they are not directly opposite one another. This simple trick works quite well and the rabbits tangle up pretty quickly.

I have used the same trick to snare rabbits as they cross over ploughed fields to get to a field of young crops. As they bound over the plough they land onto the tops of the earth furrows. I just take my foot and flatten a nice beat for them landing, then once again I stamp the top of the furrow on either side of the beat then insert the hoop into the soil which is now more compact. In perfect conditions all the snares could lie set right along the one furrow the whole length of the field, but perfect conditions don't exist. Therefore you may have to set further out or back according to the location if it is unsuitable. In latter locations or anywhere the ground conditions appear a bit soft do not set the snare from the top of the hoop as even the professionals do not get one hundred per cent neck catches. Therefore an occasional large buck or doe rabbit may be hip shared which allows the animal to assert more force and pulling pressure on the hoop which could result in the soil being loosened around the wire legs and it being pulled free from the ground. If this happens check the fence line along the field edge from where the rabbits emerge as it may have become tangled in the grassy fence line or at the mouth of a burrow.

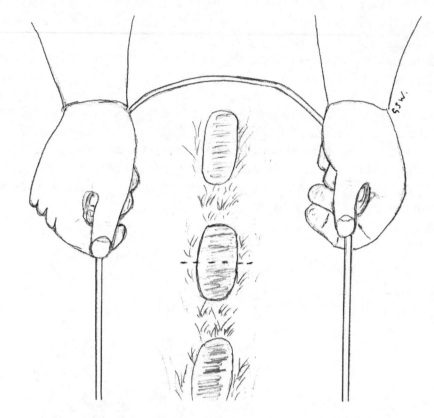

Straddle the run and hold the hoop as shown.

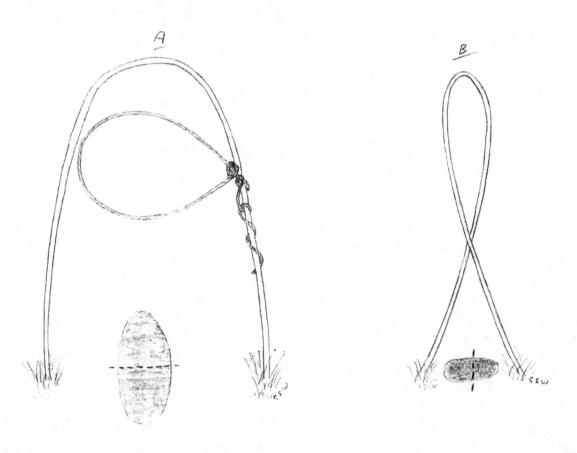

Stagger the wire legs, one forward and one slightly back to improve stability.

Therefore it is better to set the snare from the side of the hoop as the rabbits tangle up pretty quickly by wrapping themselves around the wire legs restraining their movements even more as they gain less leverage in trying to pull free. High tensile wire would eliminate any bending of the wire hoop whatsoever as it will retain its rigidity at all times due to the wire being so hard.

Rabbits inhabit large clumps of rhododendron bushes where large warrens are to be found on occasions as it offers them plenty of good security. Once again the hoop snare is most effective in controlling rabbit numbers at these locations - just set the runs as they emerge from the cover, a ring of snares can then be set all around the area enclosing the whole warren. In open areas of woodland along sloping banks and hedges the snare is very effective in controlling rabbits in and around the vicinity of the warrens themselves. Whyte showed me how effective snares can really be at these locations eliminating a lot of hard work carrying steel traps, sifter and buckets of dry earth. Smart thinking once again, using brains over brawn as the saying goes, the head is for thinking with and feet are for dancing. You and I feel extremely safe in our own homes just the same as the rabbit does in and around the warren therefore it is quite a simple task to move rabbits around their burrows. Just set the runs leading out and around away from the holes, beats will also be visible across the tops of the warrens leading form one hole to another as the rabbits creep slowly between them on emerging above ground.

This is where the big noose is very effective over a tiny obstructive loop, the snare loop should only be tensioned lightly and set lower to the ground as the rabbit is only creeping slowly between the holes as it feels safe in its surroundings. This is why the big loop is very effective due to the size of the area of the loop which allows for the dimensions of the rabbit's head and poses no threat to it as there is no resistance or obstruction as the head enters the loop. Whyte took two hundred rabbits from a hedgerow using pegged snares around and between the burrows in one week, on lamping the location later on three rabbits were visible in the beam.

The hoop snare can be used to take rabbits coming over the tops of dry stone dykes (walls) which so often borders the perimeters of woodlands (see Chapter 11). When snaring these locations I adjust the legs of the hoops by bending them upwards into the shape of an offset hook facing each hook in opposite directions I then place the hoop over the rabbit run on the top of the wall and then wedge the hooked ends of the hoop down tightly between the spaces of the stones on either side of the hoop. Rabbit sign is quite visible due to their regular crossings back and forth over the tops of these stone walls. The stone becomes polished with visible scratches from their toenails, there will also be droppings and flecks of fur present, when captured the rabbit succumbs to the snare within seconds the moment it leaps from the top of the wall which is both quick and humane.

One enterprising young fellow a friend whom I taught this method to was a builder to trade he made a small bucket of cement and anchored his hoops permanently along the tops of the walls on his ground much to the delight of the farmer who was fascinated by this method of rabbit control. Once again it should be remembered never to set snares where cattle and horses are present due to their height and reach, unlike sheep they can reach to the top of these walls and have a very inquisitive nature and a bad habit of licking wire and other visible objects which attract their attention.

Rabbits can also be snared at times as they run up the vertical face of these dykes using a slight variation of the hoop. Instead of the actual hoop, cut a length of 4 mil fence wire about 5 ft long or slightly longer depending on the distance between the spacing between the stones in the wall. The fence wire is then bent into a half moon shape and the ends are then pushed right though between the spacing or openings of the wall and bent over downward towards the ground so that it cannot be pulled back through. A snare is then attached by the double hitch method or by trapping the second loop to the fence wire which now arches over and above the vertical run up the wall. The run is visible due to the nail scratches, the polished surface of the stones and where you see the removal of any moss coverings due to the constant daily traffic of the rabbits. Once again after you secure a large noose firmly to fence wire arched over the run, the bottom wire of the noose when set should be kept around one inch out from the vertical wall face because the rabbit flattens itself tight to the wall so that it gains a secure grip with its toes and nails giving more leverage to access the wall and in doing so his chin is very close to the stonework. The rabbit is only snared on its inward journey as it jumps over the wire as it exits from the top of the wall descending on its outward journey to feed. It is good fun and tests your skill and judgement, the rabbits expire in the matter of seconds once caught and hang vertically from the wall face.

This method of snaring from the top or middle of the wall appears to eliminate any predator damage to the quarry. Set the wire hoop midway on the vertical face of the wall as the rabbit springs from the field edge a foot or more up from base of the wall with its first jump. There are no hard and fast rules as to the length of wire cut to make hoops.

My own hoops are cut to 44 inches in length then bent into the U shape, this length suits my needs in the area I use them, friends of mine cut theirs 48" long to suit ground conditions in their area of the country. In bare ground where no rabbit runs are visible then you must make your own runs leading from the perimeter out into the field. The high tensile 48" hoops are ideal in these softer conditions and holds the largest of rabbits and hares. Remember just cut them to your own requirements to suit ground conditions at the location

Chapter 15 - Hazel tealer for Woodland & Soft Ground

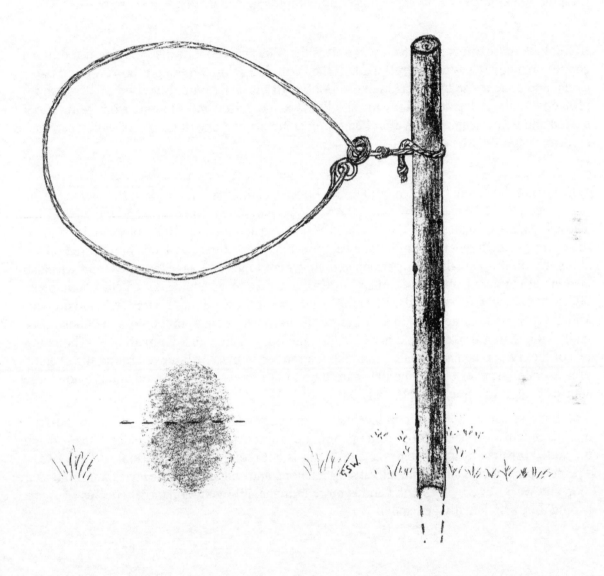

When controlling rabbits in woodlands areas the pegged rabbit snare is very effective, but as any trapper knows not every location is perfect, as ground conditions vary in different areas. At times you will come across ground that is less than perfect such as boggy and softer ground and this is where the single tealer can be most effective. Cut approximately 18" long by ½" to 5/8" thick, pointed at one end and with a tiny hole drilled through the peg, 1 ¼" down from the top. A professional rabbit snare 22 ½" long is fine and to attach the wire snare to the tealer peg, push the end of the snare through tiny hole in peg, then form a small double loop the size of a 10 pence piece. Now slip snare loop over your arm and pull the peg downwards as this motion will now form a nice little double knot at the back of the peg.   On completion of the double knot, you now tension and shape the snare noose to the correct size 7.5" x 5.5". Then pull the double knot round the tealer as shown and just bend the knot itself over the snare cable which is protruding from the front of the tealer. Push the tealer into the softer ground to the side of the rabbit run, as deep as needed sometimes 9-10". Then cock the tensioned snare loop to the required height of 6 ½" inches to the bottom of the noose over the middle of a beat as the dotted line shows, (do not ever set them between the beats). There are no hard and fast rules to the length of hazel tealers. My friend Colin is going to be snaring in longer whitegrass in a sandy type soil location and has cut his hazel tealers 24 inches long due to the soft underlying conditions.

Chapter 26 explains how to make this double knot, shape and tension a snare noose.

If you look at this illustration you will notice that this snare loop is also making use of the a copper breakaway system I developed, in the form of a small 3/4"long S hook around the eyelet and attached to the three double end loops of the snare wire. I devised this system to protect woodland deer, especially the smaller types, e.g. Roe and Muntjac from getting foot snared and then escaping with a broken rabbit snare around one of their feet which can cause a necrosis and the loss of a foot.

When using the single hazel tealer method, I only use the snare loops with the breakaway at the eyelet, all my pegged rabbit snares now have a permanent fixed stop and a breakaway eye. These breakaway snares where well tested Woodga catching over 300 rabbits in the trial, therefore two different types of breakaway one at approx 20lbs and 16lbs both tested on a straight pull, this actually increases once in a formed loop. This breakaway system was also designed to allow all animals from cats upwards to escape, as accidental catches do happen but the breakaway had to hold every rabbit and one of these pegged snares with the double knot swivel can hold up to 30 rabbits before the loop needs changing, unless the noose gets badly kinked or a broken strand happens then the noose is replaced immediately. The bottom eye of the S hoop is made smaller to make it stronger so that the big eye around the eyelet breaks open, therefore, allowing the snare loop to fall freely to the ground and the non target species walk away freely without any harm.

You can also see a knot placed in the snare at the back of the eyelet. This is to stop the 7.5" x 5.5" large tensioned snare loop from opening up and touching the hazel tealer. This is due to the added breakaway attached to the eyelet and is not required with a normal snare noose. The new breakaway snare with added stop tensions and shapes just as easy as a normal snare loop and works every bit as good and is more humane, allowing non target species to escape, should they accidentally get caught.

Improved Hazel Tealer System

As all experienced trappers know or should know that all snaring locations are not perfect therefore we must apply a little thought on how to overcome each and every problem that confronts us on the snareline. This illustration shows a tealer system consisting of a single hazel stick of $^5/_8$" in diameter 18" long and pointed at the bottom end. This tealer system can be cut 2 feet long to suit variable conditions at certain locations where extra height is needed. My friend Colin was using this system a few weeks ago, he phoned to say that the location he was asked to snare by the gamekeeper on a local estate consisted of very soft sandy type soil with long white grass protruding from the ground. Therefore 100 two foot long hazel tealers were cut to length along with 100 8" lengths of 2.5 mil galvanised fenceline wire (NOT HIGH TENSILE). A 2" right angle bend was made on every length of wire around a nail inserted into a small ¾" square block of hardwood 2" long with a 3 mil groove along the full length of one side of the block into which the length of wire is laid. Then you form the double eye around the nail, a 2 ½" long masonry nail or Hilti nail is advisable due to their tensile strength and will not bend under pressure and heat like a normal nail is prone to doing when being put under constant and regular pressure.

The hazel tealer is drilled twice to the required diameter to suit the wire tealer an inch down from the top for the first hole then a half an inch underneath for the second hole now insert the wire tealer as shown in the illustration. Once the hundred hazel tealers consisting of wire eyes were completed they were set out on location, the two foot long tealers once inserted into the soft ground worked extremely well. The proper height of the snares was attained at 9½ inches high to correlate with the height of the longer white grass and the more distinct beats. The number of rabbits snared was approximately 80 rabbits. Remember horses for courses if you learn to adopt you will become SUCCESSFUL enabling you to ATTAIN A HIGH CATCH RATE WHEN SETTING OUT YOUR SNARES.

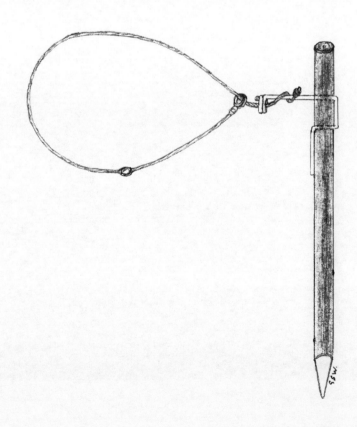

Professional Rabbit Snaring

Hazel Tealer System with Rotating Collar

A further adaptation of the Hazel Tealer system is to allow free rotation of the snare around the tealer. There are two method for this.

Illustration A1 shows nothing more than an 18" length of hazel, approximately ¾ of an inch in diameter, chamfered at the top and pointed at the bottom. Looking at this illustration you will notice a slight groove around the circumference. This created a full inch down from the top end by using a small, rat tail file which gives an all round nice smooth groove. The hazels are cut as straight as possible at the back end of the year, when the cold weather arrives. After cutting I take each individual tealer, hold it vertical in the vice and tap a 2 inch, straight length of 2 mil semi high tensile wire down into the centre top of the tealers as shown at A2. This short length of wire once inserted to its full length down into the sap vein strengthens the top part of the tealer once it dries out.

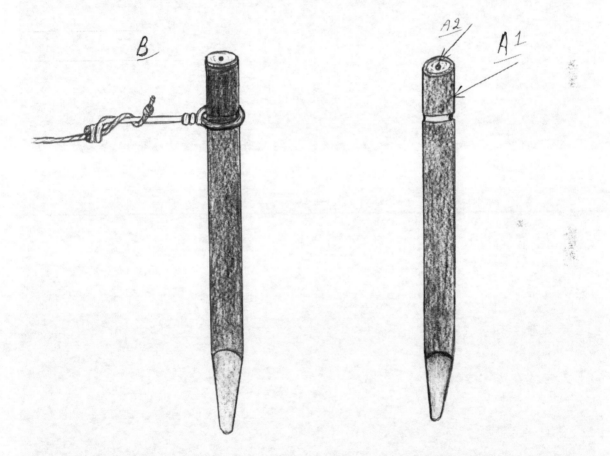

Illustration B shows the complete, fully operational system. A small extended length of semi high tensile wire with a double eye at the outer end is wound around the tealer in the groove previously created. Notice that the wire loop is not tight - it is left loose enough to allow complete 360 degree rotation around the hazel tealer, which will be inserted upright into the ground. The end of the brass snare loop, with the classic double knot, also act as a swivel allowing full rotation between snare and tealer eye.

Professional Rabbit Snaring

Hazel Tealer System with Rotating Snare

In this alternative method the top supporting wire does **not** rotate but the snare does.

What you see here is a six strand rabbit snare 25 inches long with the end of the noose formed into a loose loop around the vertical hazel tealer. In this system a small length of soft polypropylene tube has been slipped onto the end of the snare noose before it was attached to the tealer. This piece of soft pliable tube is used to hold the snare noose in place at the proper height over the middle of the small beat by pushing the tubing onto the end of the protruding wire near the top of the large pin.

Once a catch has been made the soft plastic sleeve pulls free from the extended wire, leaving the slightly larger snare end loop to fall freely down the vertical large pin. This allows for 360 rotations around the vertical hazel pin which takes the strain from the captured rabbit as it pulls and rotates in a circular manner. The reason for the larger snare loop of 25 inches is to retain the large snare loop of 7 ½ inches x 5 ½ inches after the rotation loop has been tied.

Chapter 16 - Old Style Snare System with Heeling Peg.

This illustration shows a fully assembled snare system of the old type that was in general use in Scotland. First of all let's look at the wire tealer. This was the thinner wire type tealer which was around 9 inches long has a double base with four turns around the shaft with a simple single loop at the top. It was old Sinclair Bruce that told me of a man who worked beside him with the Perth Rabbit Clearance Society who devised the first double wire tealer of this type in 1948 he was called Tam Stratton. The snare loop is attached permanently to the top of the tealer pin. The securing peg is of the type that my old friend and mentor Alex 'commando' Chisholm used, it was 6" long $1^1/_4$" broad and tapered and bevelled similar to a commando dagger blade the peg was only $^3/_8$" thick. The system is held together by the twine. There were no stops on the snares which are now mandatory under Scottish Law since March 2010. One hundred of these fully made up pegged snares weigh practically nothing they are so light and easy to carry Chisholm used to work a thousand of these wires over the northern hills of Scotland. I once watched Chisholm setting snares out on a grass field near Aberfeldy where he stayed - he was extremely fast and precise as he worked along the line, in with tealer, the peg was partly inserted in a second with the hand and then the heel of his boot pushed the peg right into ground level the whole setting time per snare was seconds he once snared around 2,500 rabbits in a week using this type of snare with the small light flat broad heeling peg. The latter years of his life Alex didn't keep well due to the fact that he stepped onto a live power line blown down in a gale one morning as he keepered a shoot, thousands of volts shot through his body he was lucky to survive and remained in ill health for years, his beautiful black Labrador died instantly.

(B) shows the full shape of this type of heeling peg made from elderberry a soft type wood easy to work with and shape these type of pegs when left to dry out become extremely hard and very robust and very light to carry they are a good snare to set out in pasture grass. These pegs can be made the same shape only longer 8" to use in different ground density.

I still use this type of tealer system occasionally except the length of my tealer is $10^1/_2$". They are used where the grass is higher although they are prone to bending that does not really matter as they are easily straightened in seconds, they are extremely difficult to see at times when set out, once again it is imperative to use marker pins at all times. The snare noose being permanently attached to the wire tealer pin after a time would become tight and this caused broken strands making the snare inoperable until a replacement noose was attached although a very efficient system. The figure 4 type tealer with the double eye at the top in correlation with double knot system on the end of the snare noose devised by Whyte was a better system to work with it had a better grip to aid with ground insertion also the simple swivelling action due to the rotation of the double know under the double eye of the tealer is a great saver of the snare noose tightening up at the tealer eye which was eliminated by the use of the double knot system which vastly improved the amount of rabbits that could now be taken with each snare noose without being replaced as often as happened when the noose was permanently attached to the old style tealer pin.

A   B

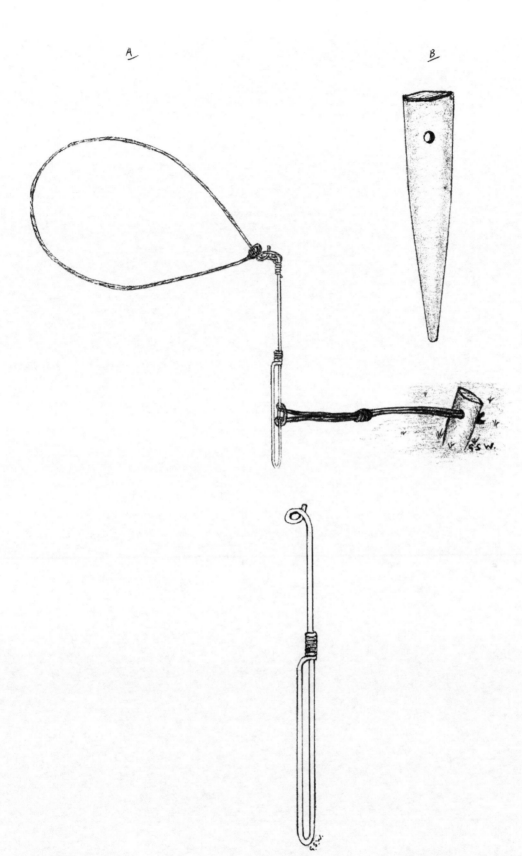

OLD STYLE
WIRE TEALER
made with
1½ milli diameter
wire - 9" long

The old tealer system was constructed from 1.5 mm galv wire

Professional Rabbit Snaring

Section 5 - Problems on the Snareline

Factors Affecting Snareline Catches

Weather - starvation

Predators - ground and avian

Disease

Chemicals

Animal waste

Disturbance

Noise

Restriction of permission area and acreage

Numbers of other trappers

Unsuitable type of ground

Food supply

Spoilage

Theft

Poaching

There are other factors which can affect your catch rate for example ground and avian predators or fighting against the natural elements. Chemicals sprayed on crops can affect the amount of rabbits that you catch, such as nitrate sprayed on grass. I once set 150 snares along a woodland edge about thirty feet out, in silage grass that was up to about one foot high. The grass was luscious and green and while there were runs showing they were not going out any distance. I was only getting about seven rabbits per morning, although the rabbits were going out into the grass and playing around they were not going out in the numbers that they should have been. The problem was that the luscious green grass had been sprayed heavily with nitrate which scours the rabbits and a lot of them were feeding on the old grass along the perimeter of the woodland, especially old does with young ones. They were also going out of the bottom of the wood into a long narrow field bordered by a stream. They were feeding in this field out in the established grazing which they preferred best. In this case I lifted all of the snares and after the first crop of silage was cut I waited until the yellow fresh colouring disappeared from the field as the second crop of hay was coming through the ground. Once it reached six inches high there were many new runs showing up nicely right along the field and the new grown grass was better feeding, I reset and took over one hundred in three days.

Another time when checking snares with Whyte, he had set snares along the grassy head ridge or headland bordering a crop field. The field on the other side of the perimeter fence was grass which was not included in the permission area, but the rabbits were running across it from a tree lined edge and feeding in the young crop field. The snares were set out in the early spring to be checked the following morning, but alas the farmer had come into the grass field later that same day and sprayed it with pig slurry, which smells to high heaven. This ruined the morning's catch of rabbits also. Disturbance and noise will upset rabbits and continual harassment is not good if you wish to snare them. Don't chase them with dogs in daytime, or with lamp or gun at night or try to ferret them, give them total peace and quiet, then on the right day with overcast blustery weather set out your snares. It will make all the world of difference to your catch rate.

Restriction of the size of your permission area is another factor preventing you from catching large numbers of rabbits. For instance you could be a skilled snareman but you are limited by the acreage of ground you have to work, so it is obvious that a neighbouring estate or farm maybe thousands of acres in size holding prime snaring locations upon it and another trapper may catch thousands or rabbits per season on it. Then again there may be more than one good trapper so the catch rate will be reduced again. The ground could also be unsuitable with a poor source of minerals and food supply. Yes there are many factors that you must become aware of when trapping rabbits which can restrict your catch rate.

Chapter 17 - Environmental factors

Weather

Inevitably the weather is one of the most important elements, at least where snaring is concerned as to the success or failure in the pursuit of rabbits. The best snaring nights are rough wild and overcast nights. A touch of rain through the wind also makes good running nights. On these gusty nights the rabbits feel secure and travel well out into the pastures to feed. Dark and dewless nights when the grass is dry are also good snaring nights. The rain is no real deterrent to rabbits, except on nights where there is continual downpour. Good catches will often follow a sequence of early evening rain showers followed by a dry remainder of the night. Rough moonlit nights with the overhead clouds flitting through the sky are also fair catching nights. On starry nights which are quiet with no wind where a heavy dew settles on the grass, also nights with a white rime frost are invariably very poor snaring nights. On quiet nights with only four hours darkness throughout the summer months, when snaring in crop fields, rabbit catches are never really excessive compared to the later months of the year after harvest where excellent catches can be taken out in grass pastures.

Types of Grass that Cause Problems

The illustration opposite shows various types of grasses you will encounter when out snaring in the countryside. These types of grasses are quite strong and wiry and springy and should never ever be left standing in front of a set snare loop, any type of obstruction should always be removed keeping the noose free and clear at all times. I have experienced firsthand the problems that are caused by obstructions partially blocking the open snare noose, due to these types of grasses being quite robust in their design.

Setting in higher growth one day, as I leaned forward to adjust a snare loop I touched a couple of strands of these types of grasses and as they bent forward they touched the top of and inside of the snare loop and actually lowered the height of the noose. I repeated the process a couple more times and the results were the same. Should a rabbit be springing up and over high growth between the beats and one or more of these higher grasses be pushed forwards and lowers the noose I found it will cost you a catch in your snare. So it is imperative to remove any and all obstructions away from the front and back of each and every snare noose.

Therefore it is most important to become observant and look carefully to become aware of small details that could make the difference of making a catch or a tripped and empty snare.

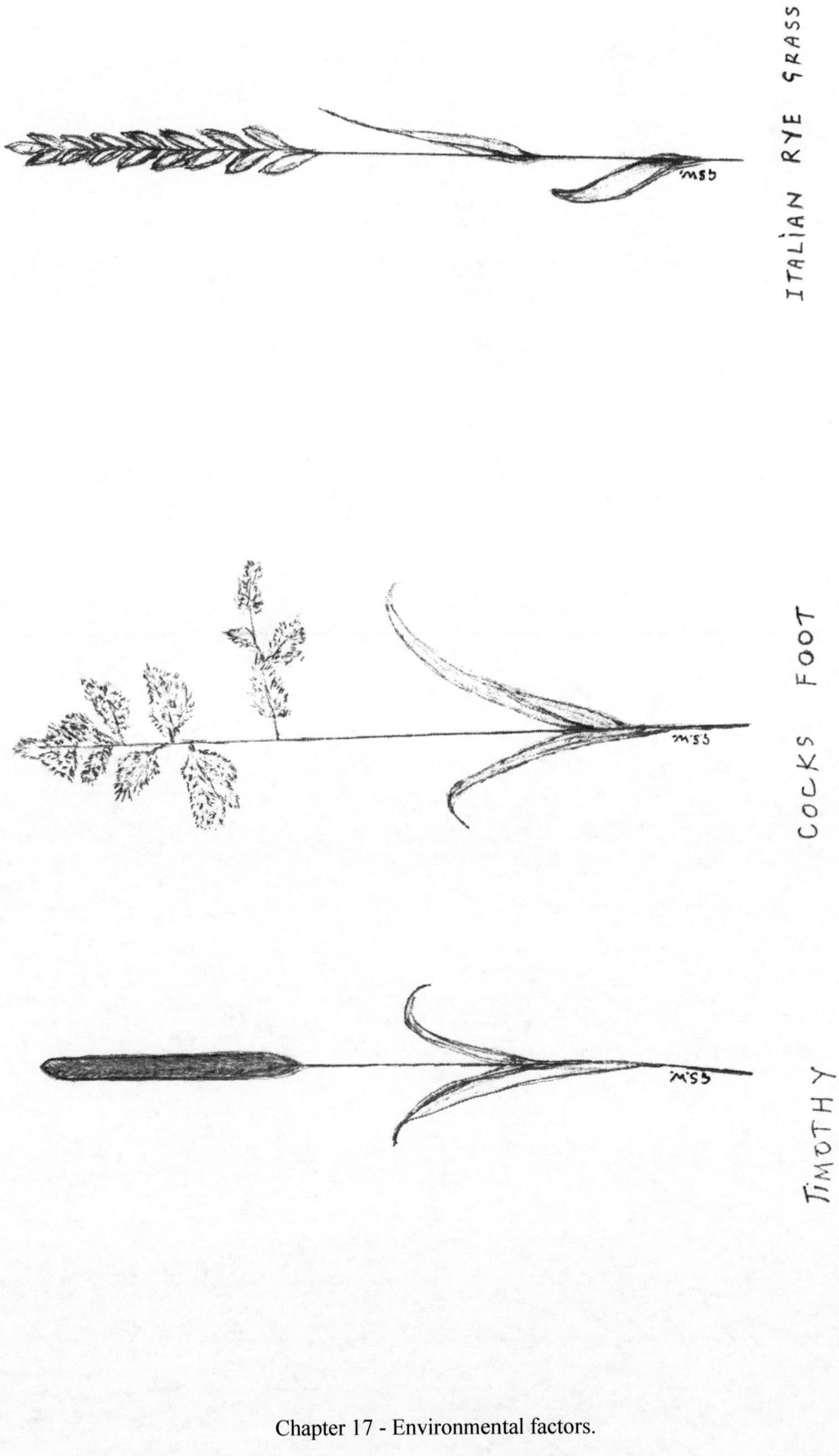

ITALIAN RYE GRASS

COCKS FOOT

TIMOTHY

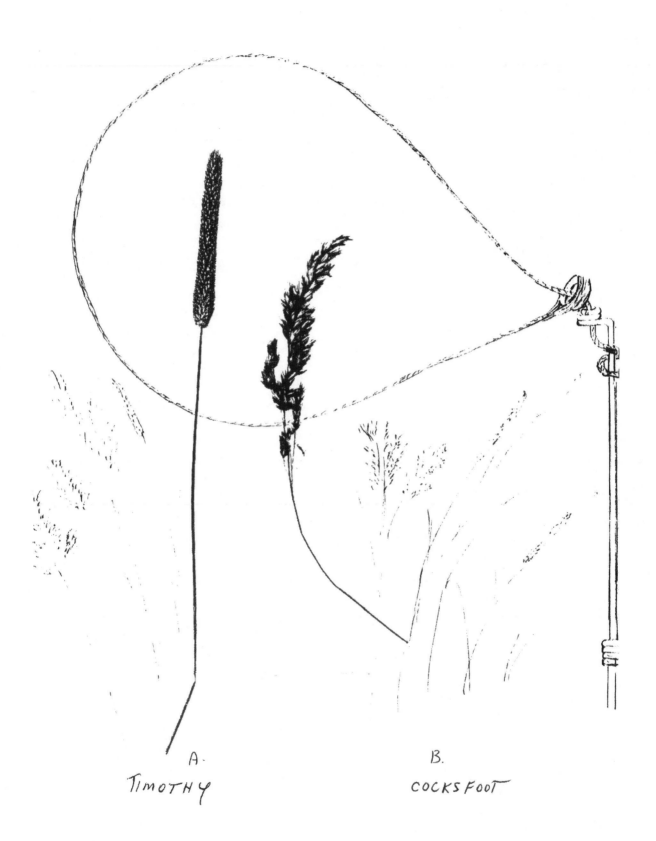

A.

TIMOTHY

B.

COCKSFOOT

Chapter 18 - Livestock

Cattle

This is where the experienced professional has the advantage over the amateur snareman. He can look at a situation and will know immediately what can and cannot happen. Look at the illustration on the following page of a cow with its head over the top of a fenceline. The top fenceline wire is loose. The cow has a mouthful of grass which the cow has gathered from the grassy bank on the other side of the fenceline, as the old adage says about the grass is always greener on the other side of the fence. Sometimes there are broken fence posts and loose and slack wires in the middle of the fenceline. These locations along the back of such poorly constructed fences are to be avoided at all times. If the runs are visible into the opposite field from the livestock this is where to peg out the snares so that the cows cannot either lean over or push their heads through between loose wires to graze on the opposite side of the fenceline where they would be liable to get their tongue caught in a snare noose causing serious damage to the said animal.

Looking at the first illustration in detail - do not set beats marked X they are far too near the damaged fenceline, if the fenceline was straight and taut with a wire strand along the top of the fenceline or a rylock square mesh fence then it would be safer to set at X beats. As the fenceline is damaged set at points A and B further out into the opposite field out of reach of all livestock.

Here is a situation I came across when the head gamekeeper asked me to snare rabbits in an almost ripe barley field bordering woodland on the west side of the field and a large grass field on the top side of the barley field which both fields were in sloping ground. As I arrived I noticed that the broad grassy edge on the barley field side of the fenceline was cropped short and flat all the way along right away I said to myself this is not the work of rabbits although there were many rabbits at this location. I put my bag down which was full of snares as I started to walk along the field edge a noticed a single strand of barbed wire stretched along fence posts parallel to the main fenceline about 4-5 feet inside the cattle field. It was 4 ft high from the ground. I thought to myself these cattle can't get to the fenceline so what's cropped the grass short and level as I reached the hill on looking over down into little valley in the cattle field there was the answer, a number of calves which were going under the single barbed wire strand and leaning through between the fence wires and cropped the grass. When rabbits eat grass they always eat in half circles, therefore the snares were set in the crop field a few yards away from the field edge at a far safer distance. When cattle graze out in grass their tongue comes out from one side of the mouth and then the other their rough tongue wraps around the grass and pulls it into their mouth cattle have no top teeth only a pad at the front with teeth at the top back half. The way cattle feed using their long tongue it's a dangerous scenario to set snares amongst cattle at any time it could lead to expensive vet bills or the beast being put down, so never ever set snares of any type along fencelines or in grazing fields, keep it safe and think safety at all times.

Sheep

Once again be careful snaring around sheep and lambs. Sheep like cattle don't have top teeth in the front part of the mouth they have a hard pad, the main problem with pegged snares set out in grass fields is that sheep will be caught by the feet. I have snared in amongst sheep many times and never had any problems. I did not use pegged snares I used hoop snares, with the wire bends shaped like an upside down U shape with only the snare noose attached to the wire hoop. The two legs of the hoop are pushed into the ground over the middle of a beat and when the rabbit is caught it pulls from the side and on occasions wraps around the wire legs. I have taken many hares with this method also large fox cubs.

When sheep are feeding they crop the grass in an upward motion of the head. They don't have a long tongue like cattle or horses. I never ever set any type of snare in a field where lambs are present due to them being smaller and smaller sized head, especially those small black faced lambs because they would have been caught by the head. I only snare among adult sheep. If they were the smaller black face adult sheep I would narrow the wire hoops to stop them putting their head into the hoops. I have often watched them grazing with their heads held low to the ground feeding with that familiar upward movement of the head and bumping the legs of the hoop they just walk around them and carry on feeding. Although I have snared among sheep for years without a single incident, I do not recommend you the reader to do it at all. So stay safe and avoid snaring anywhere in or around livestock at all times. It's better to wait until the fields are empty void of animals.

Horses

This illustration shows a horse leaning right over a fenceline cropping the grass on the opposite side of the fenceline. Remember some horses are large with long legs and necks. They can lean over a wire fence and crop the grass further out from the edge than cattle could do. A horse has teeth on the top and bottom of his mouth and remember that the horse's tongue is long and spatula shaped. Stay safe keep snares away from livestock.

Chapter 19 - Avian Predators on the Snare Line

Buzzard.

There are no eagles present in the east central Scotland where I reside, or so I thought until the farm manager gave me a call and asked me to look over a crop field with rabbit damage in the spring of last year. After checking along the bottom of the high embankment of a motorway which bordered the south side of this large field, I was crossing the same field heading north to check a hedge which bordered along the bottom of a banking of a country road. I became aware of a large dark shape about 30 yds away out of the side of my right eye. On turning to look at this large object my reaction was *"What the hell is that?"* It was the biggest bird of prey I have ever seen, except for big bald eagles in British Colombia Canada, gliding past about fifteen feet in the air it reminded me of a stealth bomber.

I stood still watching this large sea eagle as it alighted upon a branch of an old oak tree standing at the roadside fifty yards away. It didn't appear to be afraid of my presence and just sat there and looked at me as I approached it. As usual my digital Panasonic camera was left in the house as I could have obtained cracking close up pictures from 20 feet away. After a good few minutes looking at one another, as it realised I was of no threat to it, it arose and flew off across the road northwards and landed in woodland another field length away. Relating the incident to the keeper he told me he had seen it three times in the last week. He also remarked about its size and huge wingspan and said *"The bird is not doing any harm at all. It's the first time I have ever seen one"*. It was also my first sighting of a sea eagle also.

But there are a numerous amount of buzzards in the area and it's nothing to see a half dozen at a time soaring high upon the thermals then diving and wheeling around in the sky with their distinct wheeling call which often reminds me of the cry of bald eagles out in Western Canada. The buzzard is said to be a scavenger feeding on dead carcasses which it does of course, but do not be deluded in any way about this bird's catching and killing abilities. I have seen them on numerous occasions killing large full grown pheasants, partridges, pigeons. I have seen buzzards with squirrels in the woodland some mornings. I watched one kill a kestrel one morning when out snaring. Then I saw one kill another kestrel a few hundred yards from my house. The kestrel is a bird you rarely see now hovering above the fields and roadsides. The local dog walkers were aghast one morning in the local park a large buzzard swooped on a full grown seagull killing it and ripping it apart in front of them. I once saw a large buzzard swooping down into a grassy water filled ditch and emerging with a large dog mink in its talons flying about four feet off the ground and landing on a nearby thorn tree to consume its meal. Another morning on the snareline I watched a buzzard catch a large stoat and just did not grip it properly as the stoat was wriggling and trying to turn and bite the buzzard which flew up to a great height and then released its grip and dropped the stoat which fell to the ground like a stone, with the bird following its prey closely ready to retrieve the corpse on landing.

These birds have the capability to kill efficiently due to their size, with a large wingspan, powerful hooked beak and razor sharp talons. The television showed a buzzard taking an osprey chick from the nest and killing it, one also killed a white phalarope in front of dozens of twitchers while they were filming this rare bird.

On saying that every bird and animal must eat so be fair about it. When approaching the snareline just after grey light in the early morning on a few occasions buzzards have risen from a freshly killed snared rabbit leaving it lying half eaten in the wire. The early bird gets the worm as they say only this time it gets the rabbit. To stop this happening arrive earlier and get out on the snareline in the darkness before light comes in. I don't really care if the buzzards take a rabbit or two on the snareline because I fling these damaged rabbit carcases out into the field when I'm finished allowing the birds to consume what's left. The rabbits killed by the buzzards are eaten at times from the neck and shoulder into the thoracic cavity exposing all the broken ribs and flesh eaten all down one side of the carcase or both sides leaving only the skin pulled over the back or over the front legs.

When snaring up in the north with Whyte a lot of years ago there were two buzzards that caused extreme damage to a number of the snared rabbits that morning completely ruining each carcase. The damage they cause on my snareline is minimal I just wish Mr fox was more considerate when visiting the snareline.

Magpie.

The magpie is very distinguishable with is black and white plumage and long tail. On closer scrutiny the black colour gives off a purplish blueish sheen on the feathers of the wings and a glossy green sheen from the tail. They have a constant noisy irritating chatter and can be seen on a regular basis scavenging road kills.

Many people are now beginning to realise that the magpie is not just a beautiful bird with a splendid plumage but a nasty predator with a bold cheeky arrogant attitude, which has increased in numbers immensely in urban environments, pilfering garden songbirds' eggs and killing and devouring many young blackbird's chicks from their nests. They even try to get into bluetit nest boxes. I have watched them stab little fledglings that have not long left the nest to death with their sharp pointed beaks. With an increase in magpies the songbirds seem to decline due to their constant predation on the nests.

There is a lovely walkway that runs parallel between a woodland strip and a large well established hawthorn hedge that's stood there since my childhood, it runs a distance of around 400 yds. Walking my dog at night along this route in moonlight in winter nights I could count approximately 60 blackbirds roosting in the large hedge. Once the magpies started to colonise the area in large numbers the blackbirds numbers dwindled to six birds. In the spring I controlled the magpies at the end of the autumn the blackbird numbers were back up around the fifty mark again. How many more little songbirds survived the onslaught of these magpie hoards? This was one incident where magpies were the cause of the decline of the blackbird population. I don't really have much of a problem with them due to the fact that the keeper keeps them well under control.

The main problem on the snareline with magpies is that they pick the eyes out of the dead rabbits. When checking the snareline in the spring time it's a pleasure to listen to the dawn chorus with the thrushes, blackbirds, larks and many of the small finches and woodland birds singing from the tree tops in well keepered woodlands and coverts to all due to proper predator control by a hardworking vigilant keeper.

Many years ago when the milk was delivered in bottles, the magpies would peck through the silver tops covering the bottles with their strong pointed beak to get at the milk inside especially the cream which collected at the top on the underside of the cap. I witnessed this on numerous occasions. I always poured the milk down the sink due to the fact that I have watched magpies and jackdaws feeding with relish on dog poo especially ones where the dogs had meal mixed throughout their food. I have counted as many as ten birds all around a large scat taking turn about feeding on these faeces. I always told family and friends also many other people to discard the contaminated milk in case of food poisoning and also explaining these birds' feeding habits and to cover bottles to keep them safer from any further avian damage.

Gulls.

One of the worst avian predators I have encountered on the snare line over the years is the black backed gull. Over the years these birds have moved inland breeding and nesting in industrial estates upon the factory roofs. They have also become an absolute pest in the cities again nesting upon the rooftops causing a real mess with their droppings contaminating buildings, dive bombing people walking along the streets especially when pedestrians are carrying takeaway foods fish and chips and so on. They appear to have lost their fear of man. The local authorities should really be taking things in hand and having a real old fashioned cull to thin these hoards right down to an acceptable and realistic level.

They colonise landfill sites by the thousands feeding on any old foodstuffs they can scavenge and many are said to succumb to botulism due to consuming amongst all this old refuse. They also gather on abattoir rooftops scavenging any bones and meat scraps that they can find and consume. I have stood and watched them grabbing hold of young starlings feeding alongside them and swallowing them completely live and whole feathers and all. There are hundreds of them sit out all night on local playing fields. They create a terrible racket as they rise at first light awakening all the local residents in the early morning hours with their calling and wailing. After harvest they invade the open stubbles and ploughed land, free range pig units are another outdoor refuge for them.

When setting out snares I have watched these large gulls swooping down trying to catch young baby rabbits who beat a hasty retreat down their burrows. Not satisfied at missing a quick fresh meal they will actually squat low to the ground and extend their necks down the burrow entrance to try and extract a tiny victim for a meal. They also do excessive damage to the snared rabbits; they pick holes into the base of the belly and back leg area and extract all the innards before stripping all the flesh from the carcase leaving nothing but a whole skin and bones as a reminder of their presence to the trapper. The damage is at its worst when carrying out rabbit control in the summer months when daylight comes in at 3.30 am in the morning. My snares are checked three times a day throughout this period of time. The morning check is the worst. The rabbits come out and feed throughout the day in secluded and quiet areas where there is no disturbance. The damage is curtailed in the later months of the year due to daylight breaking in the later hours of the morning. Therefore the trapper is on the snare line awaiting daylight arriving.

Discussing the latter problem with Whyte about the amount of damage the gulls caused in the early summer months what he did and told me to do was to walk further out into the field and gut the rabbits allowing them to feed on the viscera which helps to satisfy the hunger and to be honest it did work in helping to curb the damage.

Sparrowhawk.

SPARROW HAWK

A small bird of prey well adapted for hunting birds in dense woodland. The cock bird has an orange tinge on its chest and belly, the female is larger with brown back and wings with brown bars underneath. They have bright yellow or orangey eyes with yellow legs and sharp talons. They are hated by pigeon breeders and become a nuisance in gardens killing the small birds in gardens that the residents are feeding. The smaller males kill blackbirds, thrushes and small sparrows, starlings and finches. The females are larger and I have seen some pretty large sized birds killing wood pigeons, magpies, young squirrels and pheasant poults. They have no predator to control them except larger hawks. I personally watched the devastation they can cause on the young swallow population day after day of course being a hawk they have favourable conservation status.

The damage they do on the snareline is minimal but on occasions over the years while controlling rabbits in woodland plantations I have seen large hen sparrowhawks killing half grown rabbits in snares and eating the heads of their victims the same scenario happens along the thick hedgerows at times.

Carrion Crows.

Like the magpie the carrion crow is one of the ugliest and adaptable of our wild birds very wary of men. They are quite intelligent and very adaptable. I watched one of these carrion crows from my kitchen window early one morning as it sat on top of my shed viewing the immediate surroundings for a little while to determine everything was safe and sound. It alighted into the garden and picked up a crust of bread in its strong pointed black beak. Before trying to consume the food it put one of its feet upon the crust to stabilize it firmly to the ground then it proceeded to stab at it with its powerful pointed beak. Not having much luck due to the crust being very hard the crow then removed its foot picked up the crust then carried it over to a dish in the garden full of water that I keep for the small birds to drink and wash in. It then dunked the crust into the water to soften it then pulled it out held it down once again under its foot where it proceeded to peck at it again and again. It carried this operation out about five times until it eventually softened the crust enough to break it down into smaller sized bits. After consuming the food it flew up and disappeared. The crow has come into the garden on numerous occasions knowing that it is relatively safe from harm and repeated the same process on occasions when it finds a piece of hard bread. This is one bird that displayed intelligence and adaptability.

Paul the keeper keeps the crows and magpies to an acceptable level with the Larsen straps and ladder type cape traps. Once again snare line damage is minimal by crows as they make an entrance hole into the belly to extract the soft innards. They also attack the anal region . They can also be extremely ruthless as I watched a pair of carrion crows pecking viciously at a myxy rabbit blind and helpless stabbing it about the head and anal region, oh for my gun on that occasion. I went and despatched the helpless creature. Last season my friend Jackie who traps foxes over a very large area of land for a number of farmers told me of an incident the farmer relayed to him about a large carrion crow that stabbed the eye out of a healthy little lamb and killed it one morning as he was checking his lambs at the time. These crows can be quite fearless and ruthless at times and need severe controlling by trapping and shooting.

My good friend Phil Lloyd in action.

Phil snared a few hundred rabbits at this location helping to stop the erosion of a sea wall.

Chapter 20 - Ground Predators on the Snare Line

There are many thousands of rabbits that live all year round above ground in the open, never entering burrows. They live out in old quarries amongst stone piles and rocks, scrub covered ground, thick bramble on briar patches within banks, heavy thick rushes, and old drystone dykes or walls. Where all these outlying locations prevail these bush rabbit as I call them are usually large, clean and healthy rabbits and are normally disease free due to their unconfined open air lifestyle. The rabbit a tenacious and lively creature, like all wild animals, are guided by pure instinct unlike man who has the ability to form theories and work out solutions. Yet the old rabbit being what he is in life, a wild animal of the countryside, takes him all his time to hang on to life even when in his prime being sound of sense and limb. Should any of his senses fail in the smallest degree, e.g. sight, sound, smell, sensitivity, feel and touch it's merely a matter of time he falls victim to one or other of his foes.

I have previously mentioned about predator damage on the snareline, how certain animals can cause considerable damage to the intended quarry. Therefore the trapper must become acquainted to the damage caused to the dead rabbits on the snareline, like a detective, and work out what predator is responsible for the damage as each and every animal who preys upon the snared rabbits each has its own trademark in its method of attacking, killing and devouring its prey. The illustration on the following page is showing some signs of the damage caused by snareline predators which comes with the job of course and how to recognise the perpetrator responsible for the carnage which really can infuriate the trapper at times.

The problem arises frequently due to the rabbits being captured as they travel outwards from their residence. Along the runs towards the feeding grounds, one minute they are bounding freely along the runs when suddenly they come to an abrupt halt on hitting a well set open snare loop awaiting their presence ready to ambush them and take them completely by surprise. The shock of their sudden capture and freedom of movement being restricted causes them to scream loudly through fear in their black nightly environment. These sporadic screams they emit as they strike the awaiting and deadly nooses time after time alerts any wary prowling predator that happens to be within the vicinity of the snaring field to their presence. Any hungry predator will take full advantage of an opportunity giving them an easy and free meal at the trapper's expense.

(A) Shows the drawing of a pegged snare with the head of a rabbit left in the enclosed snare loop. This is a classic scenario indicating the fox's presence on the snareline as it carried out its nefarious activity under the cover of darkness.

(B) Once again denotes fox activity where a rabbit is found in a snare with an elongated neck. This damage is caused by a fox killing a rabbit in a snare then trying to extract it by pulling the rabbit carcase in a vigorous manner against the already tightened snare noose to free the carcase from the snare's clutches. This is what causes the rabbit's neck to become elongated in this manner.

(C) This illustration shows a more gruesome scene that has taken place on the snareline only this time Mr Fox is not the villain of the peace. This is the work of a badger who is a dirty eater and eats a dead animal in from the backend devouring everything in the body cavity. What is usually left after a badger's presence is what you see a head with a flat clean skin with feet and occasionally a part of the spine, sometimes part of a leg bone, sometimes absolutely nothing but the skin. Even the head is gone at times but this is the most common scene that greets the trapper checking his line in the morning.

I have never really had much bother with badgers except for an odd rabbit being eaten. But don't be swayed by the bunny huggers about the cuddly badger only eating worms and berries. Like any meat eating predator they certainly do serious damage to poultry, pheasants, partridges and ground nesting birds and many small mammals etc. I have seen the first hand damage they do to lambs eating them out like a rabbit. Also where they were biting just the noses off small lambs and leaving them to die a horrible death. Like all animals that are not controlled they eventually multiply until they become a nuisance spreading disease and devouring other protected species. Therefore we are stuck with them until the blouses running this country start to get a sense of reality to do something about it by losing their Walt Disney mentality.

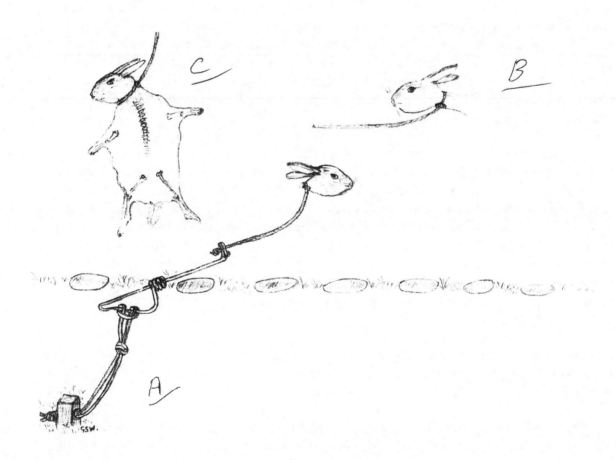

The Cat

Cats have been associated with man for thousands of years either to protect his grain against rodents which infested his storage facilities or kept as pets. Cats can never be domesticated regardless of how well they are treated they like to be continually on the prowl. Some are forced out into the elements at night by their so-called loving owner. While they sit cosy with central heating the poor cat's outside sitting on the hard frost or pouring rain. Cats are potential killers once they start hunting and become a nuisance to songbirds, rodents, rabbits, pigeon lofts and aviary owners who in turn become infuriated if their prize and valuable birds are killed by a cat. They are either trapped and despatched or taken miles away by car and released into the depths of the countryside where they revert to their wild state and live in the woodland in heavy bush or take refuge in a rabbit warren. They breed quite prolifically once they become established, then they become a potential nuisance to all wildlife especially around rearing pens and game coverts. They are very agile and great climbers. One such feral cat killed approximately five pheasant poults before he was shot in the pheasant pen. It was climbing up and over the perimeter wire at dusk. One evening the keeper was determined to get the culprit so he sat inside the pen all afternoon waiting and his patience paid off.

The feral cat is also a nuisance on a snareline especially if it is living in the surrounding woodland in the vicinity of the snaring field. His continual presence keeps the rabbit in residence and prevents them from going out in the feeding pasture. I know when a cat is around due to years of experience. They are not as destructive on the snareline as a fox can be in terms of destroying the snared rabbits as such, but they certainly affect the trapper's catch rate on occasions as the rabbits don't travel out at night due to the continual presence of the resident cat. This has happened to me on many occasions. I have set a good number of snares either pegged snares or fenceline snares and have caught only a few rabbits. On one occasion I set sixty snares on some rough grass in front of a small wood and caught nothing in three days. The runs were excellent and the beats well padded. What a surprise the fourth morning, there in the snares sat three feral cats an old female and two half grown offsprings.

On the evening check of the snares I had fifteen rabbits, the following morning I had twenty-one etc. Many lads that I have taught have told me of similar experiences on their snareline. The most rabbits I have had destroyed by two feral cats in one morning was eight. The cats were caught the following morning. Tracks of a cat are easily distinguished they walk in a straight line like the fox placing one foot in front of the other only the footprint is smaller and round with no toenail marks showing at the front of the toes. Although never set to target them deliberately, the pegged rabbit snare with the big loop can pick up prowling feral cats due to the way they walk and the height they hold their head. The double knot swivelling system is just perfect as it stops the snare wire from kinking and holds them well. The snare stop holds the cat and prevents the snare from killing.

At times I have set a 150 fenceline snares, also pegged snares and caught only six or seven rabbits with every other snare was untouched. The exact same the following morning. Knowing the problem it's only a matter of time before the culprit itself falls foul of one of the many snares. With the predator cat now gone the catch rate starts to rise. Many trappers have related exactly the same problems. The most rabbits I have had damaged in one morning from two feral cats was eight everyone was attacked and killed and eaten in exactly the same manner. The cat eats a rabbit from the back of the head. It will sometimes chew both the ears off, or on occasions just one ear then it chews from the back of the head and neck along the back. When you find a rabbit like this all eaten with the skin and fur peeled back you will know it was the work of a cat. At times you will have both cat and fox working your snareline. I have had this on numerous occasions, the cat caught in one snare along with other snares containing rabbit heads and smashed rabbits with their ribs all crushed in. Two friends of mine Alan and Trevor from Yorkshire phoned me to tell me that they had a similar experience one morning. Whilst checking their snares at first light they came across a very large feral cat in a snare, awaiting them in another snare further down the line was a Jack Russell dog sitting quite happily wagging his little tail to them after the little rascal had killed all the other rabbits and chewed them up. He was taken up to the farm and put in the doghouse. Trappers can have some funny experiences at times when out snaring.

With a cat in permanent residence your catch rate is sure to be limited once the snares have been set out. Farm cats can also be notorious wanderers. Problems arise when a female gives birth to a litter of kittens and needs to increase her food supply to feed its family.

Always keep a sharp eye when out snaring. This young Ash tree was a scratch post for a cat. There were four trees found like this in this woodland planting indicating a predator in the location.

The Fox

The fox is the number one public enemy on my own snareline and it has caused me considerable grief on numerous occasions over many years by his nefarious nightly appearances. Ron the head gamekeeper is an excellent fox controller and keeps them in check using snare and also by shooting them as he is an excellent rifle shot, but on occasions in outlying areas all of a sudden devastation.

The red fox belongs to the dog family, canidae, and resembles a collie dog. Adult foxes in the UK are the largest in the world and can stand 21" at the shoulder, average weight of dog fox 17 lbs. Vixens can also attain the same weight and heavier. It is not uncommon for dog foxes to be as large as 30 lbs plus. I have snared many dog foxes at 25 lbs in weight myself over the years and hundreds over 20 lbs in weight and can measure between four and five feet in length average tail length 18"-19". They have erect, relatively large pointed ears and a long pointed muzzle. Although only four toes show in each footprint there are five toes on the front feet, one being a dew claw. In winter fur grows between the toe pads protecting the feet. They also have excellent eyesight as the eyes of the red fox have vertical slits for pupils similar to cats. This adaptation is for seeing at night. The soft fur is long and dense and provides excellent insulation against the extremely cold damp British weather. Their colour can vary from dark red to orange and pale yellow, also pure black. Not all foxes have a white tip on the end of the tail, the legs are black same as the back of the ears, fur on the underside from chin down the belly can vary from white to dark grey and sometimes black.

They walk in a straight line same as a cat, footprint elongated toenails point inwards. The front foot has a broader heart shaped hind pad than the narrower back foot. The fox has excellent sight, sound, smell and sensitivity which makes him one the rabbit trapper's worst enemies. Although there are many predators that work on a snareline the fox is my worst at times I call him Dick Turpin. The fox plunders the snareline on a nightly basis and is a confounded nuisance at times as he goes about his nefarious activities throughout the hours of darkness on is nightly travels, leaving nothing at times but sheer carnage on the snareline which angers and infuriates the trapper as he arrives to check his snares in the morning.

A fox working a snareline on a nightly basis affects the trapper's catch rate not by just consuming the quarry but his nightly forays keep the rabbits from venturing out into the pastures. Through this continual disturbance and nightly harassment the rabbits become as cute as the fox and start to come out to feed in the later early morning hours just before daylight. Therefore I have found that instead of checking my snares right at first light I leave it until an hour later in the morning which I find at times I have a better catch rate of rabbits all live and well freshly caught in the snares.

The most common visible sign of a fox causing damage on the snareline is seen when checking the snares after first light in the morning and finding only rabbit heads in the snares. Another indication is seeing rabbits lying dead in snares with elongated necks caused by the fox gripping the rabbit and trying to tug it free from the snare. On occasions it will succeed in pulling the securing peg free from the ground therefore losing rabbit and snare altogether. Now and again the fox will get caught in one or two of the snares by the front foot and frees itself by chomping through the brass wire leaving the snare wire fully stretched and taut with uneven splayed end strands where it was bitten through. The musty telltale smell left by the fox also indicates his presence. I find the worst damage is in the early summer months at times when cubs have to be fed.

A prowling dog fox causes extreme damage. I have been checking my snares in the mornings where I have had catches of between seventy and eighty rabbits in a straight line right along a field and over thirty of the rabbits are lying stretched out dead. Every one of them has the rib cage crushed in and smashed by the fox gripping them and biting them across the back of the shoulders, with flecks of fur all around each carcase where the rabbit has been darting around with the fox trying to grab it. I know from experience that the fox is travelling a good distance away from the den. After the snares have been emptied and reset, the same fox comes back in the darkness looking for all the rabbits he has previously killed the morning before and lo and behold he finds another catch of freshly caught rabbits and does exactly the same again. He will continue to do this until the snares are uplifted. The only way to stop this is to snare or shoot it.

On another occasion I set sixty snares along a rough on a golf course. In the morning on checking the snares I had 44 rabbits, half of which were dead killed by the fox along with another twelve heads which were minus the bodies. I knew there was a den in the vicinity with all the missing bodies. It turned out the den was only one hundred yards away in a gorse and tree covered bank. It gets worse once the cubs start to hunt and they come across the snared rabbits they eat everything at times. The only visible signs are a little tiny piece of neck left or just small flecks of fur and blood in every tightly closed snare loop, or you will only find the contents of the rabbit's stomachs every other morsel is completely gone. At times you will come across a live rabbit in a snare with flecks of fur all around it. This is caused by the fox as he works his way along the snareline killing each individual rabbit but as he is trying to grab his next victim lo and behold the trapper arrives in the grey light of the morning and finds the first dead rabbits all warm and freshly killed and the fox gone before it claimed its next victim. There are many instances of this happening, which would fill the pages of a book itself. I nearly always kill the fox in scenarios like this mostly with snares.

The fox can be snared quite easily as he keeps coming back. Depending on what type of location you are snaring, check along field edges for paw prints or scat. Also tramlines, any type of edge or crop feature, even some good rabbit runs can be set until you pick it up or sit and squeak him with rifle and lamp then shoot the fox as he approaches looking for the snared rabbit he is expecting.

Accidental foot snaring of foxes used to be a problem with the old snaring system, but the larger 6 inch stop loop along with the breakaway now allows foxes to extract a foot without activating the breakaway link.

Many trappers relate the same problems caused by the fox, but the trapper gets revenge because on occasions big cubs are taken in the rabbit snares. They don't appear to have the sense to bite through the snare cable or the twine and they can't pull the 8" peg free especially out in grass fields as the peg takes a tremendous grip. I can never fathom people who use big cumbersome tent style pegs 10" long to hold a rabbit. In pasture grass the hoop snare is deadly on cubs. At times adult foxes will be caught and held in the rabbit snares especially if they are caught around the muzzle and can't bite the snare wire. Also large adult dog foxes who get caught around the top of the head in front of the base of the ears and tight up under the top of the throat at the larynx. They expire quickly as they fight the snare, on occasions the wire breaks and the fox is lying dead three of four feet away from the broken snare. A big noose and a tightly wound rabbit snare using the double knot swivelling system is an extremely strong and effective system for rabbit snaring.

Knocked rabbit snares are another regular feature of a visiting fox, tealer pins are skewed, snare loops angled and at times the snare loop is perfect except that on occasions it is angled almost straight up in the air, yes the fox can be a most destructive predator on the snareline at any time of the year many times being alerted to the snaring location by the squeals of the captured rabbits.

Classic fox damage. A dozen rabbits were all killed and ripped out of a catch of 30 in total. There was more damage the following morning. The night afterwards the fox was shot by Paul, the 'keeper, and weighed in at 24lbs.

Telltale Signs of Foxes on your Snares

This illustration shows four rabbit snares in different positions and loop shapes which indicate that a prowling animal was present in the darkness and the trapper has to establish what it was that caused these problems.

Illustration (A) presents a pegged rabbit snare still standing but knocked from the original vertical setting position to an outward angle showing that a fox came along the run and bumped the snare and tealer to the side of the rabbit run.

Illustration (B) indicates that a fox has come along the run and got caught around the muzzle showing a distinct kinked small loop, similar to the 'frying panned' loop in the rabbit snare where the rabbit has hit the underside of the top of a small low set loop and caught around the muzzle, which it has shaken off its face as it attempts to escape. The distinct kinked loop which caught the fox around the muzzle is very similar only the kinked loop is larger in diameter. On occasions I have come across adult foxes caught around the muzzle with the snare loop closed at the back of a fang therefore the fox can't bite the snare wire so he remains caught until the trapper arrives to despatch it. A lot of large fox cubs are also caught when snares are set at over 9" in high flora. At this stage in their lives when they first leave the den on their own they have not the sense to bite through the non tensile brass snare cable so they too are captured and despatched while breakaway rabbit snares allow them to escape from the snare themselves.

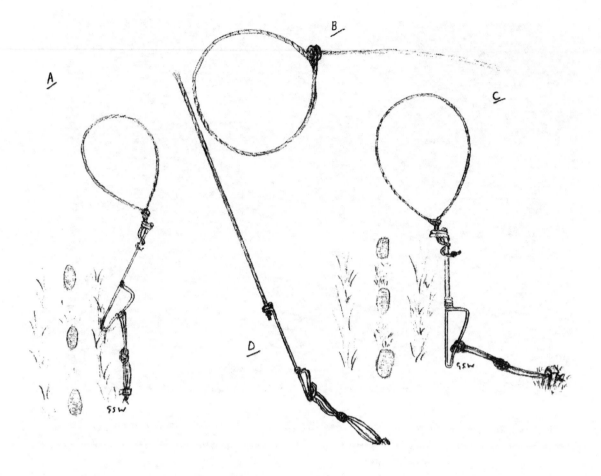

(C) This is a classic shape of a pegged rabbit snare with the loop sitting cocked up like a light bulb on a light stand. I think this may be caused by the fox going along the run with his head down going under the loop knocking it up right next to the tealer eye causing the tensioned wire to be bent upwards at this point into vertical position.

(D) This illustration is a regular scene on a rabbit snare line in the morning. This is caused by the fox being foot snared the fox then pulls it taut as it tries to extract its foot from the closed noose then it bites through the cable to free itself leaving the taut snare cable as seen in the illustration. The fox pulls the broken snare noose from its leg with its teeth. On occasions I have set fox snares on the prominent rabbit runs and snared one or two foxes in a morning, then checked their feet for broken wires which were non-existent. I have checked many many fox's feet over the years on the rabbit line and never found one yet with a broken noose on its foot. The larger 6 inch stop loop along with the breakaway now allows foxes to extract a foot without activating the breakaway link.

The Rat

Illustration (A) shows the drawing of a large rat. The field or hedge rat is an intelligent creature, quite clean looking, a good climber and swimmer. Also found frequently along stream and river banks also in and along the old broken down drystone walls covered with bramble briars, ivy and other various types of growth offering good cover and security from predators. The outlying locations usually harbour a few rats along their length.

Illustration (B) shows a rabbit's head and partly damaged face. I have been lucky enough throughout my snaring career only to have come across such damage to the quarry on only two occasions. The first snaring operation was carried out along an old fenceline which ran parallel along the front of an old broken down drystone wall which bordered on a long woodland strip of trees about 25 yds wide. It was jungle of mature trees, elderberry bushes, bramble briars around four feet high, willow herb and stinging nettles which ran almost the full length of the woodland border. Bordered by crop fields on either side this labyrinth of entanglement harboured the resident rabbit population which I was asked to control to an acceptable level due to the damage they were inflicting on the local crop fields bordering the rabbit's place of residence. A line of fenceline snares were placed the full length of the woodland border to control their numbers in short order. This was many years ago and the first time I had ever encountered this type of damage on the snareline, only three rabbits were damaged in this manner. The whole of one side of the face of each rabbit was eaten off with such clinical precision you would have sworn it had been done with a very sharp knife. There was no fur or skin on the face of each rabbit and every eyeball was also eaten clean out leaving nothing except a bare eye socket void of any meat or skin whatsoever.

This same scenario happened another time when snaring a similar outlying location a few years later.

The Otter & Mink

I have never ever observed any mink damage on the snare line even when setting in fields bordering streams and rivers but I did catch a large dog mink in the pegged snare one morning caught clean around the neck and it did not seem pleased to see me that morning. Once again the double knot system with its simple swivelling action which helps immensely in taking the strain from the noose along with the tighter spun cable allowing for free rotation helps the lifespan of the noose immensely. There was no damage to the snare noose whatsoever after despatching and removing the mink. Colin my friend from the North of England phoned me one morning after checking his snareline to say he watched a large otter out in the snaring field it had killed a fully grown rabbit, ate the head neck and into the shoulders then took hold of the rabbit ran across to the river and swam over to an island, sat and looked at him smugly and carried on with eating his stolen breakfast. Colin was laughing at how cheeky and brazen this big fellow was. Well there is always something new on the snareline to see and learn every now and again, it pays to carry a camera in your pocket to catch rare pictures of animals in one-off shots every once in a while that you are never liable to witness ever again.

The Badger

Although the fox and the feral cat are the main two ground predators that cause the most damage on my snareline, on occasions I suffer from the predation from the badger who occasionally eats a rabbit or two for a meal. To be honest I've never ever had any major problems or serious damage to my rabbit catches from one yet, over the many years I've been in the game the badger is not as destructive as the fox and feral cat who are times a constant nuisance on many snarelines. The badger may cause more damage in places where there are prolific numbers of them although I've never experienced this ever happening to me.

A member of the musteladae family its rough coarse haired coat black and silver in colour with the black and white striped face is one of Britain's easiest predators to identify and can weigh up to thirty pounds plus in weight. Although now protected by law their numbers have increased dramatically, like any animal that is not kept under control that has no natural enemies their population will be governed by road kills, Mother Nature in the form of disease and starvation. TB is now on the increase amongst herds of cattle due to the rise in their number, as they contaminate the drinking water in cattle troughs and infect the grass also with their breath, saliva, urine and faeces. The Ministry has started a culling process to regulate their numbers to an acceptable level, many more deaths occur on the roads due to their increase in numbers. Signs of badger activity are easily recognised with broad well padded runs, small bear-like paw prints and small scrape holes with scat in them. At times you will see a trail of straw from a stubble field showing where a badger exited with his bedding material.

Many people carry the misconception that the badger only digs up, roots, grubs, beetles and raids wasp nests occasionally. Don't be under any illusions; he is powerfully built with a good set of dentistry, sharp claws and powerful strong feet for digging. You will see his handiwork on numerous occasions where he has excavated rabbit breeding burrows to extract the young rabbits.

On a number of occasions I have been called out by farmers to view the nocturnal damage where it has entered into a chicken house via the open pop hole, also where one virtually chewed through and tore at the wooden boards from the hut to gain entry and kill the occupants. One moonlit night many years ago I was out waiting with the rifle along with two farmers whose lambs were being killed, the culprit turned out to be an old boar badger who was living in a small stone culvert under an old road banking.

There are always exceptions to the rule of course, but other than that the badger really has never been a problem to me on the snareline. The most damage that I have suffered at times is one or two rabbits that have been eaten and all the rest of the captured quarry were untouched. The signs of a badger that has eaten your rabbits is most obvious as there is nothing left except for a skeleton and a bare skin attached, it eats all the viscera and flesh from the back legs all the way up the belly and body consuming practically everything. At times on the head with a bare skin is left hanging in the snare.

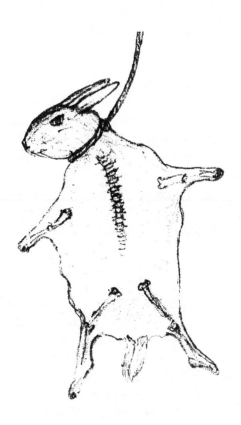

The Stoat

The stoat is a voracious little killer very lithe and agile. Although they kill a lot of smaller sized rabbits a large full grown rabbit is well within its capabilities. On many occasions when setting out snares I have had the opportunity to watch stoats hunting, chasing down and killing their intended victim. They are extremely fast when they are on the trail of a rabbit with their tail up in the air as they give chase at great speed. When woodland snaring I've stood and watched them a good thirty feet up in large beeches hunting for squirrels. One morning I had the great opportunity of seeing a large stoat coming down the trunk of a sycamore with a half grown squirrel in its jaws on hitting the ground it ran along through the woodland and into an old rabbit burrow. I could have collected a lot of good footage of stoats over the years if I had carried my camcorder with me. As usual you always seem to be without it when it's most needed.

The stoat really causes no real damage to the rabbit trapper except to kill an odd rabbit or two captured in snares. It will kill them by biting them at the back of the head and the base of the ear and many times will leave it at that but on rare occasions when hungry it will eat the rabbit down the neck to the shoulders when hungry. I have also stood and watched them at times playing tug of war with a rabbit as it tries to pull it away but just can't manage due to the snare around its neck. They seem at times bewildered as to why it won't move, probably thinking to itself my this rabbit is a strong fellow. They are also very adept at stealing the rabbits that the trapper has despatched and removed from the snares leaving them lying in a line as he moves along checking his snares in the morning. I had the cheeky little rascals standing upon their hind legs watching me from a hedgerow or woodland edge, or looking through between the spar of a gate with great interest observing my progress then they will dart out from the cover and grab a dead rabbit by the back of the head and pull the carcase backwards toward the cover. I have had as many as three taken in a morning ! I just leave them alone as I love watching stoats as they are so quick and agile creatures. They are bold and cheeky and everyone deserves to grab a free meal when they get the chance on certain occasions even the stoat.

The stoat is a fascinating creature sleek, lithe, fast and very agile. I have many great memories of their antics on the snareline. I personally think they are a fantastic creature to watch as they hunt along the many different types of edge features e.g. hedges, drystone dykes, grassy fencelines, streams, ditches, any linear structure for that matter. The stoat is also a great hunter and kills mice, rats, rabbits, birds. I have watched them attacking and killing full grown cock pheasants with relative ease. They also hunt up in the tree tops checking out nests in high thick hawthorn hedges. I have watched them hunting up in the tops of really large old beech, oak and sycamore trees after squirrels. I witnessed one coming down the trunk of a big old sycamore tree with a squirrel hanging from its jaws. The stoat was descending down the vertical tree trunk upside down. These resilient little creatures must have great strength and agility to achieve feats like this.

They like to climb up onto molehills anywhere that's elevated to secure a better view of their surroundings. When out on the snareline I have had them carry out the latter practice to gain a better view of me when pegging out snares. They will often stand on their hind legs viewing me through the spar of a gate, climbing onto the top of a drystone wall or climbing up a hedge and peering out from behind the cover for a better view to see what I'm doing, when checking snares in the morning and removing rabbits and laying them out along the snareline.

On the snareline even Mr Stoat occasionally falls victim to a pegged rabbit snare or a fenceline snare. If they are alive I stand on the snare wire close to their neck and snip the wire cable and set them free. This only happens on rare occasions. I also catch an odd stoat whilst snaring rats with whip snares on occasions I have been present when they were caught. I just cut the snare at their neck and release them

Prowling Dogs

I have only ever had one problem in my life with a dog on my snareline it came about a number of years back while snaring rabbits on a neighbouring set-aside field adjacent to one of the large rented houses on a local estate. The devastation was unbelievable every rabbit ripped to pieces and many were devoured on the spot, but it wasn't the normal devastation caused by the fox as heads were lying crushed and large lumps of skin and fur strewn around. There was something different about the scene of carnage, there was no signs of the predator that was doing the damage as the dry ground gave no clues to what it was. There was no smell or telltale paw prints, but one clue told me that it was a heavy animal - two of the snare tealers which were constructed of 2.5 mil galvanized wire were completely bent over although they are well made from good wire.

I walked over to the perimeter fenceline and hedge combined, then worked my way slowly down the edge of the field carefully scrutinising the ground for a clue like a homicide detective until I came across a large paw print with splayed toenail holes giving the indication of a large dog. A fox print is smaller with toenails pointing inwards and fur marks between the pads. As I arrived after six that evening to check the snares, lo and behold what was coming up alongside the field edge but a large fat black Labrador. On seeing me it made off and headed back towards the large estate house.

After checking the snares I drove down to the house in question and there was the culprit lying at the door as fat as a blood filled tick, it had the cheek to bark at me. I rung the doorbell and the lady in residence came to the door. I explained who I was and what I was doing then told her about the dog so he was confined to barracks after his nefarious escape. Its name was Magic and I'm glad he vanished quickly. A few months later Magic was killed crossing a busy country road.

Chapter 21 - Non-Target Species

Accidental Catches

An open snare noose is no respecter of any animal as they say. Well in my opinion it depends on the level and years of experience of the trapper concerned who is carrying out the snaring operation. The professional will be able to look carefully and assess a situation at each and every location he is going set and ask himself what can and cannot happen before the placing of any snare. I personally have increased animal welfare in the United Kingdom over the last number of years due to the invention of my humane breakaway snare system for fox and rabbit snaring. The breakaway system I devised for the rabbit snare came about quite a few years ago while snaring rabbits that were doing extreme damage in a plantation containing many young ash and oak trees.

During the course of the operation two of the snare nooses were found to be snapped and missing caused by roe deer which inhabit the surrounding woodlands. This incident upset me due to the fact these animals could lose a foot through a necrosis because of the tightened and broken nooses around the deer feet which causes death of a tissue while still part of a living body. Informing the head keeper of the latter incident he had stalked and shot them within days. I can honestly say I have never accidentally foot noosed a deer using hoop snares throughout woodland plantings while controlling rabbits.

After this incident the breakaways system was devised along with the use of a larger stop loop, with the stop being permanently positioned at a distance of 6 inches from the end eyelet at the running end of the snare. The government recommend a stop set at five inches which I have found to be too small a loop which causes rubbing on large heavy winter rabbits necks. The six inch stop loop leaves ample space between the neck and the snare noose keeping the rabbits alive and well, allowing them to sit and feed without any ill effects. The larger stop loop has also one hundred per cent totally eliminated any rubbing, choking and other trauma due to swelling of the head and oedema and bulging eyes in snared rabbits. It also keeps accidental hare catches alive and well, should the snare be fitted with a breakaway system the hare or prowling domestic cat accidentally caught will now be able to activate the breakaway link and free themselves allowing them to escape alive and well without any injury.

At times in the past I have declined to snare certain locations of higher thicker tussocky grass which held a lot of rabbits but also held quite a number of large brown hares. The problem which arose at this latter location was that the pegged rabbit snares would be set at around 10" high to snare the rabbits due to the high growth, which would also catch a lot of hares which the head keeper didn't want killed under any circumstances. After surveying these type of locations I would phone him and explain the situation informing him of the number of hares present he would direct me to some other part of the estate to snare. Therefore due to my invention of the breakaway system and the large stop loop this latter problem was solved as every hare could now free themselves in seconds by activating the breakaway link. The average circumference of a fox's neck is 10" working on this principle with regular testing between myself, Colin and Jackie the larger stop loop of 10-10 ½" allows hares to pull their head free and escape it also allows Roe deer to extract their feet also. The larger stop loop, stop, helps absorb the shock from the softer neck muscle allowing for easier opening of the snare whether it be rabbit or fox.

Over the years I have many accidental catches on the snareline. When setting out lots of snares at any one time it is inevitable that you will make an occasional accidental catch from time to time. When predators are out hunting for prey species under the cover of darkness they either stumble upon the snaring field during their nocturnal ventures or are drawn to the snaring field by the squeals that the captured rabbits make upon being snared and the sudden shock of their freedom being severely restricted by the wire noose around their neck. Therefore any prowling predator a field or two away will start to home in to the piercing screams from the captured rabbits looking for a quick and easy meal. The fox is just a confounded nuisance when he appears on a snareline wreaking nothing but constant havoc with the catch and causing nothing but grief for the trapper. He must put up with this for a couple of mornings or lift all of the snares or set out ghost snares along the field edges and upon a few of good prominent rabbit runs until the fox himself is captured and despatched. This leaves the trapper with a feeling of great satisfaction ridding the trapline of public enemy number one.

On occasions the trapper strikes it lucky, divine justice if you like, getting his own back on his old nemesis the fox who himself occasionally falls victim to a well set pegged rabbit snare as he slips along one of the runs seeking out its prey. The big rabbit noose catches the oncoming fox around the muzzle similar to a rabbit being caught around the face in a small amateur sized loop set to low to the ground. On most occasions the animal frees itself from the snare's clutches as it springs and tumbles around flinging the small kinked loop from its face which is called frying panning due to the shape which can be seem in illustration B. The size of the loop from a rabbit catch is around the size of a twopenny piece while the loop size from the fox's face is around three inches in diameter with the same distinct kink at the end of the noose.

Unfortunately for the fox with a larger and longer muzzle and large fangs of a predator the snare loop on occasions tightens up and catches in at the back of a fang which prevents the fox from opening his mouth. Therefore he can't bite the non tensile, firmly spun snare cable which rotates freely due to the simple little double knot swivel under the tealer eye. This takes a lot of strain from the snare loop therefore at times holding large dog foxes by the muzzle until the trapper arrives to check his snareline at first light in the morning. Whereupon the fox will be humanely despatched. Illustration A shows a diagram of how the fox is standing captured in a pegged rabbit snare caught around the muzzle and held fast until despatched.

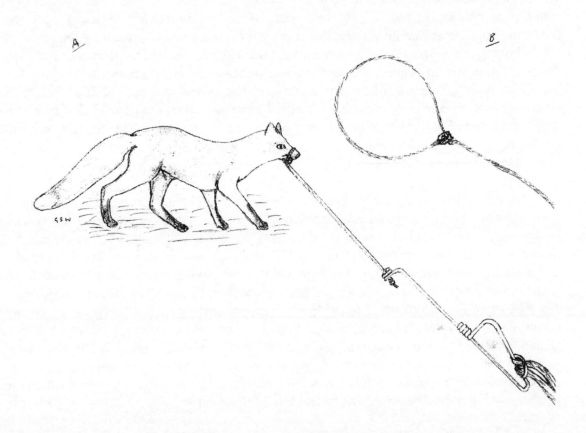

Fox catches in High Vegetation

A few large fox cubs and even adult foxes are taken in the snares at times as they too hold their head up higher when moving through the longer vegetation. Full grown cubs do not appear to have the sense to bite through the brass cable. Once again with a tight wound cable and the double knot which acts as a swivel, the snare is far stronger than one which is slack wound and more prone to kinking, splaying wire strands and breakages. Especially when permanently fixed to the tealer meaning that no swivelling action can occur during the period when an animal is captured. A non-swivelling snare wire is put under more stress. Although at times the twine itself will twist up allowing some leeway they usually eventually break anyway.

Sometimes adult foxes are caught around the muzzle and held fast until the trapper arrives in the morning, otherwise if neck snared the adults just bit thorough the pliable brass wire and are quickly freed. On frequent occasions full grown heavy foxes will succumb quickly to a good swivelling rabbit wire when caught around the top of the head in front of the ears and tight up under the chin in front of the larynx. Once again there is absolutely no need for rabbit snares to be constructed of eight and ten strands of wire its pure old fashioned fallacy. A properly constructed six strand snare is all that is required at any time.

Of the many friends south of the border whom I have taught to snare rabbits and foxes, there are many who phone me on a regular basis to keep me informed of their snaring progress and results of the numbers of rabbits being taken in their snares. They also mention about the frequent capture of foxes while snaring in higher vegetation and often remark on the holding power of the 7½ inch securing peg and the double knot swivel action which helps to retain the victims without damaging the snare itself. One such chap Bob Merrins from Cumbria set 50 snares all at nine inches plus high to the bottom of the loop in foot high hay and mentioned to the head gamekeeper that he had smelled a fox whilst doing so. On checking the snares on the following morning with the presence of the head keeper, he had neck snared thirty rabbits and two full grown fox cubs. The keeper was dumbfounded and on returning home immediately called the under keeper to come over and have a look at the catch. Before the snaring operation commenced the head keeper had remarked on the large size of Bob's snare loops and laughed, but much to his surprise he could not get over it. He also remarked about the holding power of the seven and a half inch pegs and wouldn't have believed it unless he had witnessed the event for himself.

Phil Day one of my protégés from England has permission on a large estate which is infested with rabbits on certain large areas of farmland. On snaring higher vegetation a few weeks back he pegged out a hundred snares and caught 78 rabbits the following morning and 55 the morning after, a respectable catch totalling 133 coneys in two mornings. Every snare was set at 9"plus with only about four sprung snares in the two days of snaring he just made the beats with his foot where it was necessary and set right back in the middle of them and never moved a snare either forward or back. Phil has also taken quite a few full grown cubs in his rabbit snares while snaring in higher vegetation. In one field with long grass and buttercups he and his friend Dick measured the distance between some of the beats further out along the runs and was extremely surprised to find they were approximately four feet apart, using a proper tape measure, large catches can only be obtained by using quality snares which must be set up at the proper height across the middle of the beats.

Setting snares too low, either in short or long verdure, will result in continual empty and slipped snares every morning. It is imperative that you remember this, because there is only approximately 1½ inches of the front of the neck for the bottom of the snare loop to strike before the body tapers over the chest area. Therefore if the bottom of the snare loop is too low the rabbit is through the loop in a flash and gone more so when working with normal sized tealer pins in longer grass as the snare loop has to be cocked up to a slightly steeper angle to compensation for extra height therefore eliminating the horizontal striking position of the bottom curve of the big loop which now sits in a more vertical position. This is why a slightly longer tealer pin gives you that extra height and helps to retain a better more properly positioned snare loop with the striking curve of the bottom loop ready to catch the rabbit up under the chin as it springs through the high vegetation.

Avoiding Non-target Species

An open snare loop is no respecter of animal species, regardless of what animal steps into them the open snare does not know the difference between a rabbit, hare, fox, deer, dog, etc. There is no system that is one hundred per cent foolproof. However experience can play an active part in avoiding other non target species being caught by accident, to help avoid other unwanted catches I will now convey some basic rules to help you partake in successful snaring practices.

The primary factor to be considered is that a trapper must be able to look over a location and be able to determine what can happen and what cannot happen to avoid any unnecessary situations which at the worst could lead to legal action against him. If possible snares should not be set along public footpaths or around and next to dwelling houses, unless tenants are notified in advance so that their domestic pets may be kept indoors until snaring operations are over. A little courtesy goes a long way and helps avoid any unpleasantness or friction.

The setting of rabbit snares on pastures in amongst the presence of livestock is unthinkable, commonsense must prevail at all times in latter situations. Other available locations can be set such as along the back of the perimeter fence line where the livestock are contained, and certainly not on the fence line itself. On certain types of crop fields bordering grazing fields you will find what they call the head ridge a strip or bank of land about a yard wide running the whole way along the fence line, or the grazing field may border a young plantation or woodland then snares can be set on the runs leading to and from the field which holds the livestock. But before the laying of any snare look at the latter location to see if the perimeter fence is intact, that the posts and the wires are not loose, broken or swaying to and fro. Note how high the fence is, are the wires broken or slack with no tension in them, if cattle are to be found in the grazing field look to see if there are any calves present with their mothers. Now look at the length of the grass along the headland which runs parallel with the field edge, is it long or is it cropped short, are there any hoof marks or droppings present. All of these factors must be taken into consideration any and when the latter features present themselves on occasions ask yourself the following questions. Are the adult cattle able to lean over the fence or push their heads through between the loose or broken wires to crop the grass ? The calves for certain are able to slip their heads through, on occasions they may also squeeze through the fence hence the droppings and hoof marks which may be present. The availability of these latter areas suitable for setting snares is limited by the presence of livestock and poorly maintained boundary fence lines. Although I strongly advocate not setting of any snare amongst livestock I do it on a few occasions but only amongst adult sheep, never in the presence of tiny lambs or cattle. Pegged snares are not a viable commodity to be recommended for this type of snaring as an open snare would catch the animals by the feet, therefore I use the simple and very efficient hoop snare.

Deer are also a problem from time to time when setting snares in various locations, the best way to avoid them is never to set snares near their habitat if at all possible. Keen powers of observation are necessary to be a good efficient trapper especially when controlling rabbits in young woodland plantations where deer often abound. Look for any sign of their presence in the form of droppings which are dark green oval and elongated similar to sheep. The telltale slots in the ground made by their little sharp hooves, also frayed saplings where bucks have rubbed their horns back and forth removing the tree bark.

Hoop snares are recommended where deer prevail as open pegged snares regularly catch them by the front feet and the broken snare wire can cause restriction of blood to the foot causing a necrosis and through time maybe the loss of a foot.

The pegged rabbit snare is a feral cat's nightmare and unavoidable due to snare design and the way that the cat walks and hunts carrying itself at the same height and the way it springs along runs in higher grass. Prowling and uncontrolled dogs are a very rare problem except in extreme situations, larger dogs get caught by the feet and on occasion a smaller terrier may become neck snared and released unharmed. Remember to notify any householder in the immediate vicinity of any snaring operations being carried out as it keeps a good rapport with them and saves any unpleasantness.

Foxes are a regular problem being foot snared they just bite through the pliable brass snare cable and then remove the part of the broken noose from their leg by biting it off, occasionally cubs are taken along with an odd adult fox. I have had the odd mink, stoat, polecat ferret, grey squirrel and a couple of crows which were caught out in the field away from the woodland edge. To avoid any unwanted catches use a little discretion, be observant, with some smart thinking, always remember the word KISS, *keep it simple and safe* is the motto and you won't go far wrong.

The new breakaway rabbit snare with the larger 6" stop loop which I devised eliminated all of the past problems associated with woodland deer being accidentally foot snared or livestock for that matter. This snare has also eliminated any trauma around a rabbit or hare's head increasing animal welfare greatly. The breakaway link added to a rabbit snare long with the 6" stop allows animals heavier than a rabbit to activate the b/away link to free themselves. This illustration depicts a hare caught in a pegged rabbit snare, having a breakaway link added to this snare would have allowed the animal to break free itself.

G.S.WATERS

Avoiding Pheasants.

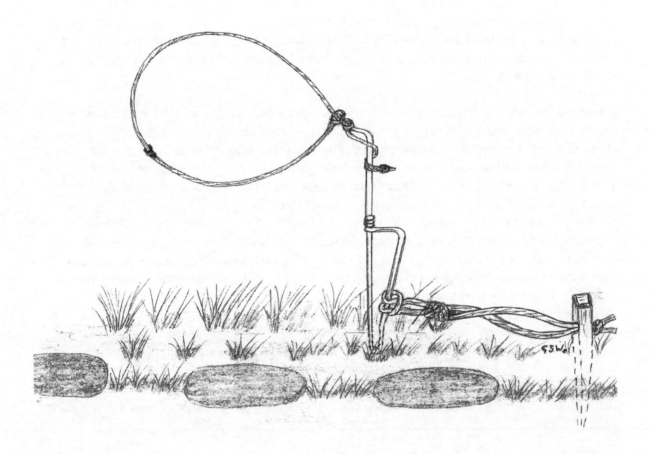

On looking at this illustration many readers will be thinking to themselves there is something amiss here with this drawing. Your assumption would be perfectly correct. First of all what you see is a rabbit run showing the prominent beats where the snare would normally be placed in the correct position with the large snare loop, placed over the middle of a beat. On this occasion the snare is set to the side with the large noose running parallel to the rabbit run instead of across the run. Let me explain why this is so.

A number of years ago the head gamekeeper Ron asked me to snare some rabbits at the back of the big wood on the west side. A grassy border approximately fifty yards wide ran parallel to the woodland edge and was lined with a high thick borderline of rhododendrons which held the resident rabbit population. Inside of the woodland at the back of this heavy tangled structure lay the main pheasant pen, a large structure which held hundreds of pheasants. In the early morning the roosting birds would fly down into this grassy pasture and make their way across it to the neighbouring stubble field. What was causing Ron a bit of concern was that the pheasants would succumb to the pegged snares set out in the grass. I assured him no harm would come to the birds in any way - as I have many decades of snaring under my belt the birds will be perfectly safe.

The plan was to peg out every rabbit run leading from the woodland all the way uphill and along the whole border of this grassy pasture, which I set around 45 yards from the woodland edge. I inserted a hazel marker pin to mark every snare. I place the marker pins a few yards further out from the snares so that they were sitting at a 45° angle facing inwards towards the snares. I do this on a regular basis when setting 30 yd to 50 yd borders of set-aside, stubble grass, etc for the simple fact a weathered wire set further out with the markers facing inwards is damn hard to see to an unpractised eye. When checking your wires just walk all the way along the outside edge of the strip in a straight line checking the snares it could not be any simpler than that.

Now how to avoid snaring the pheasants in pegged snares. As previously mentioned the snares were set out at a distance of 45 yards but instead of setting the snares in their proper position across the run I set the snare parallel to the run as seen in the illustration. Therefore the pheasants could pass to and fro along the runs throughout the day without being caught in a wire. About half an hour before the onset of darkness when the pheasants had all returned to roost I hurried up the line switching every snare from their parallel position throughout the daylight hours into the set position across the run in the middle of every beat. The snares were now all ready to catch the rabbits when they came out to feed throughout the hours of darkness. In the morning I arrived in the total darkness awaiting daylight starting to break. I then walked the whole length of the snareline, despatching the rabbits while retensioning, shaping and resetting every snare once again parallel to the rabbit runs ensuring the safety of the pheasants throughout daylight hours.

The following morning was a repeat process and the snares were lifted and counted on completion of the job. Two mornings snaring is usually enough to thin the resident rabbit population down to an acceptable level. Remember to always check your snares after every outing for broken pegs and snare strands, chewed and frayed twines, pegs needing, repointing etc.

Keep them in good condition for every new operation.

Chapter 22 - Other Problems

In connection with this part of the subject it is necessary to say before I deal with the practical aspect of it, that everyone who has participated in trapping and snaring basically encounters all the same problems on the snareline. Through the pages of this manual I feel it is my moral obligation to explain the cause of the problems and how to correct them so that the readers who wish to take part in this art will be saved from years of frustration by trial and error also from old fashioned fallacies and antiquated ideas that still haunts us about snaring even today. In explaining these problems it is hoped that all who practise this art will apply their intelligent ability as required so that they will achieve the highest level of success in the field. High levels of success which cannot be obtained by repeating and making continual mistakes therefore they must recognise when one has been made and correct it immediately, to repeat them you will be destined to continual failure. To acquire continual success one must use good equipment and top quality snares which I have covered under the heading of the big loop system. Let us assume you are using top quality snares so that any problems which may arise will be easily corrected and will generally fall into one of the categories we will now discuss.

The most common problem countered is tripped and empty snares and experience will soon tell you by looking at the loop what has happened. Using a big loop the problems are few.

If you encounter a half slipped loop the rabbit has slipped clean through, which can also result in rabbits being caught round the hips and is the result of snares set low.

A 'V' shape indentation on bottom of the snare loop usually indicates improper placement on the run and the rabbit has jumped on it upon landing with his front feet.

If the snare wire is pulled out to its full length showing a small loop the size of a one pence piece and a slight disturbance of the location it means the rabbit has been held briefly by the hind foot and pulled out and escaped once again this indicates the snare was set on the low side.

If snare loop in a similar shape as the latter one, only that the end loop is approximately the size of a two pence piece in diameter and a distinct kink in the wire at the eye of the snare indicates without a doubt that the snare loop was too low. The rabbit has struck the underside of the top curve of the wire with the front of his face below its eyes and the loop has closed around its muzzle. Sometimes it holds them, other times on approaching them they will spring into the air and somersault and fling the snare loop from their face, to correct this latter fault set the snare a few inches higher.

When snaring high grass, especially when wet, an occasional rabbit will be caught by the front foot as they tend to jump higher in wet weather conditions, this will even occur when snares are set at $9^{1}/_{2}$" high to the bottom of the snare loop as they spring up and over from beat to beat especially when they are beats 14"-18" plus apart.

Another problem which occurs when snaring in grazing fields and other locations with short flora such as woodland and rough areas with bramble patches etc is the fox who will knock our snare loop up in the air or slightly turn them at an angle or bending the tealer at a different angle.

Another clear sure sign of a prowling fox is to find a snare loop pulled straight out in a straight line with slightly uneven broken ends and the eyelet missing. The fox has been caught by the front foot and bitten through the snare wire

Another visible sign of the fox is only barely half the length of the broken snare loop attached to the tealer. This means it's been snared around the neck usually a small vixen, which has bitten through the snare wire, there are times big cubs will be taken easily, on other occasions an adult fox will be taken and held around the muzzle as it can't bite the wire. I've had full grown foxes caught around the top of the head in front of the ears and tight up under the top of the throat that have expired quickly through their struggles and found dead in the snare. Others have broken the snare and expired a few feet from the location the latter catches only take place by using a professional sized loop.

Snaring with a small loop causes a lot of snares to be tripped and empty in the mornings, or rabbits will also be caught around the top of the head at times. A narrow noose will also cause snare trips and miscatches around the head

Theft

Theft is one of the most despicable acts on a snareline and it is not always the anti-field Sports Fraternity who are responsible either. It is more often a prowler who has accidentally stumbled across the snares and taken the opportunity of the moment to steal them. On occasions they may take only a half dozen thinking that they will not be missed by the trapper, so they can try them out for themselves or just to try and copy them to produce their own snares. Other times you may have been seen while setting out the snares and once again the thief may take a few or remove as many as he can, as quickly as he can in case the trapper happens to return to the field. Worst of all it may be a fellow trapper who knows all the tricks of the trade and takes every one of your snares, these people are the lowest of the low. Most of the time it is an accidental discovery by an opportunist who may never have even noticed the snares but came across rabbits jumping around or lying clapped in the grass and on investigation discover the snares.

Having experienced the results of this despicable act myself in the past years, having practised the martial arts for 20 years I'm not shy in handing out a good spanking when it's really needed especially to Johnny Sneakum. The only tools that can be left outside nowadays with relative safely without being stolen are a pick, a spade and a working jacket I'm afraid.

Another problem that occurs on occasions is illegal lamping at night when your snares and rabbits are discovered. You will find where they have hurriedly tried to gather as many as they could but also missed a lot due to their presence being discovered, by a continual flashing light and the thoughts of someone alerting the police and being captured, maybe by a police dog handler, which has happened on a few occasions on our local estate. One lad from England who I had taught phoned me to say he had lost a percentage of his snares and about fifty rabbits one night. A reception committee awaited their return for a few nights after the theft but they never returned

Theft is one problem I am very seldom affected by, and it has been many years since I have lost a few snares, the main reason for this is that I am very careful when and where I set them. On occasion when I have set snares in high risk areas where theft is liable to be prone, I wait until the weather becomes rough high winds and rain, when the good weather hunters are in the house by the fire side or in their local. I arrive at the location in question an hour before darkness falls as the area has been viewed well beforehand and the amount of snares required for the job is taken along with me. I then scan the whole area with my little compact set of field glasses to make sure the area is void of any human presence.

I then start to set out as many snares as possible before the onset of darkness. I will move further afield from the snaring location and glass the whole area again until it's too dark to see. I will sit and wait watch and listen for another half hour, then depart from the area altogether. I will arrive at the snaring location in total darkness the following morning awaiting daylight then emerge into the field despatch the rabbits empty the snares, retension and shape them and lift the whole lot, rabbits and snares the same morning leaving no evidence of my presence. The same operation can be carried out a few weeks later to clear up what rabbits are left. This method is quite effective in eliminating theft.

These people who lift snares obviously can't make them and have no concept of time, money and skill that goes into making a top quality snare. First of all you have to purchase a drum of brass wire eyelets and a coil of 2.5 mil galvanized fenceline wire, saw ash logs and measure and cut hundreds of twines, you then start making your snares. The snares must be twisted up, tealer pins cut and shaped also securing pegs cut and shaped, and the twines must be cut to length and knotted then you must assemble them altogether which also is a time consuming process. After all the latter process more work is entailed in the setting out of the completed snares. Yes there is a lot of skill expense and hard work goes into making and setting rabbit snares, so come on lads if you want snares ask the trapper for a few or better still make your own and learn what's all involved.

Rabbit Damage to Snares

One problem that occurs now and then on the snareline caused by the rabbits themselves is the chewing on the twines as shown in illustration (A). The captured rabbit has bitten clean through the double strands of the baling twine and escaped, their teeth are extremely sharp, chisel like and bite through the twines with clinical efficiency leaving only the peg and two part strands remaining of the once complete snare system that covered the rabbit runs.

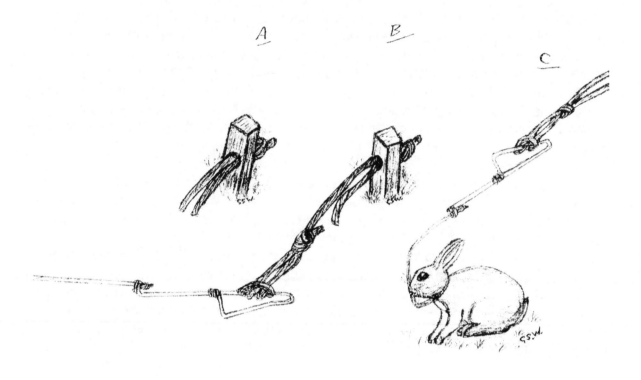

Illustration (B) shows the complete snare unit, only this time the rabbit will still be caught as it has only chewed through one strand. I always carry a few twined pegs with me so that online repairs can be carried out there and then - quickly and efficiently to keep the snareline in full operation. Should a rabbit escape due to the two twines being severed you will nearly always capture it either the next morning or the morning after. Houdini will be sitting patiently awaiting your presence with the broken part of the snare around its neck caught in another snare along the line.

(C) What you see here is a rabbit sitting chewing vigorously on the brass snare loop. I have witnessed this on a few occasions over many decades of snaring. Some rabbits will run to a different position as you approach them and keep chewing until you grip them and pick them up off the ground. I have video footage of a rabbit carrying out this same procedure. Occasionally you will get quite fractious rabbits that will jump at you and try to bite you on the leg. On one occasion I had a friend out with me while checking the snareline when such an incident occurred with an old large buck rabbit around the five pound mark who appeared to become upset and aggressive as I approached it. This rabbit leapt up with its mouth open and tried to bite me on the thigh as I sidestepped it he tried again. I moved forwards quickly and stood on the snare wire close to his neck then despatched it quickly. My friend John was completely taken by surprise at what he had just witnessed and said if I had not seen that display of aggressive behaviour I would not have believed it possible. I have been bitten a couple of times through the fingers and their sharp chisel like teeth can inflict a nasty wound to your fingers which bleed profusely. I always carry a part roll of electrical tape with me as it comes in handy now and again to fix certain incidents that occur when out snaring. While we are on the subject of snare twines, the baling twine is the best all round material to use in the assembly of snares. It is extremely strong, waterproof and very resistant to the British inclement weather conditions and lasts many many years if not damaged physically in any way. It is usually easy to acquire a large sealed drum of this baler twine from any of the farmers for whom you are catching rabbits for his farm on a regular basis.

Now I will enlighten the reader to the good points and bad points that I and some of my mentors have discovered about baler twine over the decades of its use. The twine I favoured most was the black baling twine which my old mentor Willie Mac used on all his pegged snares. Willie told me well over 40 years ago that he never used anything else because he got it free, it was strong and weatherproof, it also has low visibility due to the colour when the snares were set. This twine never appeared to be affected by the ultraviolet rays of the sun like other colours which I will explain later.

A pegged rabbit snare with one twine bitten through by the rabbit I dispatched. As I have said before rabbits seem to be prone to chewing the orange baler twine. A handful of dirt rubbed along the twines to darken them helps to prevent this.

Another good attribute about this twine is that due to its colour rabbit damage caused by chewing was practically non-existent which I experienced myself over decades of constant use. If my memory serves me correctly I only ever lost one rabbit and had one twine nipped through which can't be said for other colours of twine, like all good things in life sadly they always seem to come to an end due to progress. I suppose like many things the black baler twine got more scarce over the years until it dried up. McMaster and I stored what we could find to keep us going for future years until it was no more. Relating this story to my good friend Phil Lloyd he managed to come up with a few half rolls of similar twine and posted them up to me. I now use orange baler twine which I twine my snares with it also is easy to acquire, once again from any of the local farmers that you snare upon their land will give it you freely upon asking. Once again having a discussion with old Willie Mac we were comparing our findings with the orange baler twine Willie mentioned about the rabbits chewing through this stuff, also saying he had more chew outs in a few years with orange than he could every remember when using the black twine, another slight problem with the orange twine is that it would become slightly bleached in colour due to sunlight unlike the black twine which appeared to be impervious against the sun's ultraviolet rays. On the other hand the rabbits seemed to be attracted to the orange coloured twine although it occurred only occasionally so what we did to stop this problem was to take a handful of dirt and discolour the twine a dirty darker colour which helped immensely in curing the chewing problem, when working a trapline or snareline you must be observant and train yourself to have good visual awareness.

Disease in Rabbits

COCCIDIOSIS is quite commonly encountered in wild rabbits as small yellowish-white nodules found on the liver and sometimes in the intestines. It impairs the nutritive condition. It also resembles TB. EIMERIA STIEDAE affects the liver and EIMERIA PERFORANS affects the intestine, causing diarrhoea and emaciation. In a healthy, well nourished rabbit only the liver need be condemned.

CYSTICFRCUS PISIFORMIS - is the cystic stage of (TAEMIA-PISIFORMIS) of the dog. Is found in the peritoneal cavity of the rabbit on the mesentery, the cysts are about the size of a pea and filled with clear fluid. They rarely have any effect on the carcase.

CYSTERICERCUS-SERIALIS - cysts found under the skin round the shoulder area and back legs and inner thighs. Can vary up to the size of a hen's egg. More noticeable when rabbit is skinned. The adult worm is TAENIA SERIALIS of the dog. If the carcase is well nourished only the affected part need be destroyed. If the carcase is in poor condition condemn it.

VENERIAL INFECTION - or rabbit syphilis as it is sometimes known, does occur and is caused by a SPIROCHEATE called TREPONEMA-CUNICULI. It produces scaly crusts on the vagina of the doe and prepuce of the buck rabbit. It does not affect man. Non-transmissible.

MYXOMATOSIS - since first introduced into Britain in 1953, myxomatosis has become widespread throughout the country. It is caused by a virus infection spread by the rabbit flea. The symptoms of the disease take the form of a watery discharge from the eyes which becomes thick and the eyelids become encrusted with dry matter. Noticeable swellings become visible at the base of the ears and various parts of the body, mainly around the nasal area, under the chin, the anal region and the genital organs. Approximate period from infection to death is 11-20 days.

TULAREMIA - is an infectious disease of rodents and LAGOMORPHS (hares, pikas, and rabbits). It also occurs in domestic animals and man. In man it is characterised by sudden and dramatic onset of chills and fever. The clinical forms include infection of the lymph nodes, which become swollen and tender and often suppurate. Fatality rate is about 5%. Negligible with treatment. It occurs through Russia, Japan and many parts of Europe and the USA.

My friend, Max Seaerls, was very ill for a time with Tularemia. Max is a professional trapper who lives in British Columbia, Canada and he became ill through skinning an infected muskrat.

Large rabbit snared with a very large cyst on the back of shoulder. The exposed the cyst was full of fluid and if cut open there would be dozens of small white scolexes, similar to grains of rice. A rabbit like this is NOT SUITABLE FOR HUMAN CONSUMPTION - bury carcass.

Professional Rabbit Snaring

On Line repairs

Tightening Splayed Snare Cables.

When snaring certain problems arise now and again. The experienced trapper knows how to deal with such problems quickly and efficiently simply because he has done it many times over the years in the course of his job. The amateur on the other hand is lost and just blunders on regardless, repeating the same mistakes over and over again not taking time to stop and think to himself and ask himself questions, what has happened here, what has caused this problem, how can it be rectified.

For instance a common problem such as splayed strands of wire in your rabbit snares after a few rabbits have been caught and how to correct this problem quickly and efficiently out on the snaring field. This was a common fault with shop bought snares which were only half spun, were approximately 18" long attached to cheap thin green twine which rotted quickly due to inclement weather conditions. The snare nooses approximately five inches short compared to a professional sized noose which is also spun into a tighter cable which prevented the strands of the snare wire becoming splayed like the shop bought snares.

This illustration shows a simple system that I devised to solve any splaying problems in a matter of seconds. Many years ago I watched a man on video laboriously slipping a wooden tealer through a snare loop and trying to wind the snare cable tighter. It was slower than a year on remand watching the scene. All that needs to be done is to pull the pegged snare from the ground, check that there are no kinks in the wire, run the snare loop closed onto the cup hook inserted into the end of the no 2 thorr hammer shaft. Then hold snare cable tight at the tealer eye and then spin the hammer, its weight will spin the cable up in seconds into a nice firm cable. What I used to do was loop the snare noose over the dead rabbit's head in front of the ear then spin the rabbit round and it did exactly the same job as the hammer did, but the hook on the hammer has another couple of tricks I use it for but I'll keep that for later.

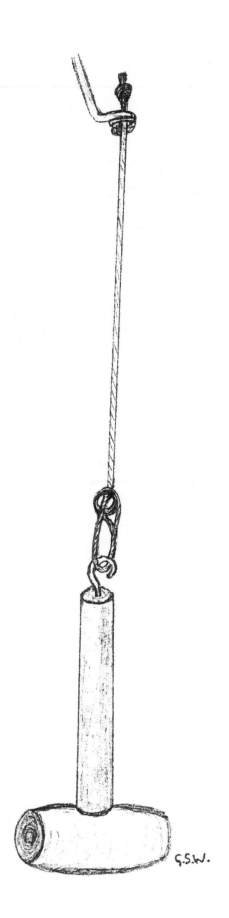

Professional Rabbit Snaring

Section 6 - Making Pegged Snares

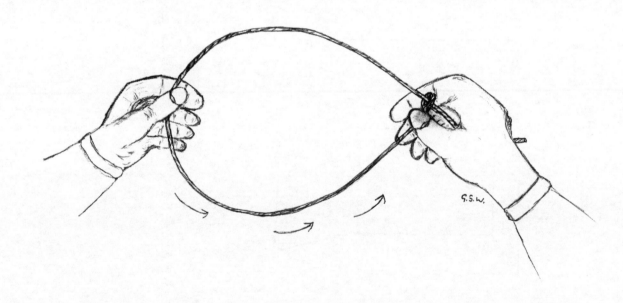

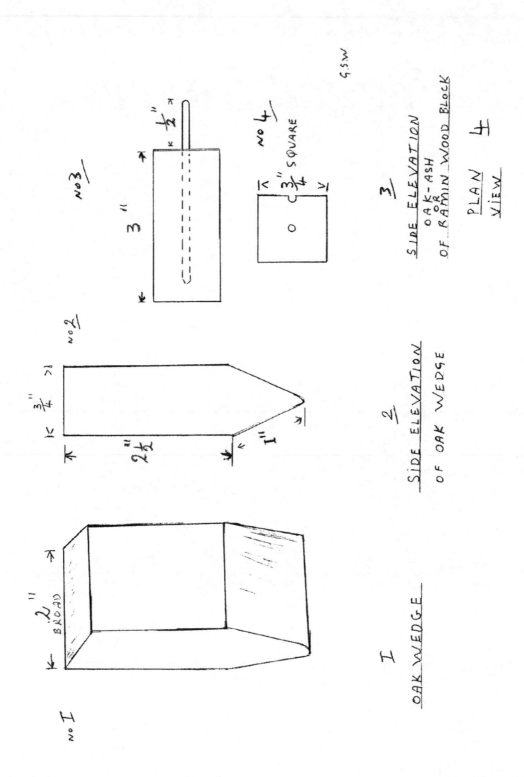

no 3

3"

½"

no 4

¾" SQUARE

O

3

SIDE ELEVATION
OAK-ASH
OR
OF RAMIN WOOD BLOCK

G.S.W

PLAN
VIEW
4

no 2

¾"

2½"

1"

2

SIDE ELEVATION
OF OAK WEDGE

no I

2"
BROAD

I

OAK WEDGE

Chapter 23 - Making a Figure 4 Tealer

Implements in Stabiliser Construction.

In order to make wire tealers reliable and consistently a set of simple templates or 'jigs' is required. These can be made from hardwood, metal or any other hard, resistant material. The jigs are used to bend the tealer wire around to form the general shape and the detail of the tealer eye as explained in the next few pages.

Looking at the illustration opposite:

(1) Shows a hardwood wedge cut and shaped from a two inch broad oak strap, taken from an oak whisky barrel. This is used to shape the '4' in the tealer base. To make these wedges just cut the strap into $3^1/_2$" lengths, a half dozen can be cut, shaped and kept for spares. One wedge will last an average snarer a long time -hundreds upon hundreds can be made from each wedge. If you use one side of the block and place the wire half an inch in from the side edge then over a period of time the constant pressure of the wire being in the vice causes a permanent groove to form. Once this side edge becomes worn just start working on the opposite side edge of the block until it becomes worn then start a new one. More recently I have started using small blocks of white nylon instead of oak. It is extremely robust, works very well and lasts longer.

(2) Gives a side elevation of the oak wedge along with the dimensions of the block.

(3) Shows a side elevation of an oblong oak block which is cut $^3/_4$" square 3" long. This is used to create the tealer eye. You will notice a nail protruding from the end of the block to a length of one half inch. This is not an ordinary wire nail it is either a masonry nail or a hilti nail $2^1/_2$" long 2 mil diameter. These nails are very strong and robust with the tensile strength to stand up to the constant winding, heating and pressure applied in the making of the tealer eyes over a long period of time. An ordinary wire nail would gradually just bend and become no use whatsoever. I would suggest that the reader make a small pilot hole in the block before inserting the masonry or hilti nail into the hard wood block to save it from splitting. Any of the hard woods, oak, ash, ramin, etc will suffice to make a block.

(4) Illustration 4 is the plan view of the 'eye block' end face showing the nail. You will also notice the end of a groove showing here because the block must have a 2.5 mil groove running the full length along the middle of the side of the block. It was I who came up with this idea of making this groove because it saves opening up the vice every time you need to bend the next tealer wire. Therefore the block sits enclosed in the vice jaws from start to finish whether 20 or 200 tealer eyes are to be formed on the end of all the lengths of wire that are cut and ready for use. The implements I use are of the utmost and simplest design and construction that can be picked up for nothing almost anywhere in your locality. A friend who is a cooper to trade supplies the oak straps he steams them nice and flat for me. My cousin cuts and shapes them to size on his table saw all I am left to do is insert the nails into certain blocks to complete the job, before that I hand sawed them and shaped some of them with an axe.

Stabiliser Construction

To make your tealers, start with showing a length of 2.5 mil diameter galvanised wire cut to a total length of 20" right angle bend at one end. (A opposite) This length of wire makes a perfect $9^1/_2$" tealer.

(B) Place the length of wire along the groove in the 'Eye block' as seen in the illustration, then insert the block along with wire between the vice jaws and hold tight. Some people I have taught place the block into the vice with the groove running along the top of the block but I prefer the groove running parallel along the inside length of the jaw of the vice. After the tealer eye has been formed you just tap the end of the wire with hammer or pliers which loosens the eye grip slightly so that it can slip off the nail more easily. To replace a new length of wire just slip it into the groove along between the side of the block and the vice jaw so for me the block remains in the vice from start to finish when making eyes.

(C) Start to wind the wire around the nail tightly.

(D) The eye has now been completed. On the final turn when the end of the wire is in the vertical position snip it off level with the nail. File the cut end with a little safe edge file then take the pliers and tighten in the turns of wire of the newly formed eye.

(E) Now that the eye has been formed and the wire removed from the block, bend the wire back on itself at a length of 9" from under the eye. The extra length gained at the bottom bend along with the turns of the eye loop gives you a tealer of $9^1/_2$" total length. Should longer tealers be required for snaring in high flora cut the wire lengths from 20" for a $9^1/_2$"" tealer to 24" + to make 11" long tealers.

(F) For the final part of the tealer construction the wedge shape block is inserted into the V shape base of the tealer. Once again it is placed firmly between vice jaws and then the long end is wound around the main shaft five times before snipping off the excess. Then file wire end smoothly and tighten the turns in more tightly with the pliers. Then set the turns tightly by giving them three light sharp taps with the hammer. If this last tightening and tapping act is not performed what can happen is this. Should you catch hares or large fox cubs the turns and the grip are pulled down the shaft pulling the tealer out of shape. Therefore once again put five turns of wire loops around the tealer shaft then set them tight with the pliers and the hammer which totally eliminates the latter problem.

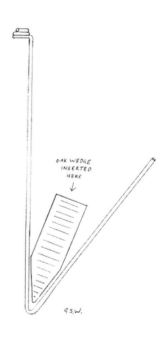

OAK WEDGE INSERTED HERE

G.S.W.

Showing a close up of oak wedge block, how to insert it into the base of the tealer pin.

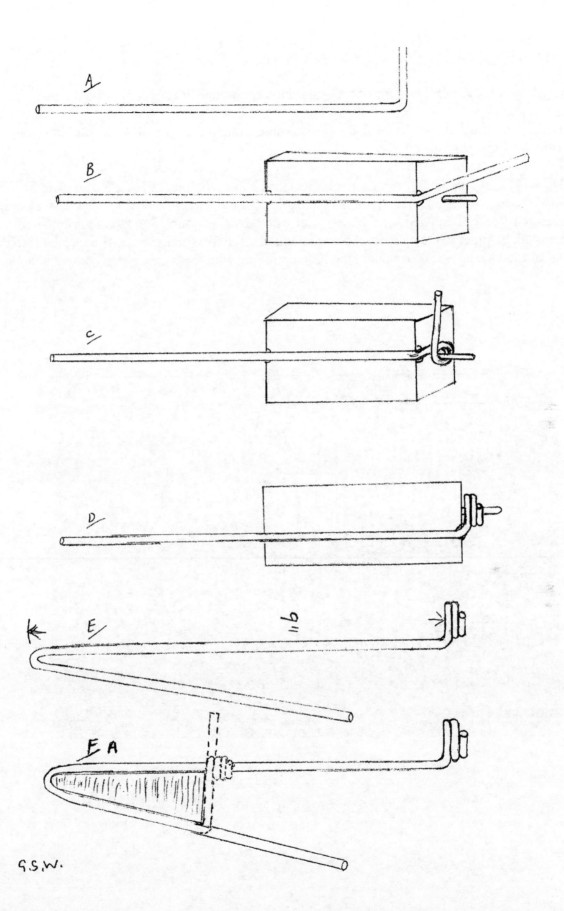

A

B

c

D

E

9"

F A

G.S.W.

Opposite:

(G)Illustration shows the shape of the tealer after the wedge block is removed.

(H) Lay the tealer (G) on its edge and tap one side straight then tap the opposite side straight also showing a V shape base.

(I) To finish the figure 4 tealer I lay it on its edge, slip a small length of 2.5 mm plate in between the wires at the base, then tap the last $^3/_8$" of the wire base down onto the steel strap. Then remove the strap and lay the tealer flat with the grip on top, then tap the grip flat with the small hammer to create a bevel for your thumb. Finally slip the base of the tealer into the end of the vice jaws and straighten the base up in line with the tealer eye to complete the job.

Figure 4, 9½ inch wire tealers all sprayed green and ready to go

G   H/   I/

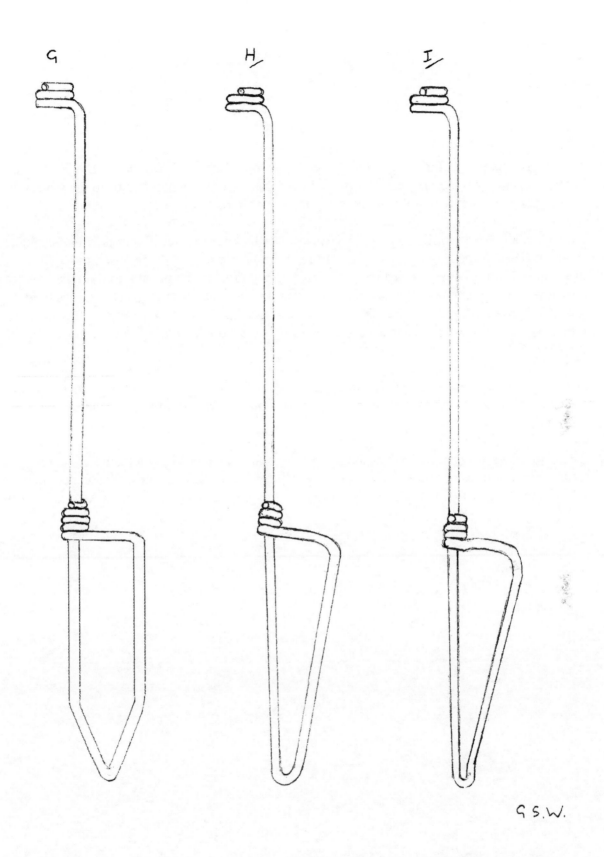

G.S.W.

Alternative Tealer Jig

This illustration opposite shows an alternative jig for forming the '4' of the tealer on a strap of wood.

First of all you must complete the double eye at the top of the tealer using the 'Eye Block' as before. Again you now measure $9^1/_2$" from under the eye of the tealer and bend the wire into a V shape, making sure that the tealer eye is facing forward away from the V shape.

Now place the partly formed tealer along the Main Block at A which shows the dimensions to shape the base of the tealer. Looking carefully at figure A you will see four nails with the heads cut off protruding in a vertical position from the block. The placing of these nails is for the purpose of stopping the wire of the tealer from bowing outwards as you bend it as they keep the wire straight and in line. Bend the wire into shape as seen then remove and keep repeating the process until you have made as many figure four shapes as your require whether it is 20 or 200.

After making the desired amount then complete the process as with the previous method using the oak wedge and winding the end of the wire around the main shaft of the tealer five times and finishing.

There are many ways of making different types of tealer pins. It's only a matter of putting your mind to it to use a method that suits you. With a little practice you will soon become adept at making them quickly and efficiently like the professionals who can make hundreds in a day.

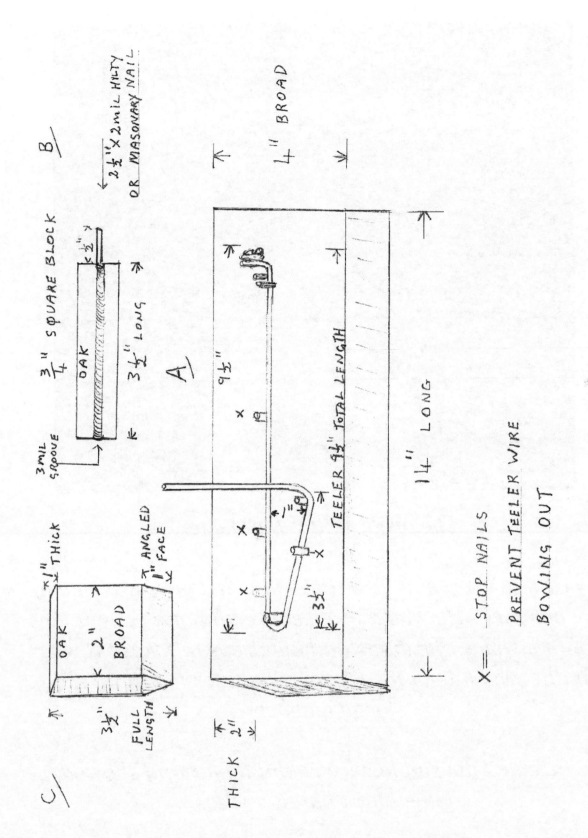

B

2½" x 2mil HILTY OR MASONARY NAIL

¾" SQUARE BLOCK

OAK

3½" LONG

3mil GROOVE

A

¼" BROAD

9½"

TEELER 9½" TOTAL LENGTH

1"

3½"

14" LONG

X = STOP NAILS

PREVENT TEELER WIRE BOWING OUT

C

¼" THICK

ANGLED FACE

OAK 2" BROAD

3½"

FULL LENGTH

THICK 2"

The great Willie McMaster,

Known to everyone as Willie Mac, this man was one of my mentors. He was a great snareman and caught tens of thousands of rabbits and hundreds of foxes. It was Willie who taught me to run road lines to kill foxes in large numbers.

He invented the single wire rabbit tealer and showed me the black baling twine.

Willie was the man who snared two foxes cubs which were hand raised for the TV film 'The Belstone Fox', using pegged rabbit snares outside the den.

Professional Rabbit Snaring

Chapter 24 - Making Alternative Tealers

Single Wire Tealer - devised by Willie McMaster.

The illustration shown here is of a single wire snare tealer, 3 mil diameter and length of $9^{1}/_{2}$" long from top to bottom including the single eye loop. To make this tealer pin cut 50 or 100 lengths of 3 mil wire 14" long. This allows ample wire to complete the whole process.

The single eye loop is formed by bending the top of the wire over into a loop and then taking hold of the now formed eye loop between the jaws of the pliers and turning it into the flat position as seen.

Next lay tealer in a flat position along a 4" x 2", 16" long strap of wood the eye being held and trapped between two vertical nails with the heads removed and protruding $^{1}/_{2}$" from the strap. There should be enough clearance between them to insert the tealer shaft with the eye loop right next to them.

Five inches long the strap from these nails there is a $^{1}/_{4}$" diameter length of smooth steel rod that has been inserted into a pre-drilled hole situated directly in the middle of the 16" long wooden strap. This length of smooth rod has been inserted to a depth of one inch to give it stability with half an inch of rod protruding vertically above the flat surface of the strap. The whole strap is held in the vice.

Take hold of the bottom half of the tealer wire bend it back around on itself around the rod, firmly and neatly forming a nice round loop in the centre of the tealer pin. To complete the job cut tealer wire to $9^{1}/_{2}$".

The centre loop constructed in this wire tealer pin is the point where the baler twine is attached by slipping the twine loop through the wire loop of the tealer the securing peg attached to the opposite end of the baler twine is then dropped through the end loop to secure the whole system together into one complete unit. You will notice the twine is looped around the spine of the loop in the centre of the tealer holding the double wires and not at the belly side marked X, this being the wrong location to insert and attach the looped twines. Although I have noticed on occasions people with their snare twine attached at this point which I'm afraid is wrong.

The single looped eye of the tealer was the standard type of loop formed on the majority of the older traditional type snares constructed with either the double or single wire tealer system. The end of the snare noose was inserted down through the top of the eye loop, then bent around the wire shaft of the tealer and threaded back through on itself beneath the eye loop between the tealer shaft and the snare wire. Once this had been completed the snare wire was slid up under the eye loop and the tail of the snare noose would tightly around the tealer shaft to complete the job of attaching the noose permanently to the tealer pin. My old mentor Willie Mac devised the single tealer system with the centre loop. It is a quick and easily made tealer, Willie formed this simple system from slightly larger diameter wire of 3 mil. This heavier gauge galvanised wire was more robust penetrated the more dense ground conditions easier and was more stable and held the snare noose firmly. Willie always set his snares from the side of the run sitting at a 45° angle with the big loop only covering the run. He also knew that the thinner galvanised tealers were not as stable when set out on open ground exposed to strong windy blustery conditions. Flying debris e.g. large sycamore leaves, small pieces of broken branches, and ash stems would strike the exposed snare loops knocking them off centre on the runs causing rabbits to be missed as they travelled outwards along their runs to the feeding grounds.

This snare unit was a simple and highly effective system many snaremen including myself using it for many years. The permanent attachment of the snare noose to the single and double wire tealer pins was the normal everyday practice. The problem was that at times the brass strands of the noose would tighten up above the eye loop of the tealer pin causing broken strands and complete breakages of the snare which had to be replaced when this happened. Chisholm also attached his snare nooses permanently to the tealer. Then Andy Whyte devised the simple and ingenious swivelling system - first he devised a figure four galvanised wire tealer system with a double eye loop at the top with a smaller diameter hole into which he inserted the snare cable once again down through the top of the tealer eye only this time the snare noose was not a permanent fixture to the tealer pin. He formed a small double knot into the end of the wire noose which acted as a very simple and highly effective swivelling device, superior to the old permanent fixture technique. Whyte's system is now widely used by the majority of today's snaremen in the UK. This simpler method used as a swivel system helps take the strain of the snare loop and increases the number of catches that can now be made from one snare loop.

A double eye loop can also be made on this single tealer system if required, allowing the double knot swivelling mechanism to be used.

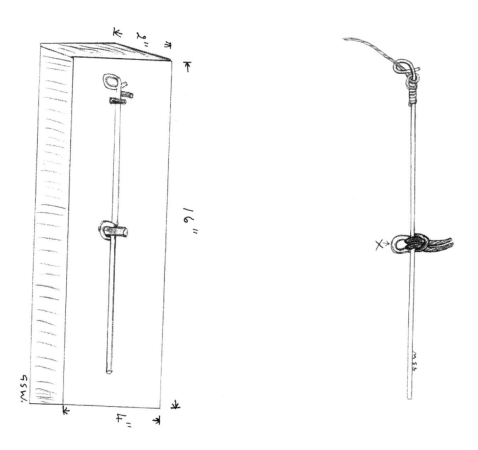

Old Style Double Tealer

The following illustration shows how to make the old Scottish double wire tealer with the single loop eye at the top. A double eye can also be formed to use with the double knot system for central swivelling action. The wire tealer pin which was 9" long and made from $1^1/_2$ mil diameter galvanized wire being of a smaller diameter this tealer was hard to see when set out in grass with a weathered noose attached. I still keep 150 of these snares only the tealers are $10^1/_2$" long and sprayed Vauxhall leaf green making them even harder to see, as they blend into their surroundings very well. I use these snares at certain locations in rough weather conditions which I would call unsafe places, where you have a chance of the odd prowler mooching about. Touch wood I have not had any stolen so far being crafty helps to avert these type of problems. Should you wish to make and try a few of these old style thinner wire tealers I recommend you make a double eye at the top to use with the double knot swivelling system. The tealer being constructed from a lesser diameter wire has a tendency to bend and in need or regular straightening when out on the snaring field. Other than that they work fine, have low visibility and when set out in higher grass using the longer tealer they are practically invisible to prowling eyes. Remember always to use marker pins to keep track of any snares as they can easily be overlooked always count them out and count then when they are being uplifted be professional in your approach.

(A) showing $4^1/_2$" square piece of clear Perspex $^3/_{16}$" thick with a fully formed tealer attached to it.

(B) side elevation showing thickness and length.

(C) showing a 20" length of $1^1/_2$ mil diameter galvanised wire with formed single loop at the top. Measure 9" from underside of eye loop bend upwards and forward into V shape then slip the tealer onto the square Perspex end as seen. Grip the tealer wires firmly at the edge of board with pliers, the jaw one on either side clamping the tealer firmly to the board. Then proceed to wind the end of the wire around the vertical main shaft four to five times or more if so required then snip off the excess wire file end smoothly. Finally tap it in neatly alongside the other wire turns then set permanently by hitting the turns three sharp taps with the hammer.

(D) showing 21" length of wire with double eye loop formed at the top.

(E) repeat the same process as described at (C).

(F) showing finished tealer.

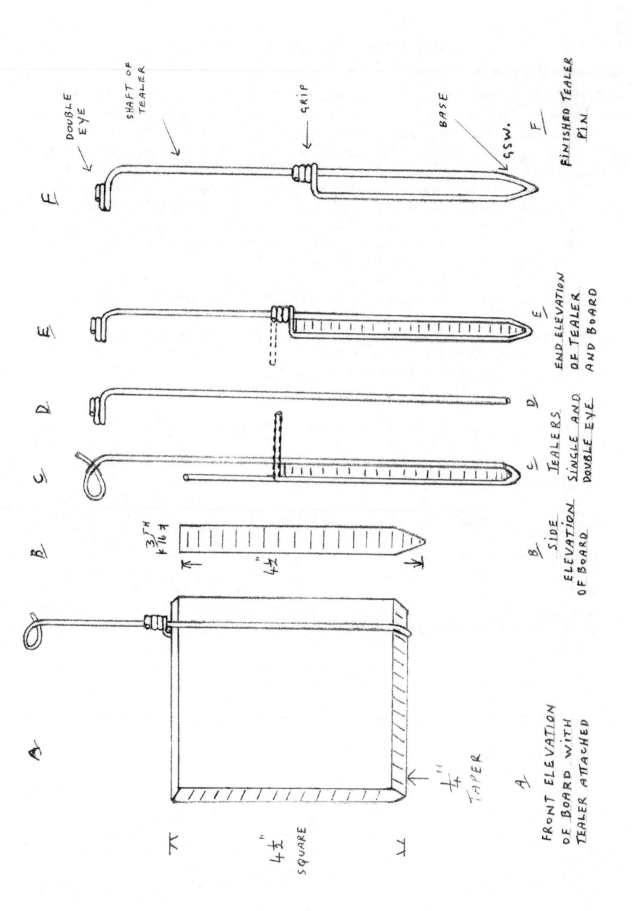

DOUBLE EYE

SHAFT OF TEALER

GRIP

BASE

G.S.W.

F

FINISHED TEALER PIN

E

END ELEVATION OF TEALER AND BOARD

D

C

TEALERS SINGLE AND DOUBLE EYE

B

SIDE ELEVATION OF BOARD

$3\frac{3}{4}$"

$\frac{1}{16}$"

$4\frac{1}{2}$"

A

FRONT ELEVATION OF BOARD WITH TEALER ATTACHED

$4\frac{1}{2}$" SQUARE

$\frac{1}{4}$" TAPER

Chapter 25 - Making the Loops

Preparing the Wire

Making your own rabbit snares is a very simple process, and there are a number of various methods devised on how to make them. All professional snaremen make their own snares as it is without doubt they can be made at a fraction of the cost of the commercial ones advertised for sale in gun shops and local sporting goods shops. I have already stated the latter snares are inferior in design compared the professional ones designed by trappers themselves which are by far a more superior quality snare altogether in design and catching ability. Just as the true professional knows from hard won experience that a poor quality product results in failure and poor catches out in the field, he also knows from years of field craft and a study of his target species bodily characteristics, that his snares must comply with the dimensions of the quarry in mind and construct them to the proper length so that they will perform perfectly once snaring operations commence. To make your own snares the brass wire must first be purchased either in 5 or 8 kilo drums or in coiled hanks from 1 lb upwards.

The diameter of brass wire recommended to be purchased to make good quality six strand rabbit snares is .457 or .455 do not accept thinner wire of .375 diameter as the former is the proper thickness to acquire to produce a good quality six strand snare . This is more than sufficient to hold the heaviest of rabbits and hares, any additional strands are an extreme waste of wire and eight or ten strand brass snares are too thick, I do not recommend them at all. In this line of work the secret of a good snare is to make it long enough and to wind the six strands into a nice smooth, even, tight, cable. The strands need to be tightly wound, I say tight but do not overdo it - after a little practice in making a few snares you will get to know by experience the proper texture required. When the brass strands are wound in this latter fashion forming a nice snare cable which is far strong, with a light tension incorporated into the formed noose the least pressure will close it quickly.

The big snare loop also sits very well in the proper catching position retaining its shape and position over the run should it be knocked or even in the presence of high winds. The cable also beds well into the rabbit's neck fur and on being spun tighter than a commercial snare it causes practically no problems with loose and open splayed strands which are consistent every day with snares that are slack and only partly wound. This poor quality adds further burden to the snarer's daily work of having to constantly lift and rewind snare after snare.

Should the brass snare be purchased in 1 lb coiled hanks many people appear to have a problem with it springing up and getting themselves into a tangle, which can easily be avoided by a little forethought. First of all take the coil of wire unwind the wrapped end and make sure that it is going to uncoil from the top of the coil and not from the underside which causes the problem as people appear to try and pull it up through the coil from the base. Another simple trick to keep the wire neat in its nice round circular coil is to take an old plastic flower pot, one that tapers narrower at the base, and turn it upside down and place the coil over the now upturned base. It will now retain its proper shape and will pull off its now stable base given by the upturned flower pot in a relatively easy manner without causing any tangles or kinking. The heavier drums of wire due to their design and weight offer far more stability when unwinding the brass wire, once the stability of either drums or coils of wire has been established regardless of the manner the making of the snares can now commence.

We shall start with the most common and simplest method of making rabbit snares, the way in which many professionals make their own equipment. First of all you will require a length of hardwood strap 26 inches long approximately 2" broad, $^3/_4$"thick. You then insert two 4 inch nails, $1^1/_2$" from the ends which will be 23" apart.

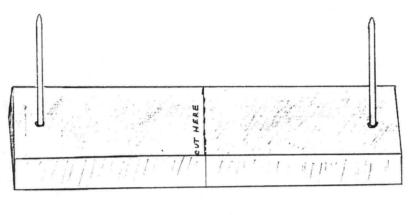

WOODEN STRAP

LENGTH   50"   CENTRE LINE To CUT WIRE

BREADTH   2"   NAILS   4" LONG

THICKNESS - 1"

NAILS - 46" APART

Now cut yourself two or three elastic bands $^1/_2$" broad from an old motorcycle wheel inner tube - check them for size but don't put them on the strap yet. Having done this put an X mark beside one of the nails as a starting and finishing point.

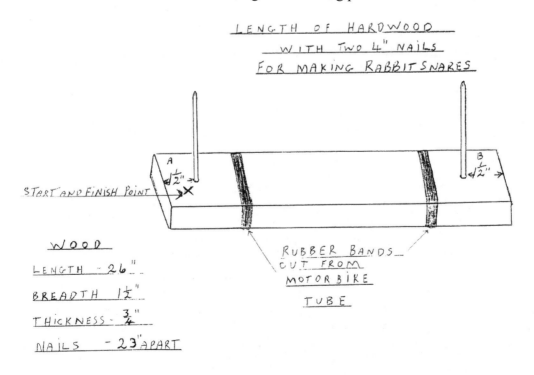

LENGTH OF HARDWOOD
WITH TWO 4" NAILS
FOR MAKING RABBIT SNARES

A $\frac{1}{2}$"

B $\frac{1}{2}$"

START and FINISH POINT   X

WOOD

LENGTH - 26"

BREADTH 1½"

THICKNESS - $\frac{3}{4}$"

NAILS - 23" APART

RUBBER BANDS
CUT FROM
MOTOR BIKE
TUBE

The following diagram explains how to wind the brass wire. Take the loose starting end of your wire coil or drum and form a small one inch loop and place this small loop over the nail marked X the starting point. Now take hold of the wooden strap in your left hand with the X mark in the downward position and proceed to wind the brass wire around the nails until they are full. You can count the turns as the wire comes over the top nail - for instance counting one hundred and fifty turns of the wire will give you fifty snares due to the fact each snare is made if six strand and three double strands make six. It's very simple.

To finish just snip the wire strand off an inch past the nail at the X point and bend it around the nail. To hold the wire stable slip the rubber bands over the brass wire and nails from each end this stops the wire slipping over the top of the nails. (A)

Now look at illustration (B). Take a large pair of scissors and insert the sharp point at the base of the nail at point X, in between the loops of the wire strands. Then slip so many at a time over the top of the nail and cut them clean through until everyone is severed. The rubber bands which had been placed over them beforehand prevents them from slipping upwards.

Illustration (C) which shows clearly how to insert a snare eyelet. To do this go to the opposite nail from the cut end and pull three double strands from the top of the nail. Insert the eyelet between them and then hold the six strands firmly and give the eyelet a couple of quick turns in an anti-clockwise fashion (if right handed) to hold it tightly in place. You continue this practice until every triple set of strands has received an eyelet

To make double the amount of snares at any time cut a length of board 50 inches long, insert two nails at 2 inches in from the ends, leaving 46 inches space between the nails. A pencil line is drawn across the board at the halfway mark between the nails which is the point where the wire strands are cut through. This gives you two bundles of wires to be made into snares each 23" long which makes an excellent snare.

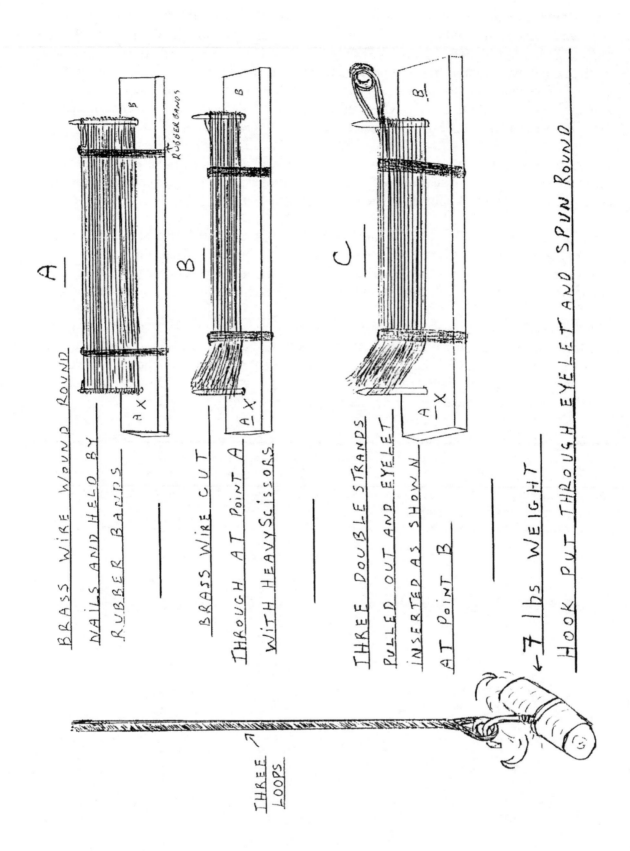

A

BRASS WIRE WOUND ROUND
NAILS AND HELD BY
RUBBER BANDS

B

BRASS WIRE CUT
THROUGH AT POINT A
WITH HEAVY SCISSORS

C

THREE DOUBLE STRANDS
PULLED OUT AND EYELET
INSERTED AS SHOWN
AT POINT B

←7 lbs WEIGHT
HOOK PUT THROUGH EYELET AND SPUN ROUND

THREE LOOPS

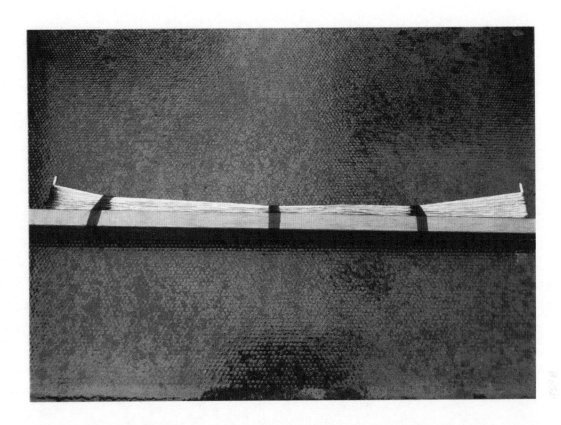

Brass snare wire wound around two nails 23" apart, bands cut from motorbike tubing hold wire firm and neat. 75 couple strands gives you 25, 6 strand snares. The reason for 23 inches is that you lose approximately half an inch in length once the strands have been spun into a nice smooth cable, giving you the required length of 22 ½ inches.

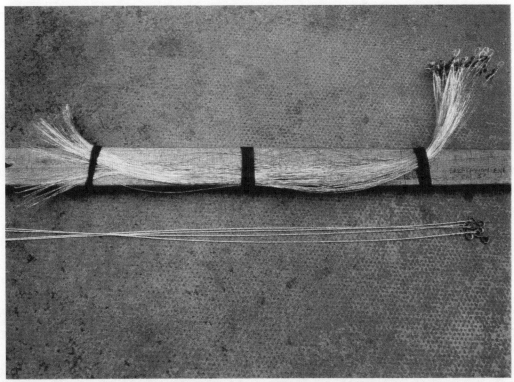

Snare wire is cut at one end at the nail. Sets of 3 double strands are attached to eyelets ready to be spun into 6 strand snares.

On completion of this task take hold of an eyelet, starting with the top one of course, and proceed to pull the six loose strands from the end of board. Insert the eyelet onto the hook attached to your weight, then take hold of the opposite top loose ends between the jaws of a pair of short narrow-nosed pliers which will be held in the left hand with the weight suspended at the bottom. Make sure that all of the vertical strands are firm and taut "not any slack in them". You then run your forefinger and thumb firmly down the loose strands to keep them smooth and even and after doing this you now spin the suspended weight in a clockwise fashion until you end up with a nice firmly wound snare cable which only takes a few seconds to make.

Hold pliers in left hand then grip 7 lbs weight as seen between thumb and fingers then spin the weight in a clockwise fashion if left handed apply this action from the opposite side. Just take your time when spinning the weight do not jerk it you want a nice smooth spinning action. The first spin that you do the weight will spin quite quickly when you see it slowing down take hold of the weight again then repeat the process for a second time. Once again take hold of the weight and spin it for a third and final time this will give you a nice smooth snare cable. You repeat this process until all the snares have been made. The finished product now consists of a nice straight smooth tight brass cable measuring approximately $22^{1}/_{2}$"long each and every snare is exactly the same length and consistency. In Scotland you must also add a stop to the cable.

The weight used to spin the snares into a nice cable can be made from any suitable object, e.g. a short length of thick steel bar, small thick steel flanges, a clutch plate, the head of an old bricklayers mash with the shaft sawn off at the head and a cup hook screwed into the remaining part, an empty soup tin filled with lead or cement with a length of thin galvanised wire inserted before it solidifies then a hook bent into the protruding end. The variety is endless. One good tip to remember is to use a weight of 5 to 7 lbs which keeps the snare wire taut and spins the strands even and tight. If you use a very light weight it's not got the density therefore instead of keeping the strands taut it's more liable to dance on the end as it's being spun around causing ripples.

Spinning up the snares using the suspended weight by hand is how I like to sit and make them helping to retain the old style handcraft, although I have a small geared winder which can be attached to an old table within a minute or so. These old winders were used in conjunction with small sized circular sharpening stone attached to a steel shaft. The gears can be of a ratio of one complete turn of the handle to 6 or 12 turns due to the appropriate type of gears within the enclosed housing of the machine. My own winder turns the shaft 12 times to one complete turn of the handle which should always be at the six o'clock position when attached to a table or bench. The end of the steel shaft is drilled with right angled piece of thin steel rod or steel nail protruding in an upward position.

The fastest homemade method I have seen in use is one made by a friend of mine - an engineer - consisting of a 1 horse power little electric motor with a couple of pulleys and a small drive belt assembled upon a two foot square board with a foot pedal to operate it. One small touch of the pedal using three triple strands from three drums of wire and the snare is complete in a nanosecond. He made this snare making machine for an old man who was employed by a company who sold field sports equipment. This machine produced over a quarter million snares annually until old Charlie died and my friend George has this machine in his shed where it now lies.

When spinning snares over the years I have noticed that at certain times of the day especially around noon and the afternoon the weight looks as if it's lethargic at times as it turns slowly which is noticeable to me. I have noticed that if I am sitting spinning snares in the early hours of the morning around one to two am they look as if it is motorised and spins with extreme speed so that the snare cable is ready with barely two separate spins of the weight. In my opinion I think this anomaly is due to the magnetic polarity of the earth at certain times of the day and month more so with the phases of the moon. I have discussed this with Colin on occasions. I have never heard of this ever being written or talked about by anyone ever before absolutely never. Even government officials I have asked couldn't give me an answer.

Once the required amount has been made, each individual snare is lifted and the end is inserted through the large sized hole face of the eyelet to form the snare loop, on accomplishing this insert the thumb of your left hand and run the new open snare loop into a closed position then open it up slightly, always do this with all new snares for the very first time, which ensures proper closure.

After this task is completed hang your newly made snare loops up to weather. Don't just tie them up in a bunch and hang them up, spread them along a length of wooden dowling or a length of plastic coated wire but never hang them on rusty nails or plain galvanized wire in case of oxidisation. Spreading the snare loops out from each other this allows the elements to dull each noose completely and naturally.

I've heard it said to bury them in dung middens but I would not want my brass snares corroded or tainted with ammonia and acids, just to be on the safe side in case it affected the wires by weakening their strength.

One method I would most certainly advise against, it putting brass snares into a fire of any kind to blacken them, another fallacy the same as the fire is supposed to burn any scent off them. This silly idea will almost certainly ruin the snares by seriously weakening them they will also be tainted with smoke. I have also read where the scribe stated to soot the snares over a candle flame. Could you really imagine sitting sooting five hundred to a thousand nooses over a single candle flame you would be there until the millennium, honestly what next, these silly old antiquated ideas die hard with some people who still believe in them even today. Forget all these misconceptions because it makes not one bit of blind difference when setting brand new shiny snares, at least they will be strong and unweakened, the only problem with new snares is with their visibility making them much easier to view by any prowlers snooping around. Therefore weather the snares naturally and just wash your hands in a stream or trough and rub them with grass and set them out well beforehand in the morning and you will have no trouble whatsoever with any scent being left on the snares.

POINT TO NOTE - when a 23" snare is spun into a cable it loses approximately $\frac{1}{2}$" in length making a $22\frac{1}{2}$" long snare when formed into a loop with the double end knot it gives $7\frac{1}{2}$" x $5\frac{1}{2}$"to correlate with the characteristics of an adult rabbit's head.

Chapter 26 - Putting it all Together

Making the Tealer Knot

The double knot you see under the double eye of the tealer is as simple a swivel as you can get. Your snares will last a hell of a lot longer using this method, than if they are permanently attached to the tealer. A number of years ago I snared 1500 rabbits doing a little test while just working at times with 100-150 pegged snares and I only had to replace 4 nooses but to be fair I had no problems with foxes.

(A) First of all take the end of the snare loop and insert it down through the top of the double eye of the tealer pin, then bend it up into a U shape at the base approximately one and a half inches.

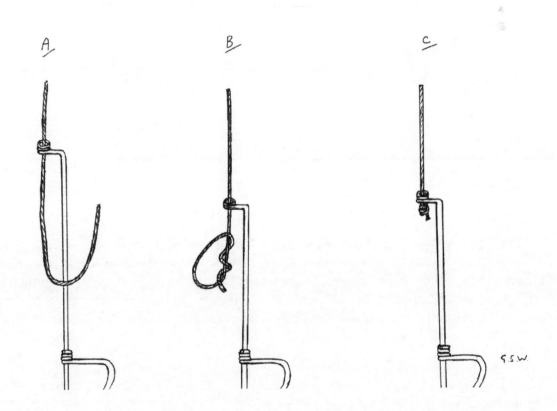

(B) Take the tail of the snare loop and bend it back over on itself and wind it through twice - to form a little loop with the small tail end of the wire cable protruding.

(C) Let the tealer pin slide down the brass snare cable until it stops and rests on the small loop as seen in illustration (B), then slip the brass snare loop over the wrist or some smooth object e.g. a piece of two inch diameter doweling of wood or a short length of plastic pipe 2" diameter

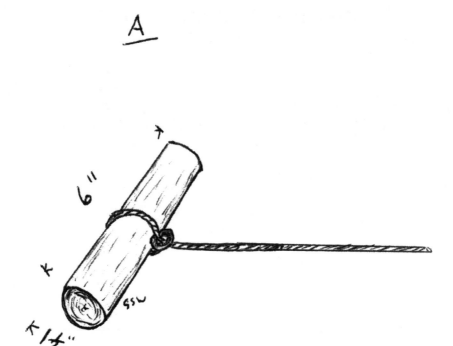

Once this has been done take hold of the double eye of the tealer pin firmly between thumb and the middle knuckle of the forefinger of the right hand and pull down firmly to close the loop into a nice double knot. Then slide the tealer back up the brass snare cable an inch or two and pull down again from a different angle, doing this gives the knot a nice even shape so that it will twist freely acting as a swivel below the double eye of the wire tealer in illustration (C).

This swivelling action is most effective in saving snares from kinking and I highly recommend the use of this type of pegged snare.

Different ways to secure the snare

This illustration shows three rabbit tealers with the snare wire attached permanently using the double knot in the end of the snare loop which allows complete rotation of the snare loop once an animal has been captured. Looking at these three drawings I am going to explain what can and cannot happen and how to avoid certain problems depending on how the end of the snare cable is formed around the shaft of the tealer. To the inexperienced and an unpractised eye looking at these illustrations one may say that they look fine but over many years of continuous use of these snare systems I noticed a certain fault that occurred on occasions but not all the time. Therefore as I have said before it pays to be observant and develop good visual awareness while practising the art of snaring because it can mean the difference of success or failure at times. As I have mentioned before *the wise man's eyes are in his head while the fool walketh in the darkness*.

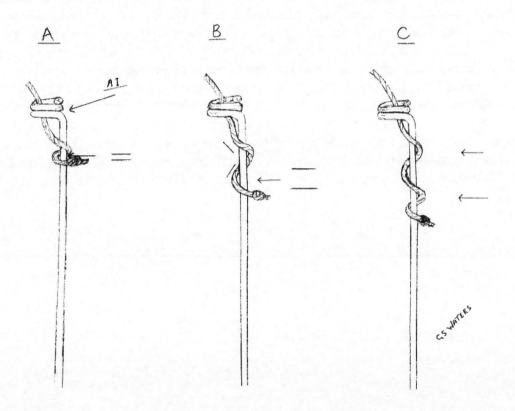

(A)   Illustration shows the end of snare cable with one complete turn around shaft of the tealer. The arrow points to narrow gap or space between the turn of the cable and the knot - they lie practically parallel with each other as the two strokes show. Forming the end of the cable in this manner with a tight gap as shown, creates a little problem that I began to notice over the years. It happens now and again when a capture is made and the knot end of the cable is pulled with great speed from the tealer shaft due to the forward motion and body mass and weight of the rabbit. This causes the snare cable to slide up the tealer shaft before it has fully unwound causing it to jam under the base of the tealer eye, where the arrow at (A1) is pointing. This could cause the cable to snap due to the inability of the cable to rotate freely as it normally would. What may save the wire snare cable from breaking is being good quality wire firmly spun. Do not over tighten snare wire when spinning up snares as this causes the wire to become rough and brittle and very awkward to tension and shape the noose. There is little stretch and play left, in over spun snares therefore they can't stand up to the regular abuse when catching large and heavy winter rabbits therefore they are prone to strands breaking leading to snapped snare cables and lost quarry which is to be avoided at all times if possible.

(B) This is a similar illustration only this time there is a larger gap left between turns of the snare cable around tealer shaft, and the end knot. The two strokes under the tealer eye shows a 45° angle of the snare cable attaching the end of the snare noose in this latter manner appears to eliminate the problem of the knot becoming jammed as shown in figure (A) due to the angle and the slightly wider gap before the end knot as shown.

(C) When using a 24" snare cable compared to the normal 22½" snare, this obviously allows for a larger snare noose but also allows for another couple of opportunities when using this length of snare. First of all should you prefer to use the normal loop size of 7.5" x 5.5" the end of the snare noose can be wrapped around the tealer shaft twice at a 45° angle as shown in illustration (C). Should you wish to snare a hare or two the loops can be extended by forming only one turn of the snare cable around the tealer shaft. The longer 24" snare can also be used to its advantage of allowing the trapper to gain extra height while snaring in higher grass, by leaving an inch of snare wire above the tealer eye then forming the actual snare loop itself. These little tricks can help solve little problems when out on the snareline should they arise, another simple trick to gain extra height for a snare is to cut a small thick piece of turf a few inches square lay it down to the side of the run then compress it slightly with the ball of the foot to stabilise it then insert the tealer into it, it works every time. Forget all the old fashioned nonsense that we were subjected to over the years by scribes who tried to capture people's imagination over the years, always writing about the secrets of this and the secrets of that. Well there are no secrets, it's just a case of pure old fashioned commonsense and simplicity.

Tensioning the snare loop.

First of all before tension is set into a snare loop it must be fashioned to the proper shape. To achieve this the loop must be opened out until it is fully extended, with the brass eyelet resting on top of the double eye of the wire tealer pin. The open loop must now be retained in this position, by holding it firmly between the bent forefinger and the thumb of your right hand, if right handed of course. You now place the large open loop over your left knee, still retaining your firm grip of eyelet and tealer pin in the right hand. The top of the snare loop should now be on the bottom part of your kneecap. Still keeping a firm hold of the loop in the right hand, you now take hold of the snare loop on the far side of your knee, between forefinger and thumb of the left hand. Hold the wire firmly, then pull the forefinger and thumb around the bottom of the loop back towards your right hand which maintains a firm grip throughout this process. You should now have a small half moon shape of wire on the underside of the snare eyelet due to the left hand pulling in the slack along the bottom of the wire loop.

Now hold the snare loop directly in front of your face and place the four fingers of your left hand through the snare loop, so that your fingers are now pointing towards you. Now take hold of the bottom of the snare loop so that the wire is held firmly between thumb and fingers and proceed to squeeze the snare wire of the loop down and around the bottom of the loop towards the right hand which is still retaining its grip of eyelet and tealer pin. You then push and squeeze this small half loop of wire toward the eyelet until it's straightened out. Once this has been achieved your left hand works around the firmly held noose fashioning the smooth wire into the desired shape of either a nice deep oval loop or into a pear shaped noose depending on each trapper's preference.

It is hard to describe this simple and quick process in written detail as it only takes seconds to shape and tension a snare loop. To the novice it may appear an awesome task but after a few practice sessions they will become quite proficient in mastering this simple technique. The most important point to be observed under this heading is that all snare loops when set in a catching position shall not sag, spring or lose their shape or form, but will hold firmly in a stable position. A properly shaped and tensioned snare loop if struck from the underside of the noose by a small rabbit hedgehog or other small mammal the bottom of the noose lifts up from the top of the tealer wire where it rests and immediately returns back to its proper position still retaining its proper loop size and ready to intercept its intended quarry. If no tension had been installed into the wire noose the snare would have remained tripped and unable to catch until the return of the trapper the following morning. A well shaped and tensioned snare loop can withstand a fair knock from a human foot or any passing animal as long as they don't enter in the open loop itself.

There are also quite a number of various types of birds that wander about out in the fields in their daily quest for food such as pheasants, partridges, crows, seagulls, curlews, on occasions blackbirds and thrushes which usually inhabit the field edges. Over the years I have caught a few crows in pegged snares set well out in the fields, twice I have caught partridges and released them, the same with an odd pheasant or two. Once I found a mallard drake in a snare. But prowling foxes are a damn nuisance on a snareline for tripping, knocking and breaking the rabbit snares when foot snared but on numerous occasions over the years a good few cubs and adults have succumbed to a well set pegged rabbit snare. Therefore it is not just rabbits that trip your snare loops on occasions, so that it is imperative that you tension all of your snares, which is the routine practice to the professional as he is well aware of the many problems that can occur on occasions when setting snares. A well tensioned snare loop will just spring back into its original catching position, should it be accidentally knocked or brushed by any of the latter creatures. It's still ready to catch any outgoing rabbit travelling out to the feeding grounds. A well set pegged rabbit snare set well out in the field is usually a very selective method employed for capturing wild rabbits.

There are many people who have participated in rabbit snaring for many years and are supposed to be proficient in the art yet they cannot and do not know how to incorporate proper tension into a snare noose. All they do is open up the loop until it's fully extended to the top of the tealer then put a distinct kink in the snare cable to try and hold it open and hope for the best. This is not the way to do it at all, a high wind or the least knock the loop just slips forward in a half closed fashion unable to reset itself and once sprung will not catch at all until the operator returns the following morning to reap the same silly setting. I have also read that dropping the securing peg through the loop, this also is supposed to help tension a snare noose. I'm afraid it's another fallacy one of the many. Tension can only be inserted into the snare loop by the operator himself and no other way.

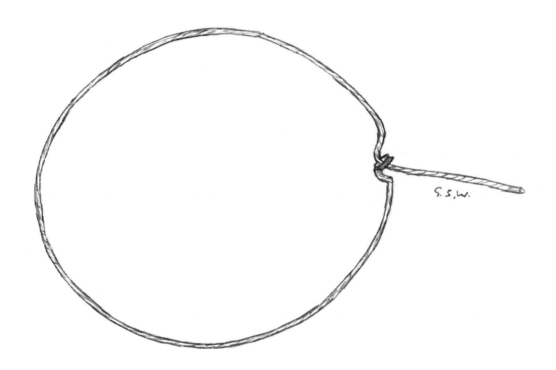

The illustration of this snare loop shows how a lot of amateurs and even gamekeepers still set a snare loop, with a distinct kink in the wire above the eyelet, because they do not know how to set the tension into a rabbit snare properly. This small loop if struck by an animal or bird out in a field will spring half closed and catch nothing, because it has not been tensioned properly which would enable it to reset itself if knocked. This is how snares are still being set today and I know of instructors at colleges who are still showing students to snare with a small noose set low to the ground, the same goes with their fox snares, will they ever learn. People hate changes and pride is a great thing.

Professional Rabbit Snaring

How to Shape and Tension a Snare Loop Alternative Explanation.

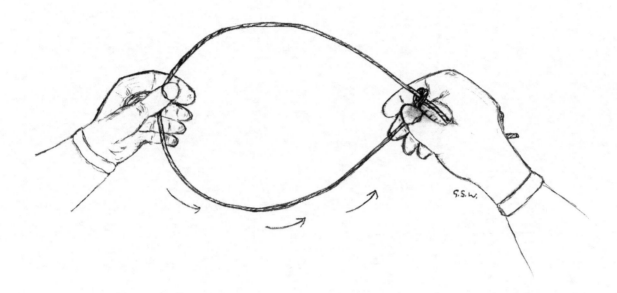

This is one of the few different ways to tension a rabbit snare loop properly so that your snare loop will spring back into position if brushed by a bird or reset itself if knocked from underneath the loop. To be shown by a man with experience takes a few seconds to accomplish this simple feat, but to be only told takes longer which is most obvious. So to save any confusion I have drawn an illustration to accompany the wording, as they say a picture is worth a thousand words. Therefore if you hold a snare loop in your hands as seen in the picture, first of all I would suggest that you use an amateur size noose around 4 inches diameter until you become familiar with it then progress onto the professional size noose. Once the skill of tensioning a large noose is attained the more you just sit and practice with it the more proficient you will become.

1. Hold noose between hands as shown. In fact I have shown you the eyelet on the open snare loop but in practice the right thumb should cover the eyelet as it must be compressed firmly between thumb and fore finger until the job is done.

2. Squeeze or compress the snare loop slightly inwards in a concertina fashion, still holding snare loop open with right hand at all times between thumb and first joint of forefinger.

3. You now work your thumb and tips of your four fingers down and around the loop pushing slack and squeezing straight with thumb which moves always on the underside of the wire loop in an anti clockwise manner as arrows show direction right along bottom of loop until your left thumb & fingers have reached to your right hand.

4. Release eyelet with your right hand and just hold snare wire with same hand

5. Take forefinger on left hand and push snare wire upwards just under eyelet, now pull left forefinger back and the eyelet should now spring backwards towards your right hand or back onto top of tealer eye if using a pegged snare.

6. Just repeat the process until you get the hang of it by squeezing or compressing loop and work in an anti clockwise fashion down around the bottom of the snare loop.

7. Once you get the hang of it and tension set, you then start and shape a nice big oval snare loop similar to what you see in the illustration.

People who are left handed hold the snare loop in left hand and work round the loop in a clockwise fashion.

Section 7 - The Snarer's Life

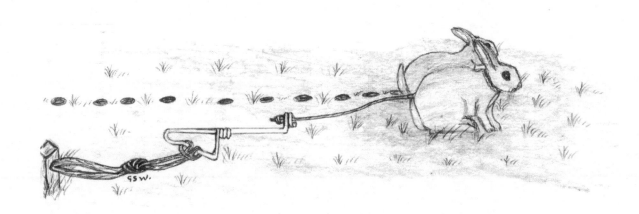

Chapter 27 - Tools for Snaring

In addition to the actual snares, the trapper working them requires a few other accessories which he would do well to carry along with him. Particularly when first commencing operations as a better standard of work achieved with their aid rather than without them. The tools in most regular employment are a bag, a trapper hammer, a pair of good quality sharp steel snips, a pair of short narrow nosed pliers, a wooden toggle, also a good sharp strong reliable pocket knife, spare pegs with twines attached, spare nooses, a bricklayer line pin lengths of twine, roll of electrical tape, and a small compact lightweight pair of field glasses. With all this latter equipment at hand the snareman may now be considered well provided for most occasions.

The trapper bag is most essential to carry bundles of snares - it must be light in weight made of strong material with separate compartments to carry separate items, a strong broad strap makes for comfortable carrying when transporting daily catches of rabbits. It also helps if the inside of the bag is constructed of washable material as dried blood and spillage of urine and faeces can cause an ordinary canvas bag to smell and rot if left unwashed for a period of time.

The hammer is a most essential piece of equipment and it must be robust and well made it is very efficient and labour saving when properly applied in the nature of the work to be done. I use a Thorr No. Two which consists of a barrel shaped head with cow hide protruding from each face, a hickory shaft with a brass cup hook screwed into its end. On purchasing a new hammer I make an automatic adjustment to it. By inserting it into a vice it is held firmly, then I take a hacksaw and cut the excess hide off each end leaving only a half inch protruding from both sides of the barrel head. It is then submerged into a pail of hot water to soften the firmly coiled hide which is then taken and each side of the hide end is beaten on a hard stone surface to mushroom the hide face over the sides of the barrel shaped head. This latter action ensures a nice malleable surface suitable for driving snare pegs into the ground without undue damage. The brass cup hook inserted into the end of the shaft serves the simple and effective purpose of rewinding an occasional snare which shows splayed strands through constant use and abuse from its victims. Pull the complete snare from the ground, insert the wire snare loop into the hook and close it tight. Hold the end of the noose at the eye of the tealer firmly in one hand, with the weight of the hammer suspended in the air, then proceed to spin the hammer round with other hand until a nice firm snare cable is formed then slip if off the hook and reshape and tension the loop. I devised this method many years ago as it takes only a few seconds compared with the old fashioned method of slipping a hazel tealer into the closed noose then by putting a foot on the opposite end of the snare to secure it one would then take the strain and laboriously proceed to rewind it by hand.

The snips are used to remove snares with broken strands. The short narrow nosed pliers are a valuable asset especially to bend the extended neck of the tealer eye back to its original right angle bend shape due to it being distorted and elevated by the continual daily abuses from captured rabbits, occasional hares, foxes etc. The little wooden toggle previously mentioned is such a simple tool yet it is also very valuable on the snare lines it consists of nothing more than a four inch length of an ash peg square or round in shape with a tapered point at one or both ends. The purpose of this latter object is to smooth out the snare cable once the rabbit has been despatched and removed from the snare. Stand on the securing peg with one foot and by inserting the fore and middle finger of the left hand into the snare noose pull it closed and taut to straighten out the snare cable and keep it taut, you then proceed to run the wooden toggle lengthwise up and down the wire this ensuing action smoothes out and firms up the snare wire. This handy little device saves a lot of daily wear and tear on the hands as its compact size enables it to be carried in one's pocket allowing for easy access. When it comes to lift the snares the little toggle is slipped in-between the double snare twines at the back of the knot between tealer and securing peg. Held between the middle finger of right hand it is used to withdraw the embedded snare peg from the ground with relative ease.

My pocket knife was purchased in Spain many years ago its overall length when closed is 4". It's a cheap knife but made of good steel and quite robust and still holds an extremely sharp edge today after years of cutting gutting and skinning tens of thousands of rabbits, foxes and many deer. How many manufacturers of today can justify a pocket knife ranging from forty pounds upwards to over a hundred pounds is nothing short of extortion and greed, the French opinel is an ideal product and costs less than ten pounds.

The bricklayer's line pin is also a valuable asset to the snare line. With its spear like shape which is sharpened on both sides to make it double edged and its flat enlarged circular nail like head it is an ideal tool to carry in one's pocket. When carrying out rabbit control throughout the dry summer months when the ground is hard and parched due to the lack of rain the line pin or a small flat faced screwdriver is pushed in to break the hard surface of the ground first which then allows for easier penetration of the wire tealer and the ash securing peg.

The carrying of extra twines and prepared snares are in case of fraying and breakages, the roll of tape is carried for emergencies such as accidental cuts and general little everyday upsets and repairs of the vehicle, broken bag straps or cracked hammer shafts etc. The tiny rubber coated binoculars of 10 x 25 magnification are invaluable for scanning the setting, location and surrounding area in the event of any nefarious prowler in the vicinity, or strange cars stopping on nearby roadsides. I recommend their use.

To be able to carry out any type of activity a person must be physically fit. Novice or professional each will require warm and durable clothes to suit the occasion, especially the harsh British climate which can be extremely unforgiving at times. I used to visit army and navy stores also local retail markets where some good attire can be purchased at a pretty reasonable price. I don't use waxproof jackets because of the smell. I find them unsuitable due to sweating and the rain runs off them and soaks your trousers. I use a good close fitting cap of the German military made from a soft olive green warm material with ear flaps which I purchased for less than three pounds at the local market. A product is now popular in this country is clothing from an American company called Realtree who manufacture a wide range of goods to suit every occasion in field sports, their products are of excellent quality produced to an exceptionally high standard and very fashionable. I find the quilted jacket light and very warm allowing good ventilation and free movement when fully clothed. In Realtree you are very well camouflaged while out snaring in either woodland or arable land. I fully recommend this new clothing to anyone who participates in field sports as much thought and design has been incorporated into producing this new range of garments. This attire allows for a more comfortable feeling and an easier and speedier setting pace when laying out a line of snares. A pair of Polaroid sunglasses are worth carrying along in your pocket as they are ideal to wear on bright or sunny days as they cut out the sun's glare and faint runs and tiny beats can be seen more clearly, trappers are very innovative people and I for one am not slow in incorporating modern equipment of any kind into this line of work to enhance any future success.

(A) - This is called a tapping stick I devised this tool which is nothing more than a length of hard wood ASH OR OAK cut to a length of 10" long and ¾" diameter. This stick is used on wet conditions should the ground at the snaring location be of a softer density. Instead of holding the head of your hammer in your hand and knocking the securing peg into the ground with the hammer shaft which becomes dirty, wet and slippery. It also chips the end of the shaft. That's why I use the tapping stick to tap the snare peg down deep into the soft ground (see illustration in Chapter 5). This keeps your hammer shaft clean and tidy. The tapping stick is only carried and used in wet weather.

(B) - Bricklayer's line pin, it has a few purposes of use. The line pin that I use I sharpened the two edges similar to a double edge knife which I have on occasions gutted rabbits with it. Its main purpose is to break the surface on hard ground to insert tealer pins especially in dry conditions, once again I hammer it in to the hard dry ground to make a slot before I insert the heeling peg which is 6" long 1¼" broad and $^3/_8$ths of an inch thick before the small peg is inserted and hammered into the ground. I pour a little water into the hole this little trick creates suction once the peg is down as the water slides up the peg giving it great holding power. Whyte showed me this method many years ago I have used this method many times over the years. I have also used the line pin similar to a wooden toggle to slip it through between the snare twines at the back of the central knot to extract the snare pegs.

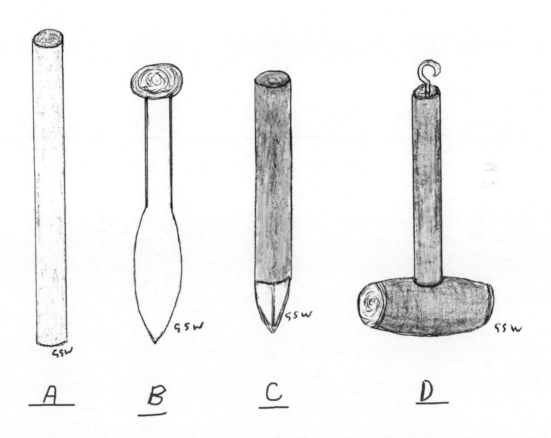

A   B   C   D

(C) Is just a length of hazel or ash, approx 5" long, ½" in diameter and pointed at one end. It is used to extract rabbit snare pegs from the ground by slipping it through the twines behind the central knot. It is also used to smooth out the snare cable after any catches. I have also used it to extract tealers from frozen ground by slipping it through the grip of the tealer and pulling.

(D) Thorr No. Two hammer with barrel type head with cow hide inserted into each side of the hammer head. An excellent tool for inserting securing pegs into the ground without damaging the tops of the pegs. The hammer shaft can also be slipped through between the twine to extract the pegs from the ground and as a lever to pull stubborn pegs from the ground. Insert the shaft between the twines from below. Let them slip down the shaft so far, then holding the hammer shaft in a vertical manner cup both hands around the top and then lever the pegs out. It can be used compact the ground before placing a snare or to smooth out snare cables. The hook in the end of the hammer shaft can be used to hang it up in the shed, to hang it from the snare bag, to spin up splayed snare strands in the cable or to pull the frozen in tealer from the hard ground after a few early morning frost. The use of all tools is endless if you apply a little thought into whatever you are doing.

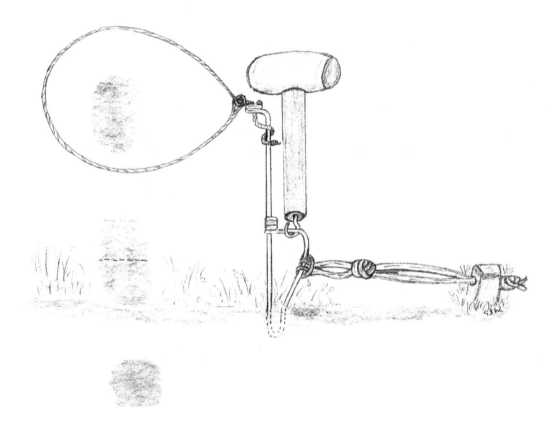

This illustration is a pair of ladies size secateurs only 7 inches long they have green rubber sleeves on the handles. They are very robust and of good quality steel, very sharp, compact and light to carry and fit into a jacket pocket with relative ease they can be purchased from the pound shop. I have three pair they are ideal for pruning back branches of bushes, weeds, especially hawthorn when setting hangers or fence line snares along old railway fence lines. They are an excellent little tool to carry when setting traps for rabbits, fox snaring, also when rat snaring to cut back briars or weeds of any type, even cutting twine and soft plastic tubing for tealer sleeves for fox snares. I purchased a couple of pairs of these little secateurs and took them over to Canada for my pro trapper mate Peter out in BC Canada he was very impressed with them and used them every day while beaver trapping and coyote snaring. They are easy to acquire and within everyone's price range.

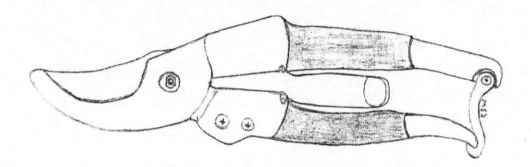

(B) is a small pair of pliers less than five inches long rubber coated handles very light and compact they fit perfectly into your hand and picked. I keep a pair in early every old jacket that I use when out snaring they are handy to bend the snare tealer necks back into place should a larger animal like a hare or a fox get caught in a rabbit wire and slightly elevates the tealer eye. I really don't have much of a problem with this because the neck of my tealers are short and tight which practically eliminates this problem. I even use them on occasions to slip them between the twines at the back of the knot to pull securing pegs from the ground these little pliers are only for light work on the snareline. These little tools can be purchased at the Saturday markets from 75p to a pound.

(C) is just a set of small nippers - like the rest is small less than five inches long light and easy to carry fits into the hand and pocket with ease. They are a handy little tool to cut off a damaged snare noose should any breakages of the cable occur a new snare noose can be attached in seconds while carrying out the line repairs out in the field once the new snare noose is applied the snare can be reset immediately without having to lift it and carry either one or more home to repair when it can be done right away, so remember to carry spare nooses, and twined pegs with you as it saves valuable time and problems while on the snareline.

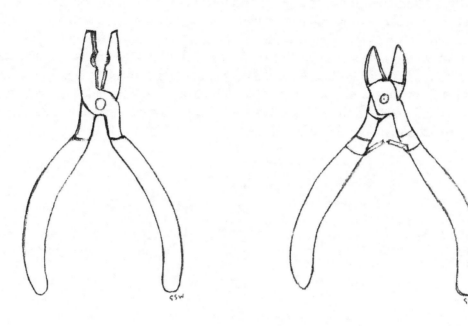

(D) This illustration shows a top quality pair of wire cutters. They are Knipex and German made this tool is designed and manufactured for hard work. I always carry these cutters with me all the time. I kept two pairs of these cable cutters one for cutting rabbit snare and fox snare use they cut steel fox snare cable as clean as a whistle. I have one pair left. The other pair packed in after 20 yrs the jaw snapped due to pure metal fatigue. I cut all my 2.5m wire rabbit tealers with them and 4 mil galvanized wire also 2.5 high tensile wire. I got them from a friend of mine. They are extremely robust and a top quality product. To buy products of this brand name are not cheap but well worth the money.

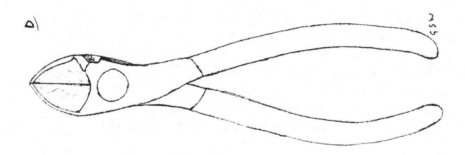

Chapter 28 - The Rabbit Snarer at Work.

This illustration shows a trapper setting a snare over the middle of a beat on a rabbit run. Once again notice the big loop which allows for any margin of error, this noose while moving to and fro in the wind will still catch effectively. Should a rabbit going outwards past a rabbit which is already caught on the same run, it is likely to return by another run and be caught on the way back. The experienced trapper can tell this by the position of the snare around the rabbit's neck.

Notice the marker pin at the side of the rabbit run. It is imperative that marker pins are used so that every snare counted out before setting can be accounted for when the snares are lifted. It is only pure laziness not to use them.

To carry snares, cock all the snare loops upwards and then drop the peg through the opened, tensioned snare loop, and carry them on your arm as this trapper is doing. Carrying snares like this keeps them from becoming entangled. All of my pegged snares are tied together in bundles of twenty five, easily set and accounted for.

Keep your hands clean and rub with a handful of grass or soil before setting. Keep your snares away from oil cans, rags etc in your car boot. Don't handle scented soaps, aftershaves or anything that has a lingering smell about it.

These 5lb to 6lb rabbits from 20 caught in 25 snares in Scotland. Note the snares are all tagged with the police ID numbers.

Professional Rabbit Snaring

Removing Fleas from a Game Bag

This illustration shows how to eliminate rabbit fleas from your game bag in a few seconds.

A. Take a couple of handfuls of nice dry soil from a mole hill or under a hedge bank, etc.

B. Put the soil into the open game bag.

C. Close the flap over the bag.

D. Hold bag tight and give it a few firm shakes.

E. Hold bag firmly in an upside down position.

F. Ejecting soil and fleas together.

G. You are now left with a nice clean empty bag, flea free.

Gutting Rabbits

After removal from snares and before gutting, 'thumb' every dead rabbit and squeeze pee from carcase. Gutting rabbits is a very simple job that must be carried out as soon as possible to avoid the body gassing up and the flesh from becoming tainted as the carcase will start to decompose quickly especially in hot weather. A greenish discoloured taint appears along the back of the kidney area, also around the belly due to the bacteria passing from the viscera to the flesh. There is also the task of having to carry all the extra weight of the intestines, therefore the object of the exercise is to eliminate and avoid giving yourself as much extra work as possible. Some people dig a hole and bury the intestines. There is no need to do this as again its work that can be avoided. I leave them for the gulls and crows to mop up.

There are a number of various methods used in the gutting of rabbits. The first and most important requirement is a nice sharp knife, it does not have to be a large one either. Another extremely useful implement is a miniature replica of a butcher's steel only 4 inches long. I purchased a few of these at a knife stall at the Scottish Game Fair for £2.50 each. They are an excellent buy. A few of my stalker friends also purchased them as they keep a fine sharp edge on your knife after a few downward strokes. I hold the rabbit around the hips with my left hand, the carcase is upside down allowing the viscera to drop downwards. I hold the knife in my right hand and then insert the tip of the blade into the abdomen and make a downward incision along the belly, being careful not to cut into the intestines and contaminating the flesh with faecal content and also unnecessarily contaminating your fingers at the same time minimising any mess. After every rabbit has been incised along the belly I insert my fore and middle fingers along with my thumb of my right hand and feel the stomach which is located just below the liver, on taking hold of the abdominal contents I then pull down and away from the carcase leaving the liver still contained in the body along with the offal.

When snaring throughout summer months dead animals gas up quickly with the stomach becoming distended. With this happening I use a different method of approach when gutting, I lay the rabbit on its back and pinch the belly skin between the forefinger and thumb of my left hand, I then take the knife which is held in the right hand and place the blade in a flat position against the belly then slit the pinched skin and open up the small incision with my fingers to avoid puncturing the distended viscera and any further contamination of the contents on removal from the carcase. After gaining a bit of practice at this exercise it won't be long before you get the hang of it and once the knack is obtained it will become an extremely simple task in the future.

A rabbit carcass has 12 ribs, but the right kidney lies slightly forward of the left one. A cat has 13 ribs but the kidneys lie opposite each other. This is so that you can tell the difference if offered a skinned and gutted carcass.

16 Rules for Safe Snaring

1.   Do not set pegged snares or fence line snares where livestock are grazing.
2.   Check perimeter fence lines for slack and broken wires and fence posts which will allow cattle to access grazing along the back of fence lines.
3.   Horses are quite large animals and can lean over fence lines to crop grass on the opposite side further away from the fence line than cattle.
4.   Do not set snares, pegged snares or hanging snares in the vicinity or on fence lines around game rearing coverts.
5.   Keep snares away from public footpaths.
6.   Always use good quality and strong snares. Use good quality materials, wire, tealers, twine and pegs.
7.   Never use badly kinked snares or ones with broken strands which are liable to break and cause needless suffering. Change any snares that become kinked or broken.
8.   Secure all snares firmly and properly.
9.   Count all snares set out and snares in when uplifting them.
10. Use a marker pin to account for every snare to avoid missing snares.
11. Avoid snaring near dwelling houses, to do so would endanger domestic pets, or ask owners to keep cats in for two days. If snaring around or near dwelling houses cannot be avoided notify tenants beforehand of how long the operation will take and to keep pets indoors until finished.
12. Despatch all animals quickly and humanely.
13. To avoid being scratched by rabbits, hold them firmly over saddle area in front of the hips to despatch quickly and remove snare loop.
14. Check all snares every day at daybreak.
15. Rabbit control throughout summer period, check snares three times a day morning, afternoon and evening.
16. Do not ever set snares and leave them unchecked.

101 General Snaring tips to Remember

1. The professional snare is approximately 23 inches long with a brass eyelet inserted at the end.
2. It consists of 6 strands of .455 or .457 wire spun into a tight smooth cable.
3. There is no wind down from the eyelets which ensures quicker closure and more humane as there is no ends protruding to cut into rabbit's neck.
4. A tightly wound cable is far stronger and more robust.
5. Slack wound snare cable does not tension properly, they kink more easily and are more prone to breaking readily due to the loose splayed strands kinking.
6. A professionally made large snare loop needs only a light tension incorporated into the tight wound cable as it runs smooth and closes very fast. It also retains its proper shape and form and sits in its catching position proudly.
7. The tighter wound cable is very strong and holds rabbits and hares with relative ease and beds well into the rabbit's neck fur. It also holds large fox cubs and also adults on occasions.
8. Eight and ten strand snares are a fallacy just a waste of extra wire, they are slower to close especially with wind down from the eyelet.
9. The professional deep pear shaped loop is $7^1/_2$" by approximately 6" deep and is designed in comparison to the dimensions of the rabbit's head.
10. The large snare loop covers a run properly and allows for any margin of error and catches rabbits easily, regardless of their direction of travel along the run.
11. A tiny loop does not cover a run properly, allows no margin for error and is prone to continual tripping and misses due to the rabbits knocking it over with its chest. May occasionally catch rabbits around the nose and top of head. Setting with a narrow loop causes misses and also odd catches around the top of the head in front of the ears.
12. Always make sure that the eyelet sits straight and slightly cocked forward to help eliminate any drag with no twist to left or right.
13. Professional sized loop offers no obstruction whatsoever on the run, unlike a tiny loop. The big loop offer a far larger kill area allowing plenty of room for the rabbit's head to enter more freely and due to its size is practically invisible, which allows good catches to be taken even in daylight hours.
14. Always set the snare loop at an angle when snaring sloping ground on hills and banks, tilt the noose to the angle of the bank slope.
15. Always set the snare on a straight section of the run. Never set where the beats are angled such as the last beats before a fork or the first beats on the fork itself. Make sure the beats are straight in line with each other. Face outwards along run when setting a snare.
16. Set snares out in the morning, especially in winter when darkness sets in during later afternoon, to let them air out properly. In summer months in longer daylight hours they can be set out later as the air is warmer.
17. Remove any stalks of grass or vegetation from the front and back of the snare loop to give rabbit's head a clear entry. Check snares at first light in the morning.
18. Remove any flecks of fur from the snare cable especially in wet weather as it clings to the wire and your hands and will impede the closing action of the snare.
19. A teardrop bead of water seen hanging dead centre from the base of the snare loop indicates that the noose is set perfectly in position on the run.
20. Wash or rub hands thoroughly with grass before setting and handling snares.
21. The pegged rabbit snare with the double knot is by far superior to other snares due to the swivelling action which helps eliminate kinking and breakages, compared to

snares where the loop is secured permanently to the tealer pin. Working with 100 to 150 swivelled snares to test the catch ratio to snares, out of 1500 rabbits I only had to replace four nooses due to only a strand or two braking. I had no breakages in the test period due to predators.

22. Snares should be set directly over the middle of the smaller sized beats.

23. Do not set snares in between the beats.

24. Do not set the large squatting beats as this denotes a stopping place.

25. Polaroid glasses are very useful in helping to recognise beats in short cropped grass especially on bright days. A peaked cap is also good in cutting out day glare.

26. To remake a beat after a catch is made out in the shorter grass, use the ball of your foot to tap the grass down and reset directly across the centre of it.

27. The presence of new growth such as tiny new shoots of grass and weeds on beat indicates the absence of any rabbit traffic along the run, so refrain from setting them.

28. Newly formed ill defined runs are always productive, more so than old established ones with new growth and old dry droppings usually have a dead look about them.

29. Where no runs are available at certain locations just make them by scuffing your boot along in the soil, or short crop and grass, or use a garden hoe.

30. An early morning survey will also reveal runs out in dew covered vegetation making them visible so that they can be marked out to set later.

31. Keep snares clean and away from abnormal odours, petrol, diesel, creosote, scented soaps, aftershave, tobacco. Also avoid handling ferrets. Wash hand and keep from being tainted.

32. Rabbits are prone to chewing red baling twine, dull it by rubbing it with a handful of dirt, the sun also bleaches it a lighter colour.

33. Black or brown twine is less visible and appears to be unaffected by the ultraviolet rays of the sun and less prone to chewing.

34. To cut twines in large numbers, quickly wind it around two nails on a board 12" apart and cut through at one end.

35. Make knot in twine three-quarters way along its length away from peg. This allows extra room to slip hammer shaft or hand toggle through when uplifting snares.

36. Do not attach long twines to a pegged snare. It only needs to be long enough to clear the point of the peg.

37. Change snare twines if signs of chewing or fraying is visible, therefore always carry spares as replacements. Always use twine that is weatherproof strong and non-shrinking, at times you will catch animals larger than rabbits.

38. Melt the ends of nylon twines at the knot at the peg top to stop splaying and fraying occurring.

39. To restrict a snared rabbit's movement on approaching it, stand on the snare wire first then stoop to retrieve it.

40. To eradicate fleas from your game quickly and most efficiently, open the bag and drop a few scooped handfuls of dry soil from a mole heap, hedge bank, or rabbit hole, or under a tree root, into the bag, then close the flap over and shake up and down then empty out the contents, it will be flea free in seconds.

41. To control a rabbit while despatching it humanely, hold it over the saddle or base of the back in front in the hips with the left hand, and dislocate the neck with the right hand in a split second down and forward movement.

42. A snare loop should be constructed to the dimensions of the rabbit's overall head size, six inches from below the jaw to the tips of the ears, and seven and one half inches for the breadth of the whiskers.

43. Rabbit snared around the top or the head or muzzle while using the proper loop size indicates the set is set too low and needs to be set higher.

44. Rabbits will only slip through a big snare loop if it is set too low, the noose must be set up to take the rabbit under chin.

45. Two rabbits can be taken with the one snare at the same time especially when the doe is caught first and a buck tries to mount her. The length of the remaining snare wire occasionally becomes wrapped around its back leg securing it also.

46. Buck rabbits caught in a snare will sometimes be attacked by other bucks, flecks of fur will be visible beside the victim, and in wet weather you can see the small bare patches more visibly over the back of the snared rabbit more so than in dry weather. I have watched this happen on occasions.

47. After despatching a rabbit thumb the abdomen to dispel any urine from the body.

48. Eviscerate snared rabbits as soon as possible as bacteria will pass from gut to belly flesh causing deterioration. A greenish colouring due to the gasses building up in the intestines causing the stomach to distend especially in hot weather.

49. Discard any rabbit carcase with enlarged liver with white ill defined spots and distended stomach (coccidiosis) if carcase is thin and emaciated. This organism is found in the soil.

50. An indication of myxomatosis in an area without seeing any rabbits with the disease is by viewing the droppings which are thin and an elongated pear shape instead of being a nice round or saucer shaped.

51. Snaring in longer grass helps hide the rabbits from certain predators.

52. Foxes and cats can affect your catch rate of rabbits by keeping them from travelling out at night due to their persistent nightly presence.

53. Use marker pins when working snares to avoid leaving any behind especially in longer grass in warmer weather, grass is growing daily.

54. Natural marker pins can be cut from hazel, willow or snowberry bushes as the branches are nice and straight they can also be made with crow feathers and wire.

55. Inserting marker pins at a low angle to the ground pointing out towards the snare makes them less visible to prowlers.

56. Crossing marker pin in an X fashion indicates a snare to either side.

57. Double wire tealer pins $9\frac{1}{2}$" long are ideal in length to give height and proper stability to a snare. Tealer pins ten or eleven inches long are ideal in longer vegetation to gain extra height and still keep the striking curve on the bottom of the snare loop in its central position.

58. A big loop also allows the tealer pin to be inserted into the ground well back from the edge of the run, avoiding any contact with the rabbit's body.

59. To construct tealer pins use 2.5 mil (English) galvanised wire it's by far stronger and does not flake. Do not use high tensile wire it is far too hard to work with.

60. A double eyed tealer is better if using the double knot swivelling system as the snares last much longer.

61. Degreasing and spraying wire tealers with Vauxhall leaf green auto paint camouflages and also cuts any oxidisation between the brass snare cable and the plain galvanised wire tealer.

62. To gain extra height with the snare in softer ground in higher vegetation stamp foot down at side of run to firm ground up, or slide eyelet up cable slightly reducing loop size or cut a small square of turf and bed it at side of run nice and stable then insert tealer pin into it.

63. Tealer pins can either be set in a 45° angle or in a vertical position.

64. When uplifting snares and on pulling the securing peg from the ground, hold it in right hand, then use the shaft of the wire tealer pin to scrape the soil from peg keeping it clean.

65. When carrying pegged snares the securing pegs should be slipped through the snare loop, then the nooses slipped over the left arm this keeps them neat and tidy and free from tangling and easy to select from the arm and to work with.

66. After a catch pull the snare cable taut and rub hammer shaft or ash toggle up and down snare wire to smooth it out before retensioning and shaping the snare noose.

67. A snare peg of approximately 8" long is sufficient to hold any rabbit or hare and even foxes on occasions.

68. Chamfer the edge of the peg head to help repel water and splintering. Drill a $^3/_{16}$th hole an (1 $^1/_4$") from the top for the twine to be inserted. A round peg can be pulled free in wet weather.

69. A longer more tapering point on a peg is easier than a short square peg, as the long point can penetrate the soil easier giving a tighter fitting grip especially when the ground is moist to create good suction, flat broad pegs don't turn.

70. Inserting a peg into bone dry ground offers no suction, after a heavy fall of rain the pegs can be extracted easily, so watch weather forecast and pull snares up beforehand. A smooth peg retains less soil.

71. Snare pegs can be cut from elder, ash, hazel, larch, holly or oak.

72. Check over all snares after each operation, and replace any broken pegs or repair others. Also check twines for chewing and fraying, also for broken or badly kinked snare strands and broken snares.

73. Carry spare snare nooses, twines and pegs for on the line repairs every day.

74. A bricklayer's steel line pin or a small flat faced screwdriver are handy tools to carry, to break the surface of dry hard ground to insert either tealer pins or pegs.

75. When setting pegged snares try and avoid any slack in the twine location between tealer and securing peg which eliminates any play.

76. A tealer pin inserted in a vertical position gives more stability and holding power than one set at an angle.

77. Avoid using soft white treated wood for snare pegs as it just bursts and splits.

78. When looping snare twine through the central loop in a single wire tealer catch the double wires at the back of the loop, not the single wire at the front of the loop.

79. A single wire tealer will turn in dry ground in high winds especially if struck by large blowing leaves, e.g. small twigs, sycamore and ash steams.

80. Where runs are extremely faint along hedgerows and field headlands, just make them more prominent with your foot and set them, it does not put the rabbits off from using them whatsoever.

81. In high weed or grass stamp on a faint beat with your boot and set the snare directly in the middle of the new made beat, it gives the rabbit a good landing and take off point and works every time.

82. In fenced off areas set snares along the back of the perimeter fences as the rabbits follow along the length looking for exit holes.

83. To give a shorter peg better holding power in softer ground stamp it down, then hammer in the peg below ground level. Then hold head of hammer in hand and drive the peg deeper by striking it with the end of the shaft, also slide twine down double tealer to the base and insert it this allows the peg to be driven in deeper.

84. In woodland in softer ground conditions a length of a pliable dead branch can be broken off and inserted between the twines deep into the ground. This holds very well. Where legal a length of branch can also be inserted further along the run to act as a kill stick, this also takes the strain of the snare peg.

85. A Thorr No. Two hammer with rolled hide ends has good weight for inserting securing pegs without damaging their tops.

86. Should any wire strands become splayed on a snare cable pull it from the ground and loop noose over end hook on hammer shaft and spin up tight in seconds, either that slip noose over top of dead rabbit's head, or both back feet and spin the body round. This also tightens up loose strands. Then reset snare, this eliminates old laborious method of hand winding with piece of stick.

87. Setting fresh ground, set snares as far out as possible take a kill the following morning, and then lift snares and set further back nearer field edge take another kill the following morning and repeat this process for a third morning, then lift the snares. This method takes rabbits wary of their own kinds screaming every night when caught as the others become reluctant to advance outwards into the field.

88. The hoop snare consists of a length of 4 mil or high tensile galvanized fence line wire bent over your knee there are no hard and fast rules as to length, just cut it to suit ground soils and density. Normal length 44 inches long. High tensile wire can be used also.

89. Hoop snares can be used to snare amongst adult sheep only, not amongst tiny lambs. When grazing the sheep bump wire loop and walk around it, an open pegged snare loop would catch them by the feet. Do not set open pegged snares amongst livestock (absolutely never).

90. The hoop snare can be set to snare rabbits coming over the top of dry stone walls or running up their vertical face. They will also hold hares, they can also be used to snare squirrels and mink.

91. When woodland snaring the hoop system helps to avoid deer being caught by the feet, a larger version can be used to hang fox snares.

92. Do not set pegged or hoop snares indiscriminately. Always set in a straight line or in some sort of pattern. They are far easier to check and collect when finished.

93. Count all snares before setting them out and recount when finished snaring, by using marker pins of some sort every snare will be accounted for.

94. Occasionally a snared rabbit will have the snare cable tangled around a back leg, should any blood and hair be attached to the wire pluck a small handful of grass and run it back and forth along the snare's length until removal, then smooth out cable and reset.

95. Do not hang snares up on rusty nails unless they have twine loops through the nooses to suspend them, otherwise it would corrode the brass wire.

96. Straighten out any kinks in the snare cable before smoothing it out with ash toggle or hammer shaft, running kinks into a snare weakens it by leaving only a few strands to take the strain instead of six.

97. On hard stony gravelly type ground I have used six inch nails to secure snares, where pegs would not suffice.

98. Length of garden wire can be used to secure snare loops to branches and briars on occasions at certain locations.

99. In fields of grass grown for silage it is often heavily fertilised with nitrate making the grass luscious green colour. Rabbits do not like it much as it scours them so it is best to wait until the first crop has been cut, then set it with snares, rabbits prefer established grazing fields.

100. When snaring golf courses where the grass is cut very short and rabbits are coming out onto the grounds where no runs are visible, ask the greenkeeper to let a border of grass grow 4 ft wide 4" long along the edges of rough ground where broom, whin, rhododendron banks grow, once the beats become visible the rabbits can then be snared quickly and the grass recut.

101. Wildlife and Countryside Act states that all snares must be checked daily BY LAW.

Keeping Snares in Good Working Order

The pegged snare is the main instrument in the trapper's armoury as he wages war on a daily basis with his old adversary the wild rabbit. Man has tried every devious means to eradicate this humble creature from the land. Where rabbits reside in large numbers serious damage will occur especially to crops and in young woodland tree plantations etc. The order of the day is to control their numbers to an acceptable level not total eradication of any creature which in my opinion is negative thinking as there are many other animals or birds whose survival depends upon the rabbits. Lest we forget this same creature helped save us from starvation throughout the war years therefore it deserves a bit of respect and consideration as it is a very resilient and is a natural born survivor. Everyday of its life it is fraught with the danger as every man's hand is turned against it as it battles to survive all the ground and aerial predators, disease and severe inclement weather conditions.

Therefore the humble rabbit deserves respect. It will be a sad day to walk in the countrywide without seeing a few rabbits sitting out along the hedges and field edges on a summers evening. As there is many people of all walks of life derive much pleasure in viewing them and watching their antics as they walk in the countryside. All countrymen like myself who pursue the rabbit as their quarry have the highest respect for it. It also helps many people in employment such as gamekeepers, pest controllers and rabbit trappers and many others who enjoy a bit of sport, ferreting, lamping, long netting, bushing and snaring. It also keeps field sports companies in permanent business supplying all the equipment deemed necessary for rabbit control work. Getting back to the snare which is one of the most efficient simplest and deadliest cost effective tools ever devised to catch large numbers of rabbits over a short period of time. Like all working tradesmen the trapper is no different in his line of work.

He also needs tools to apply them daily to complete the job in hand. While the snare being the preferred unit to suit his line of work whether it is pegged snares or fenceline snares, the professional trapper always keeps his wires in good working order showing humanity and respect for animal welfare. This is only right as there is no place for cruelty, ignorance, idleness and sheer downright laziness in the line of work. Neglect can't be tolerated at any time which is bound to create hostility with the media, which we field sportsmen can well do without. All snares should be well looked after and kept in good condition for the job in hand, check the number of snares before settling them out in the field, recount them when uplifting the snares after every operation. Check all snare nooses individually for kinking, splaying and broken strands which needs immediate replacement should this occur. Check tealers for any elevation at the neck also checking the swivelling action is in working order and straighten out any visible distortion in the wire. The twines should also be checked for clean bites, chewing, fraying, fatigue caused by continual use out in inclement weather and bleaching due to the ultraviolet rays of the sun.

Pegs should be checked for any splitting, breakages, burst and splayed points, cracks near the twine hole etc. Another simple trick I do is to melt the ends of the twine at the knot end protruding from near the top of the securing peg. This action keeps the knot clean and of a neat and tidy appearance as shown in illustration (B) while illustration (A) displays an untidy splayed and bushy effect similar to a shaving brush. This poor finish retains more stoor, dirt and grass and weed particles, which must be removed on checking after every snaring operation. Carry spare nooses, twine extra pegs, extra breakaway links when using breakaway snares, carrying out these regular checks keeps your snares in good working order ready for immediate use on the next outing.

Chapter 29 - The Life of a professional Snarer

General Little Tips & Tricks to keep in Mind

A QUICK REFERENCE SEQUENCE FOR THE READER

1. When snaring in higher grass along fencelines, hedges, field edges, or pegged snaring in higher growth in various locations, always check weather conditions due to the fact should heavy wind and rain arrive creating wet conditions, the longer wet grass falls over onto the snare loops particularly blocking and lowering them therefore preventing you from making a catch.

2. Snaring along smooth galvanised wire fencelines, pluck some soft grass and wind tightly around fenceline wire. Then attach snare noose tightly around grass on the wire, this helps prevent the rabbit pulling the snare noose along the full length of the fenceline wire between the posts taking the rest of the set snare nooses with it reducing your catch rate. The grass helps snare cable to secure a better fenceline grip.

3. Snaring rusty fenceline wires check for beads and blisters of rust on the wires if they are present a couple of quick rubs with a small file or a piece of rough sandpaper cleans the wire strand making it more smoothly or once again I found that winding some soft grass around the rusty fenceline wire cushions the snare, always leave a gap between the first and second snare loop while winding the snare cable around fenceline wire before trapping the second loop with the third turn of the snare cable as this allows play and freedom of movement of the snare cable as the captured rabbit moves to and from. Should the snare noose be attached to the rusty fenceline wire with beads of rust being present and no gap left between snare cable turns on fenceline your snares can snap and the quarry lost.

4. Pull all standing grass and weed stalks away from the front and back of all snare loops whether pegged snares or fenceline snares keeping the snare loop free from any obstructions at all times.

5. When snaring rylock fencelines with the square mesh always make a little halfmoon shape outward bending the snare cable behind the eyelet this is to allow a little clearance between the running eyelet of the snare noose and the coils of the fenceline wire at the top right hand corner of the square mesh. If left handed it will be attached on the left hand side.

6. Remove your empty snare bag place it on the ground and kneel upon it when setting fencelines where there are nettles, thistles, stones or briars growing where you may have to reach under overhanging tree branches to set snares in awkward locations kneepads can be used if so desired. A small pair of secateurs are very hand to trim back any protruding briars, nettles, thistles, weeds or overhanging little branches causing any obstructions.

7.   It pays to carry a few basic simple little tools with you on the snareline such as secateurs, snips, pliers, knife, wooden toggle, hammer with cup hook inserted into the end of the shaft, roll of electrical tape as each and every one of these tools has its daily use out on the snareline, to carry out on the line repairs, right there and then when required, to keep snareline operations flowing smoothly at all times. Replacing nooses with broken strings, straightening tealers, repointing pegs, or replacing them along with chewed or fraying twines, toggle for smoothing out snare cables after a catch, hammer and hook to spin up any splayed snare cable strands, pulling out frozen tealers and securing pegs, electrical tape to cover cut ringers or repair broken straps etc.

8.   Railway lines are great strongholds for holding large numbers of wild rabbits, where a rail line passes through arable flat ground and you can see over from either wide of the line always set both sides of the line with snares within both fencelines or if they are too thick and overgrown and impenetrable set out peg snares on either side in the surrounding fields where the runs exit from the railway bankings. Why set both sides you may ask. Well it's like this. First of all should the actual fenceline wires be snared the rabbits will squeal with the actual shock at being caught and restrained they start pulling to and fro, the fenceline wires will rattle and twang after a night or two of this commotion other rabbits not knowing what the unseen danger is will then start going out to feed in the field on the opposite of the track where they too will be captured. So it pays to always set both sides, the same with woodland strips also thick bushy hedgerows. Should a railway banking be of the type where the lines run along the top of a steep; rising bank for quite a long distance then one side only may be set unless you so desire to set out both sides of the line.

9.   Many fencelines erected nowadays have the wires tensioned and the staples are inserted only to a depth of halfway which allows the fenceline wires to twang and thump against the vertical posts inserted to hold the whole structure of the fenceline. This causes extra noise along with the captured rabbits squealing in the hours of darkness which is heard all along with the vibrations the full length of the fenceline, then many rabbits will refrain from exiting through the fenceline to venture out in the surrounding fields to feed, to help reduce the twanging and thumping of the fenceline wires, take a hammer a few days beforehand and drive every second staple tightly into the posts all along the fenceline which helps to reduce any disturbance at night under cover of darkness.

10.   In wet weather rabbits will often prefer to go out from under hedges or roadside banks and fee along roadside verges where the grass is cut short rather than venture out into longer grass or crop fields than get wet.

11.   In locations of clear cut woodland where rabbitproof fencing has been erected around the designated area set pegged rabbit snares all along the inside at the back of the perimeter wire to catch the enclosed rabbits as they travel all the way around the enclosure looking for an exit. Snares set at 25 yd intervals will account for many rabbits in situations like this.

12.   Along the edges of crop fields rabbits eat the cereal in half circle patches these irregular shaped eaten places often vary in size which I have personally paced them out at a distance from five yards in length to 25 yards plus in length. Therefore if you look carefully a few yards out from the field edge you will see runs that lie parallel to the perimeter which I call visiting runs similar to railway lines which run between

these heavily cropped locations around the field connecting each location as rabbits pass along these trails to and fro from these interconnecting feeding sites set these runs with pegged snares as many rabbits can be taken on a daily basis from them, when setting these parallel runs stagger the snares one forward and one back to prevent a captured rabbit tripping the other set snare should it be set too close.

13. When snaring in wet weather conditions always remove any flecks of fur from the snare loop before resetting as it could impede the fast running action of the noose.

14. When pegging or rabbit snares on open runs always face outwards the same way as the rabbit is travelling, this gives a more accurate placement and setting technique also a higher catch rate.

15. When setting certain locations, at times the runs may not appear to be very prominent to the naked eye. A trick I use is to look into the sun, this appears to make the runs stand out more easily to see. Do not look directly at the sun. It's the ground itself that it being viewed. Should a slight shower of rain occur this makes the runs stand out better and more visible to the eye.

16. At times I have been asked to set pastures that had been grazed by cattle, then sheep were put into this same field for a week or so to crop what grass was left and to put it mildly it was not much as it was more like a bowling green. The head keeper even remarked to the farm manager do you think this man has x-ray eyes. I looked the field over and left it for a week to see if there would be more growth would generate. It was October and the weather was quite nice and not cold. Although rabbits were in residence throughout the small larch wood bordering the motorway banking the field was not showing great rabbit signs such as runs etc. The field faced south the sun was up so I went over to my vehicle as I had an idea again. I had a good pair of Polaroids which I collected and wore when I re-entered the field. I walked along the front of the south facing woodland with these glasses on checking out the ground. I started setting snares around 40 yds out I was actually following the droppings out and started to find faint signs of beats which I made more prominent with the ball of my foot. On occasions I found a few faint runs that I also set. I managed to get fifty wires set that morning. The keeper asked how I fared and I explained the situation not expecting many rabbits. The next morning I had snared 30 rabbits out of the fifty snares set. The Polaroids worked well cutting out the glare giving good clarity of the ground. I have used Polaroids for a few decades now on certain occasions and found they worked well and most suitable in the latter type conditions.

17. The use of a longer tealer pin is most advisable when setting in high growth as it gives good height to the snare noose and helps to retain the striking curve on the bottom of the loop across the middle of the beat. Unlike a shorter tealer where the loop would be cocked up at a higher angle to gain height.

18. Don't be afraid to straighten out a rabbit run at times take your boot and just stamp the part of a run straight then make the beats with the ball of your foot. I do the same along hedges, field edges, bankings along fencelines. When a catch circle destroys a run in longer grass join the run up again by kicking a straight line through the circle to join the run upon the opposite side, then stamp new beats out with the ball of your foot. In setting locations where there are no visible runs just make them it works every time.

19.   Use a bricklayer's line pin or a small flat faced screwdriver to break a hard ground surface to insert tealer pins in dry hard conditions.

20.   Make a pilot hole in the ground using a half inch diameter steel spike with a nice tapering bullet point. I use this trick in dry hard ground due to the fact it saves broken pegs. I also carry a couple of 500 mil Coke bottles full of water to pour about one inch of water into the hole which creates good suction and holds the peg well in the ground, to extract the peg quickly in seconds just hammer the steel spike down into the ground next to wooden snare peg give spike a couple of light taps to each side pull it out, tap the peg lightly on opposite side from hole and simply extract it from the ground.

21.   When making wire snare tealers I spray them with dark grey primer, once primer has dried I respray with Vauxhall leaf green paint applying the paint helps camouflage pegged snares from human eyes. It also saves the ends of the snare nooses which is wrapped around wire tealers from oxidisation which can occur on occasions between the double knot end of the noose the plain galvanized tealer wire.

22.   Remember when setting pegged rabbit snares insert the tealer pin at the side of the run allowing only the large snare loop to cover the run itself, keep the twines straight between tealer pin and securing peg so that the whole system remains tensioned from loop to peg ready for that initial strike as the rabbit hits the snare noose. This system of setting allows for high catch rates of rabbits as the strain is taken immediately due to the fact there is no slack or play in the system.

23.   Despatch rabbits quickly, on removal from snare noose, thumb urine from carcase immediately, eviscerate as soon as possible to stop bacteria passing from gut to flesh and flanks.

24.   A snare peg with a long tapering point has good holding power once it is inserted into the ground due to the fact of its shape and cuts through the soil like a knife which clings very tightly to the whole of the peg creating good suction in normal ground conditions.

25.   A snare peg with a blunt short tapering point pushes the soil downwards underneath it as it is inserted in the ground which is harder to drive down into the ground due to the shape of the peg's point it does not hold as tight like a longer tapering pointed peg does.

26.   A four or five inch ash or hazel toggle a half inch in diameter is lighter and more easily carried in a pocket than your hammer when it comes to uplifting your snares, as the small uniform shaped toggle pointed at one end slips through between the snare twines behind the knot with relative ease making it easier to extract the snare pegs. On certain occasions though the hammer itself is needed for greater leverage.

27.   When forming the middle knot in the snare twine place the position of the knot nearer the tealer pin leaving a larger space between it and the securing peg which allows for easier access of wooden toggle or hammer shaft.

28.	Short flat broad elderberry heeling pegs with a double edge tapering point similar to a commander dagger style are extremely hard, light and very robust once they are cut and dried dimensions are 6" long 1¼" broad ³/₈" thick, they are excellent for use in pasture grass being broad and flat they don't turn in the ground and have good holding power for rabbits, hares and large fox cubs.

29.	Snare stabilisers have various names that they are known by in Scotland, e.g. tealer pins, set pins, star pin.

30.	In the winter months when the onset of darkness is around 4.30 pm in the late afternoon set snares out in the morning and be off the snaring field before 2 pm due to the relative humidity in the air to allow the set snares to air out. Throughout summer months when carrying out pest control when the weather is warn and drier the snares can be set out morning and afternoon. I check my snares three times a day throughout summertime.

31.	Should you find it difficult to see runs out in the grass or in young grass crops look carefully for dirt on bent leaves from rabbit's feet or take a bag with marker pins and go to the said field early in the morning. There you will see the runs in the early morning dew, place a marker pin at the side of each run then take your wellington boot and stamp along the dewy run for a few feet then make beats with the ball of your foot to make the runs more visible to your eye then set them a few days later, don't be afraid to make runs where they are needed even in flat bare ground.

32.	The ultraviolet rays of the sun appear to bleach various colours of baling twine except black twine. Over a few seasons of use the black coloured twine appears to be rarely chewed by rabbits compared to other colours especially orange and red.

33.	To gain height with a snare cut a small square of turf out of the ground and place it by the side of a run then give it a slight press with your foot to stabilise it, then proceed to insert the tealer pin into the block of turn to gain extra height.

34.	When snaring in high growth on a regular basis make and keep a couple of hundred snares with longer tealers up to 11" long to gain height and to keep the striking curve over the run.

35.	Straight hazel pins cut at 18" long to 24" long are excellent for snaring in high flora where the ground is soft, the hazel tealers should be ⁵/₈" diameter and pointed at the bottom. This type of tealer can be inserted then tapped down into the softer ground giving a firm and stable grip. Allowing for good height to set snares in the higher growth insert a short wire tealer pin lengths through the hazel peg one inch down from the top, see illustration on this type of tealer pin.

36.	Staggering the wire legs of a hoop snare on either side of a rabbit or hare run gives better stability and holding. Using the wire hoop system in woodland if the ground feels soft stamp ground on either side of run with heel of your boot compacts the soil and firming it up before setting. Small lengths of twigs a half inch in diameter stabilises hoop snares immensely by inserting them down into the ground alongside the wire legs.

37.   When spinning up snare nooses by hand it is better to use a heavier weight of around seven pounds as it keeps the wire strands taut and stops any movement or dancing while the weight is spinning, which can be caused by light weight making ripples in the snare cables. Remember also all strands must hang straight and taut together before spinning commences. Should a strand hang loose heavy rippling will occur in snare cable. Do not over tighten the snare cable.

38.   Do not set snares on large squatting beats covered with droppings as this donates a stepping place on the run these beats can be from 10"-12" long.

39.   Set snares over the middle of small beats four inches long or look for small daps a couple of inches in diameter set right in the middle same as an ordinary beat.

40.   Make sure snare loop sits straight across middle of the beat, not at a slight 45° angle, many beginners and amateurs make this mistake not realising they are doing this, setting a snare loop at this latter angle is a bad mistake which will result in knocked snares.

41.   Do not set snares over grass in between beats on the jump, always set across the middle of small beats.

42.   Do not set snares on angled beats misses will occur.

43.   Pick beats that are running in a straight line as you will get a more accurate setting and a higher catch rate.

44.   Should you come across angled beats stamp them into straight line with your foot then remake beats with the ball of your foot.

45.   Set snares higher in wet weather as the rabbits rise slightly higher keeping their bellies dry.

46.   Learn to establish viable rabbit runs from runs that are no longer being used by being observant and developing a keen eye.

47.   A viable rabbit run with regular rabbit traffic is prominent the beats are well padded sometimes down to the bare earth, toenail holes will be visible so will moist fresh droppings on grassy beats that are well padded the grass will be flat with dirt showing from the rabbit's feet as it travels along the run bounding from beat to beat all the way along its length.

48.   A rabbit run that is dead with no regular traffic passing to and fro along its length looks dull and lifeless, droppings are dried up and with no visible moistness with a dead appearance. The beats will have new found growth appearing through the ground such as tiny fresh grass shoots around ¼" to $^3/_8$" in height along with fine tiny weed leaves also appearing alongside the new grass shoots similar to minute chickweed, called speedwell. This fresh growth will also appear growing in the rabbit's scrapes nearby the runs. Therefore develop good visual awareness and well practised eye like the pros or you will be checking empty wires in the morning.

49.   If you want to make large catches of rabbits forget the old traditional system with the four inch loop and three and four fingers high nonsense. Using the large loop system is the way to go forward your catch rate will rise tenfold. The big loop system is certainly not a new method as it was used by my mentors eight decades ago and by their mentors before them. These professionals earned their livelihood from catching large numbers of rabbits therefore their methods were kept secret from the public. The choice is yours, you can be happy with about a dozen rabbits from a hundred traditional snares in a morning or 80s and over 90 out of 100 big loop snares set higher.

50.   Always keep this in mind to attain LARGE CATCHES.

        A. PATIENCE
        B. A KEEN EYE
        C. PRECISION SETTING
        D. EQUALS DEATH

Unusual Snaring Locations

Over the decades I have been asked to snare rabbits in one or two unusual places. I have snared cemeteries where the rabbits were eating newly laid and freshly planted flowers. They were scraping and digging on the short grass all over the border their droppings were everywhere the grass was burned brown with urine and droppings, graves were being tunnelled into. The rabbits can be quite destructive. Long nets and stop nets are good in these locations. Should the cemetery be enclosed by a boundary wall a place I found that they like to hide is behind large gravestones that lie close to the inside of the boundary wall. I netted a lot from these locations as I made my spaniel, Bell, hunt along the bottom edge of the wall and she would mark any rabbits hiding behind the gravestones which were easily netted. Check all the shrubbery, bushes and any surrounding woodland. Parts of the cemetery sectioned off with beech hedges look for runs here. Remember discretion is important in and out as quickly as possible. At a church fête I was asked to go over to look at the lawn which was at the back of this really old country church and there was a single rabbit run like the M6 motorway stretching right over the full length of the lawn in the short grass. The rabbits once again were eating the flowers and shrubs and their usual scrapes and diggings. The next day I pegged three snares along this run on the lawn the beats were padded to almost dirt, five rabbits were snared from this run alone and more that were entering through the bottom of the surrounding privet hedge.

Football grounds were other locations I have snared. One location a player almost broke his leg in a deep scrape on the pitch, a lot of the rabbit runs are already made for you where the lines are already marked out around the pitch edge, the penalty boxes, the halfway lines etc. Look along these places and you will see beats and droppings all along many of these manmade runs. Short heeling pegs are ideal at these locations out on the short grass. Some pitches are bordered all around with an ash track surrounded by steep grassy banks where you will at times see well defined runs. Where the rabbits usually live in burrows and rough ground at the back of these bankings they emerge at night from their residence to travel up and over the top and down the other side to feed out on the short grass on the playing field. Walking along the edge of the pitch you will at times see single beats where the rabbits spring from the track up onto the short grass. Set a wire on each of these single beats and also the downward runs on the surrounding grass bankings and set the man made lines on the playing field itself. After the snaring operation is finished any burrows can then be ferreted. My cousin Chick was the groundsman on a local football ground. I taught him to snare and he was catching over a hundred rabbits every season. He enjoyed eating rabbits and he would share them out to local pensioners like himself. The secretary of the local football grounds asked me to go and look over their playing field as it had been relaid a couple of years back with Astroturf the rabbits have been going out onto this Astroturf and eating it. There were a number of bare patches hundreds and hundreds of droppings and the damage caused to this fake turf was a mess. I know exactly where the majority of these rabbits are in residence therefore the next few dry days the rabbits will be ferreted by my friend Alex and I. The last time it was ferreted over thirty were accounted for in a very short period of time as they are burrowed into the back of one of the steep grassy bankings which are a pleasure and easy to net and ferret. Other locations I've snared are roadside bankings, motorway bankings, railway bankings, canal bankings, river and stream bankings, hospital grounds, private grounds, walled estate gardens. In 60 years of snaring you name it and I have snared it.

Unusual Catches

Catching Two Rabbits with one Snare

Catching two rabbits with one snare as shown in the illustration occurs every now and then. Some people have never had this experience. This can happen only once in a while especially at the turn of the year in the months leading up to springtime when the rabbits become amorous in milder weather and the bucks turn their attention to the opposite sex. On the ground you will notice the rabbits are beginning to 'mark', a term used by pro trappers to indicate rabbits' presence on the ground by diggings, and shallow scrapes, fresh droppings and flecks of fur lying around which indicates the presence of bucks chasing does. What happens is a doe will be caught in the snare by the neck and along comes a buck with amorous intentions and tries to mount the doe rabbit and in doing so the doe is running around in the snare which wraps around one of the buck's back legs it then becomes tangled by the snare wire and it too becomes trapped therefore the trapper gets an extra bonus when checking his snareline in the morning.

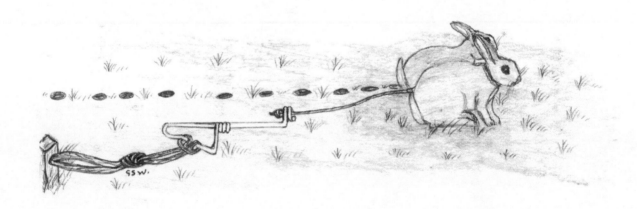

Snared and Tangled

Whilst checking rabbit snares in the morning you may on occasions come across a scene such as depicted in this illustration. As I have previously said all rabbit runs should be set according to conditions some of which are similar and there are others that differ due to the type of terrain at that said point of the snaring location in question. There would be small undulations, rough grass, longer tussocky grass and so forth the amount is endless. Therefore many snares can lie set roughly at the same height and a number of others will be set higher. On most occasions all rabbits will be neck snared but little variables happen now and again such as a rabbit caught around the neck and shoulder, one may be caught around the hips.

The rabbit in the illustration was neck snared but as it was running somehow the snare cable has become tangled around its back leg. Different things happen out on the snareline that just can't be explained at times even though the pegged snares were well set with the large noose sitting proudly covering the run properly across the middle of a small beat. These little quirks can happen to anyone even the professionals it's just a fact of life even although we strive for perfection it doesn't always work out the way we want it.

A Spiritual happening on the snareline

Many years ago while out on the snareline I experienced a rare spiritual phenomenon. It was a beautiful September morning. It was warm, the sun was splitting the sky, the birds were all whistling from under the still leafy canopy on the trees, the only other noise that could be heard was from the early morning motorists as they passed by on their way to work on the country road which bordered a woodland strip of trees on the west side of a large field. There were quite a number of rabbits in residence in the wooded location. There were a mixture of mature oak, ash, sycamore and beech. The undergrowth was a labyrinth of bushes, stinging nettles, willowherb and bramble briars and old broken dry stone dyke run the full length of this woodland strip, this dilapidated structure was held in place by an equally old wire fenceline it was an ideal structure for stoat and weasels of which I have seen on many occasions working their way along this old edge feature whilst carrying our previous snaring operations in the past.

This day I'm referring to was just one of these lovely days, it was great to be alive and enjoying the tranquillity of the countryside. I parked my vehicle in an old open gateway which led to the woodland strip of trees to a large short cut stubble field which ran away downhill to a woodland at the bottom. The previous day I had pegged out 70 snares approximately 50 yards out from the field edge, as I approached the start of the snareline I could see a fair number of rabbits sitting clapped in the snares all the way down the field. I worked my way down the snareline despatching rabbit after rabbit and thumbing them then placing each and every rabbit beside the marker pins marking the snares on every run. About three quarters of the way down the line, I noticed a black shape clapped in the stubble in the last snare on the line at a first glance thought that it was a large feral cat then realised that it was a large black rabbit. I had another five rabbits to dispatch before I got to the black one.

Suddenly I became aware of a full bodied spirit person standing a few yards from me out in the stubble, as I have mentioned before I come from a psychic family these type of happenings don't faze me at all. I said good morning to my spirit friend, who was a tall beautiful elegant lady from the Victorian era, middle aged she wore a long light blue coloured crinoline dress with a matching wide brimmed hat which sat at an angle on her head covering part of her shiny black hair. Helen was her name she was well educated and very well spoken and in a soft and pleasant voice she said *"Glen do not kill that black rabbit because the Lord loves to see beautiful creatures that he has created"*. I said to Helen, *then the Lords will, will be done*. The moment I spoke these words she disappeared completely leaving me alone standing in the stubble field.

After dispatching the other rabbits, I walked over to the last snare which held the black rabbit and stood and admired him. It was a large rabbit over five pounds in weight, its coat was glistening as if it had been washed and blow dried, its large brown eyes were shining like the Cullen diamond in the morning sunlight. It had an all over radiant appearance it was just a picture of health in perfect condition. I said to this rabbit *you are a beauty and the Lord said you must be set free*. As I leaned forward to remove the snare noose from its neck it clapped down tight, on removing the noose I said *you're free my friend* but it did not move. I picked it up and checked it over it was fine. I laid it down gave it a clap and a wee pat on the backside then suddenly it sprang to life was off running like the wind heading for the woodland strip. Suddenly a few yards from the old drystone wall it stopped turned round and sat upright, we both looked at each for about ten seconds then the large buck was gone over the broken wall into the undergrowth.

A few weeks later half a mile north of this field I was checking a line of snares above a valley, lo and behold there were another two black rabbits caught. It was a Sunday morning and jokingly I said *Lord these two lads should have been in the Kirk and they would not have been caught this morning but I take it that these fellow's have to be freed also* which they were of course. I never killed a black rabbit since that day, every black rabbit I snared has always been set free. I believe I was being tested by the Lord that day to see if I would obey his instructions and his will which I did. I still always think about that day and will never ever forget it until the day I die, then I will probably get the answer on the other side.

Conclusion

Snaring is not a new method in trapping wild rabbits, it's been around a very long time. The main focus of this book is to portray the proper use application and construction of the rabbit snare. As seen the modern snare plays an important part in efficient rabbit control. Forget the primitive traditional snares of the past, we must learn to go forward and adapt to new modern techniques, ideas and equipment.

Through many years of fieldwork and practical experience in the application of snares, I have displayed the faults and weakness of small loops when low set and their improper placement. I have also shown the maximum capability and strength of the big loop system, how it outperforms the old traditional methods every time and continually commands permanent success. Those who are stubborn and unwilling to change their antiquated ideas and adapt new methods are blind ignorant to the facts. They will never have the ability to become proficient in the art of snaring and will only ever obtain a very limited rate of success. The detailed instructions techniques and methods I have set forth in the foregoing chapters of this book are designed to give you a sound working knowledge in the true art of rabbit snaring. This combined with your own practical field experience should help you achieve a most acceptable standard in the use of snares in a very short period of time.

The cruelty that snares inflict is always grossly exaggerated by those who know the least. The true professional treats his quarry with the utmost respect, handling and despatching it humanely and checking his snares daily at the required times to coincide with the seasons. He totally condemns those who are his exact opposite, the antiquated, idle, ignorant and lazy, who lays snares and won't check them and bring the name of field sports into disrepute. If the person is too lazy to check them don't set them.

Keep an open mind learn all you can about snares and the quarry you intend to catch and remember smart trappers remain students. It's really amazing how much we have to learn to realise how LITTLE we really know.

About the Author

I was born in December 1946 in the Old Stewartfield Rows - three parallel lines of back to back dwellings built to house workers of the local mines and Broxburn Oil Works.

The village sat on a hill nestled under the shadow of the large Stewartfield shale Bing. There were many of these large local Bings where much game abounded Hares, rabbits, partridges and pheasant. The village overlooked the small town of Broxburn which was surrounded by farms and game estates to the east and north. The people from Stewartfield were good, down to earth and kind Godly people. A poor but tight knit community where everybody looked after each other, even tramps who came to the village were given tea and something to eat. This is where I grew up into the World of Poaching.

My father was a professional boxer so was his older brother my Uncle George. Jimmy Waterson who was a long time family friend of my father was also a professional boxer. They were miners and also notorious poachers, purloining game on their regular nefarious night time outings to help supplement their meagre wages. Gate netting, long netting, snaring and setting gin traps were the order of the day. Gate netting along with snaring was the main method at catching hares for the dinner and a few to sell. Tommy Brechney a top class football player was another good gate netter, a good friend and neighbour of my father and Jimmy. There were a few other men in the village who participated in the night netting game. I was well schooled from a very early age on setting gate nets, long nets, snares and traps. There were quite a good few netting dogs in the village that kept the people well fed and with a couple of extra bob in their pocket.

Growing up, climbing the bings and sliding down them on old tin sheet, fishing in the local quarry for perch and swimming in the local canal were our regular pastimes, as well a guddling (tickling) trout in the local burns in the summer time. We would make catapults and some of the village lads became really deadly with them and still use them when out walking today.

As I grew my thoughts began to turn to the local rabbit population instead of playing games and my father taught me to make snares and set them. I was out with him checking snares on a regular basis and one day two pheasants were caught which he gave to me to carry. I was about five or six years old at the time. When we came to the end of the field he was carrying the rabbits and he said to me *"Where are the pheasants son?"* I said *"I flung them away, I don't want to carry chickens it's the rabbits I want"*. He just shook his head and went back and got them. My mother laughed when he told her.

I caught my own first rabbit in a fence snare when I was around 8 years old, I can still see that old dark grey buck yet, lying in that snare. I couldn't wait to get home to show my mother - that was me hooked and where my snaring career began. My father and Jimmy taught me how to snare the hares that lived on the bings using old building bricks which were picked up on the bings. They were attached to the snare cords and buried in the shale alongside the runs with a stalk of willowherb holding the big noose in place over the run. It was a very simple but deadly effective method of catching hares.

The late Sandy Livingston who taught me to snare foxes and rabbits

As the years progressed I met really good pro rabbit snarers like McMaster, Livingston, Chisholm and Whyte who helped further my career in the snaring game immensely. I emigrated to Canada in 1968 but came back home and got married to my wife whom I was dating before I left. We were going to get married out in Canada but came back home.

I continued snaring and my own son and daughter used to accompany me when they were younger. They just drifted away from it, but my oldest granddaughter used to go out snaring with me regular and became proficient in setting and catching. I still went back to Canada on a quite regular basis and met my good friend Peter Alan from Vancouver where he lived at the time. Peter taught me how to process my mink pelts to Canadian standards, my father had taught me how to put up my fox pelts as he too was out in Canada for a time. Peter was a professional Government Predator trapper in lower mainland B Columbia, later he went to work full for time himself still doing a lot of government work trapping beaver and nuisance bears , and raccoons. He also ran his winter trapline snaring coyotes, trapping fisher, marten, bob cat and lynx he moved up to the north near McBride he became the official Wolf trapper up there where I was up staying with him. We had 20 years of great trapping exploits him and I, but sadly he passed away a few years back. His Son and Daughter still live out there. Aubrey his son is also a proficient trapper, but like all good things in life they always come to an end sooner or later.

I don't smoke or drink and beat cancer and two heart attacks. But a tough life and many years of hard training I'm still here on the Earth Plane and with God's will I might just get another ten years of good rabbit snaring.

The Quickset Long Net

Not just a snarer, Glenn has turned his hand to most forms of rabbit catching over the years.

These photos were taken in 1979 and show a 33 year old Glenn demonstrating a quickset long net system he had devised as a young man five years earlier. At the time long nets were deployed in the field from separate parts, needing endpins to hold the head and foot lines and the poles set in the net as it was run out. Glenn's idea was to attach the net and the lines to the poles before you went out to use it.

When carried with the poles together the netting hangs down in long loops and originally Glenn would push this into hessian rice sack, obtained from one of his Chinese neighbours, to stop it getting snagged or tangled. After a while this idea was dropped as it added no real benefit.

As well as fixing the net permanently to the poles, Glenn also came up with an idea to tie the bagging between the poles into fixed pockets. Each section was tied into 4 pockets, each 2 yards long.

This innovative longnet could be run out single handed in under two minutes and was highly effective along field edges and when ferreting. On its first use in the field Glenn caught 27 rabbits and many thousands of rabbits over the nights that followed.

In carry mode - the net lifted and tied in position ready for the next operation.

Starting to set a long net: My own method starting at point A and finishing at point B. No back pegging involved at the net is permanently attached to fibreglass poles.

Half way along - notice how the stakes are held in my left hand and inserted into the ground with my right. The running cords pull each stake out in sequence. This 100 yard net can be set by two good men in 45 seconds.

Professional Rabbit Snaring

Woodgas' Professional Rabbit Snaring DVD

In this DVD Woodga takes you through the whole process of making and setting rabbit snares using the wire tealer and large loop method championed by Glenn Waters. A long time friend of Glenn, Woodga has regularly collaborated on the development and testing of the rabbit snare.

With this DVD you can literally start with a spool of wire and end with simple, light weight and highly effective snares. Also covers the use of hoop and fence snares.

Since this DVD was made, new best practice guidelines on the use of snares have been introduced. In Scotland the 2010 Snare Order has made some of these guidelines a legal requirement. All users of snares have a responsibility to keep up to date with changing advice and legislation in their region, which is usually published on government websites.

Available from Fourteenacre £15 plus postage.

Fourteenacre Ltd, PO Box 14552, Dorridge, Solihull, B93 3EA
Tel 07530 788061.   Email: sales@fourteenacre.co.uk,
Website: www.fourteenacre.co.uk

Professional Rabbit Snaring